THE LYTTONS IN INDIA

THE LYTTONS
IN INDIA

*

*An Account of
Lord Lytton's Viceroyalty
1876–1880*

*

MARY LUTYENS

John Murray

LONDON

First published 1979
by John Murray (Publishers) Ltd
50 Albemarle Street, London W1X 4BD

Printed in Great Britain by
Butler & Tanner Ltd, Frome and London

British Library Cataloguing in Publication Data

Lutyens, Mary
The Lyttons in India
1. Lytton, Robert Bulwer, *Earl of Lytton*
2. India – Governors – Biography
I. Title
954.03'5'0924   DS479.5
ISBN 0–7195–3677–4

Contents

Contents

Illustrations

Illustrations

Reproduced by courtesy of the India Office Library and Records

Foreword

This is the story of four years in the life of my maternal grandfather who was thrust into a high position he had never sought, and who was to meet disaster in trying to do what he saw as his duty. Robert Lytton did not go to India as 'a Party man', to use his own words, and 'never treated any Indian question as a Party question'. Unfortunately for him, however, Disraeli's policy for Afghanistan, which he was sent to India to implement, became the leading political question in England and Lytton was abused by the Liberals as few men in public life have ever been abused. I have tried in this book to assess how far he himself was responsible for his failure. But essentially it is a personal story, showing Lytton's relationships—with Queen Victoria, with his wife and other women, with his staff, colleagues and subordinates in India, and with friends and members of the Government in England.

I did not go to India for the purpose of writing the book. I had been there for several months in the twenties when official life was little different from what it must have been in the eighteen-seventies, whereas when I returned there ten years after the British had left, everything was so changed that my youthful impressions were in danger of being obliterated. In the twenties I had stayed with my uncle, Victor Lytton, Governor of Bengal, and with my father, Edwin Lutyens, who had a house in Delhi for twenty years while the new city was being built; above all I had the wonderful good fortune to travel with my mother all over India in the wake of Mrs Besant, spinning cotton for Gandhi, staying with Indian families and making many close Indian friends. I witnessed several instances of that behaviour of the British officials and army officers in India which the Prince of Wales had so complained of to Queen Victoria in 1875, and I was disappointed to meet so few Indians socially in Government House circles. After a garden party given

Foreword

by my mother in Delhi, one British official declared that he had met more Indians in a social way in that one afternoon than in the whole of his previous twenty years in India. Yet after writing this book I feel more sympathy than I ever thought possible for those men of good will who went out to India determined to rule justly and failed simply because it is impossible to be just to a subjugated people.

The spelling of Indian words has presented some difficulty. For well known names and places I have adopted modern spelling— Jaipur for Jeypore, for instance, Karachi for Curachee, Ambala for Umballa—but for lesser known names and places I have retained the spelling used by the Lyttons.

Disraeli's Offer

To Lord Lytton   2, Whitehall Gardens, S.W.
Confidential   Nov. 23, 1875

My dear Lytton,—Lord Northbrook has resigned the Viceroyalty of India—for purely domestic reasons— and will return to England in the
spring. If you will be willing, I will submit your name to the Queen as
his successor.

The critical state of affairs in Central Asia demands a statesman, and,
I believe, if you will accept this high post, you will have an opportunity,
not only of serving your country, but of obtaining an enduring fame—
                                         Yours sincerely, B. Disraeli[1]

Robert Lytton, who was just forty-four, was British Minister at
Lisbon when this totally unexpected letter arrived on November
29. Disraeli had defeated Gladstone in the election of 1874, and was
anxious to replace the Liberal Viceroy with a nominee of his own
who would carry out his imperial policy. Northbrook's resignation
gave him the opportunity. Lord Lytton was not, however, Disraeli's
first choice; Lord John Manners, Lord Powis and Lord Carnarvon
had all been approached and declined the offer for one reason or
another before Lytton's name was put forward. The Queen was un-
likely to disapprove of Lytton. She had met him on his appointment
to Lisbon in March 1875, and had noted in her journal, 'Lord Derby
presented Lord Lytton, whom I had never seen and who is a
miniature likeness of his father, only far more pleasing.'[2] Lord
Derby, the Foreign Secretary, had married a first cousin of Lytton's
wife, Edith Villiers; Lord Salisbury, the Secretary of State for India,
was a neighbour of the Lyttons in Hertfordshire and had known
and liked Robert since he was a boy; Disraeli, moreover, who had
been indebted to Robert's late father, Bulwer-Lytton,* for many

* Bulwer-Lytton, the novelist, had been born Edward Bulwer in 1803, the youngest of the

kindnesses in the early days of his career, was delighted to be able to offer his son this high honour.

Robert Lytton was appalled at the idea of going to India. When his father had died in January 1873, he had made up his mind that now he had inherited the family property at Knebworth as well as the barony, he would retire from the Diplomatic Service at the end of his time at Lisbon and devote himself to what he believed to be his true vocation—the writing of poetry. The year before, he had declined the Governorship of Madras on grounds of health, but it was not so easy to turn down this far more important post. He had a strong sense of duty, and, besides, he knew that his acceptance would be a tribute to his father whom he had venerated. His reply to Disraeli, dated December 1, 1875, began, 'No man was ever so greatly honoured ...' and went on to stress his 'absolute ignorance of Indian affairs', his '*total want* of experience in every kind of *administrative* business' and his fears that his health, never very good, might 'break down at some critical moment'. In particular he had suffered for many years from 'a painful, and distressing complaint' which occasionally incapacitated him altogether 'for the most ordinary mental labour'.[3] When he had consulted the eminent surgeon, Prescott Hewett, about the possibility of going to Madras, he had been warned that nothing could be worse for this complaint (piles) than the climate of India.

On December 20 came a telegram from Disraeli: 'We have carefully considered your letter and have not changed our opinion. We regard the matter as settled, but it must be kept secret until you hear from me.'[4]

Quite apart from his health, there was no man less suited by temperament and circumstances to fit into the British colonial system than Robert Lytton. Born on November 8, 1831, an only son with a sister, Emily, four years older, he had been a very sensitive, delicate child. He had suffered from the turbulent break-up of his parents' marriage when he was five years old. His father was too busy earning a precarious living writing novels and plays and carry-

three sons of General William Bulwer of Heydon Hall, Norfolk, and his wife, Elizabeth Lytton, heiress of Knebworth House, Hertfordshire. When Edward inherited the Knebworth estate from his mother in 1844 he adopted the additional surname of Lytton. He was created a baron in 1866. Although he is referred to here as Bulwer-Lytton to differentiate him from his son, he dropped the Bulwer with his peerage and became simply Lord Lytton.

ing out his duties as a radical member of Parliament to care about his children, and their mother, a beautiful Irish girl, Rosina Wheeler, whom Bulwer-Lytton had married in defiance of his mother's wishes, did not want them. If it had not been for a family friend, Miss Mary Green, who made a kind home for them at Cheltenham, their childhood would have lacked all affection except for the deep love they had for each other. Their father paid them short visits once or twice a year, and perhaps because of his very remoteness he was to Robert the embodiment of romance, to be adored to the point of worship. His father's love and confidence were, he afterwards wrote, necessities of his being.[5]

On one visit to Cheltenham Bulwer-Lytton brought with him a younger friend, John Forster, drama critic and afterwards editor of the *Examiner*. Forster took to Robert at once and thereafter acted as a real father to him. When Robert was nine he and Emily were taken away from Miss Green's care. Emily, who had spinal trouble, was sent to a clinic in Germany and Robert to a private school where he was so unhappy that he became ill. He spent his holidays partly with a tutor and partly with Forster in London. It was Forster who saw that he had new clothes, who took him to dine with Dickens and other literary friends, and to the theatre for which he conceived a passion. Above all, Forster opened his excellent library to him. From the age of twelve, when he started to write verses, Robert had only one ambition—to become a poet.

In 1845, when Robert was fourteen, his father sent him to Harrow. Disliking games, he was also very unhappy there and, much to his father's disappointment, showed no intellectual distinction. (The only thing Robert did not regret at Harrow was learning Greek.) In 1846 his much loved sister, just returned from Germany, died in London of typhoid fever. This was the cause of a bitter feud between Bulwer-Lytton and his estranged wife, who declared she had been kept away from Emily's death-bed. Bulwer-Lytton wrote to Robert at Harrow to say that if he ever saw his mother again or so much as opened a letter from her or accepted a present he would disown him.[6] It was a cruel ban to put on a boy of fifteen, but reverencing his father and hardly remembering his mother, he submitted to it.

Bulwer-Lytton had decided that Robert should enter the Diplomatic Service. With this end in view he took him away from Harrow after three years and sent him to a tutor at Bonn to learn German. The following year Robert's uncle, Sir Henry Bulwer (afterwards Lord Dalling), Minister at Washington, offered him a post as unpaid attaché at his Legation. Robert was delighted to accept, and with his father's approval and an allowance of £80 a year, he sailed for New York shortly after his nineteenth birthday. He was described when he first arrived there as 'a boy eccentrically dressed with abundant velvet cuffs and collars, and shiny boots, but even at that age witty and original, a most amusing and charming companion'.[7]

Robert was also very good looking, though rather short. He had his mother's Irish colouring—dark curly hair and blue eyes. He continued throughout his life to dress eccentrically in the fashion of his father's day with bell-bottomed trousers and square-cut toes to his shoes and a good deal of jewellery. He was very happy in Washington, and he and his uncle became devoted to each other.

When, in the spring of 1852, Sir Henry was transferred to Florence, then the capital of the Grand Duchy of Tuscany, he took Robert with him, still as unpaid attaché. Through John Forster, Robert was introduced to the Brownings, and soon became their intimate friend and a member of their circle. He did not need Mrs Browning's encouragement to write poetry—he had never ceased to do so—but he was able to show her what he wrote and benefit from her criticism. His first volume of poems was prepared for the press while he was in Florence and many of the poems in his second volume were written while he was there. He lost his heart to Italy, came to loathe Austrian rule and to consider Garibaldi the greatest of heroes. He also fell passionately and romantically in love with a married woman, five years older than himself—Harriet Wilson, the wife of Captain Fleetwood Wilson, a retired officer of Hussars, who had come to live in Florence, then the cheapest civilised town in Europe, as the result of a financial crash.

Judging from the poems Robert wrote at the time, which seem to have been largely autobiographical, his love was reciprocated, at any rate at first. 'Midnight, and love, and youth, and Italy!/ Love in the land where love most lovely seems': how those lines from one of his lyrics evoke the atmosphere of those early Florence days. Later, the hopelessness of this frustrating passion, which lasted some years, brought back all the melancholy of his boyhood. All his life he was to suffer periods of 'almost intolerable hysterical depression', to use his own words.[8]

Robert had now begun to read greedily—poetry, philosophy, drama and history in English, French, German and Italian, as well as the Classics. His extraordinarily retentive memory would have been a boon to a scholar or a statesman; to a creative writer it was a handicap in that it sometimes led him into unconscious plagiarism. He had come to a stage in his development when not to try to publish his poems felt like 'the suicide' of his 'own identity'. He wrote to his father: 'I feel that all those glittering prizes [in the Diplomatic Service] which allure others, would, even if I were to obtain them, greatly diminish rather than increase my happiness: each step forward would be a step further from my ideal, and would have to be trodden over some relinquished dream or some strangled instinct.'[9] How well he knew himself already. He was to be haunted all his life by the relinquished dream of becoming a dedicated poet.

In contrast to Forster, who offered to see his first book through the press and give it 'a favourable breeze', his father was not only totally discouraging but wounded him deeply by writing: 'I don't think whatever your merit, the world would allow two of the same name to have both a permanent reputation in literature. You would soon come to grudge me my life, and feel a guilty thrill every time you heard I was ill.... No, stick close to your profession.... As to your allowance, I should never increase it till you get a step.'[10]

To this Robert replied, 'What you have said is *enough*. I shall only recur in thought to those suggestions for the future with regret that they were ever made.... I am quite willing to abide in the Profession and work as well and as cheerfully as I can in it.'[11]

Bulwer-Lytton eventually agreed to the publication of Robert's first book on the understanding that he brought it out under a *nom de plume* and promised to publish nothing more for two years. These conditions were accepted with the sweetness with which Robert always submitted to his father, however much he was hurt by him. *Clytemnestra and Other Poems* by 'Owen Meredith', was published in 1855. Forster reviewed it seriously though rather coolly in the *Examiner*. It was praised, however, by Matthew Arnold and Leigh Hunt; the anonymous critic in the *London Review* ranked Owen Meredith as third among living poets, while Burne-Jones and

William Morris at Oxford hailed him as a successor to Tennyson. The poems show a strong influence of Tennyson and Browning.

At the end of 1854 Robert was transferred to the Embassy in Paris. This was definitely a step up. Although he was still an unpaid attaché he was no longer under his uncle's wing. After two years in Paris he was moved to The Hague. In 1856 it became compulsory for unpaid attachés to pass an examination. Robert studied for this at The Hague, passed it in 1857 and became eligible for his first official salary of £250 a year.

The two years being up in which Robert had promised not to publish anything, he brought out his second book, *The Wanderer*, still under the *nom de plume* of Owen Meredith. The book was very well received by the critics and the public. It contained a hundred quite long poems, much more Byronic now than Tennysonian.

Later in the same year, 1858, Bulwer-Lytton, who, having changed his political loyalties, had been Tory member for Hertfordshire since 1852, was made Secretary of State for the Colonies in Lord Derby's Government. His wife, Rosina, took the opportunity to attack him publicly. Robert, to save his father further scandal, offered to take his mother abroad. When both parents eagerly caught at this proposal, Robert took his mother to Luchon in the Pyrenees. For the first time he heard her side of the marriage story and, feeling deep compassion for her, attempted to make peace in letters to his father. In doing so he was accused by Bulwer-Lytton of treachery and gross disloyalty. His mother too turned against him when she found she could not poison his mind against his father. After three intolerable months he parted from her in Paris, never to see her again although she did not die until 1882, aged eighty.

The only creative result of those months at Luchon was the composition of a long narrative poem, *Lucile*, which was published in 1860, again under the same *nom de plume*. It became very popular, especially in America where it is still quite well known.

Robert's next appointment in the spring of 1859 was as Second Secretary of Embassy at Vienna where his Chief's wife, Lady Blomfield, who was to become his aunt by marriage, could hardly have treated him more warmly had he been her own son. Having become reconciled to his father at a happy meeting at Baden, Robert's income was made up by Bulwer-Lytton to £500 a year. Robert's four years in Vienna were hallowed by his friendship with Julian Fane, a son of Lord Westmorland, who was to die young of consumption. (Robert wrote a memoir of him.) This was the first close man friend fairly near to him in age (Julian was four years older) that Robert had ever had. Julian gave delightful, merry little dinner parties at which the conversation was as good as the food and wine. After the opera or an official reception Robert would return to find Julian alone in dressing-gown and slippers, and the two men would talk intimately of life and literature, often until dawn. It was at these long night sessions that Robert became addicted to smoking and late hours.

During this time in Vienna Robert was sent by the Foreign Office on two special missions to Belgrade and Constantinople which he conducted so successfully that he was highly commended by both the Vienna Embassy and the Home Government.

Promotion to First Secretary of Legation at Copenhagen came at the beginning of 1863, to be followed the next year by transference to Athens. But before taking up this new post he was given four months' leave. One of the first things he did on arrival in England was to call on Mrs Edward Villiers, Lady Blomfield's sister, whom he had met briefly ten years before in Paris. Mrs Villiers had been Elizabeth Liddel, one of the sixteen children of Lord Ravensworth. Edward Villiers, a brother of Lord Clarendon, the Liberal Foreign Secretary, had died of consumption in 1843, leaving his widow very badly off with four small children, the youngest of whom were twin girls, Edith and Elizabeth. Lord Clarendon had put at his sister-in-law's disposal a small house on his estate, The Grove, in Hertfordshire, so that by letting her own house in London and wintering abroad Mrs Villiers managed to live in a certain amount of comfort.

When Robert had first seen Edith in Paris as a girl of twelve she had impressed him 'with a peculiar sense of tenderness and reverence, strangely like the *atmosphere* of love'.[12] She was now twenty-two. Her elder sister Theresa (afterwards well known as the author of *Pot-Pourri from a Surrey Garden*) had recently married Charles Earle; her only brother was in the army, and her beloved twin sister, Lizey, had been married for two years to Henry Loch, Governor of the Isle of Man. (There is a legend in the Loch as well as the Lytton family that Henry Loch had proposed by mistake to Lizey instead of Edith. Although almost identical in appearance,

Edith had far more charm.) The girls had received no formal education apart from visiting masters in drawing, dancing and music. Theresa was an accomplished water-colour artist while Edith, who loved music, played the piano rather well. Their winters in France, Germany and Italy had broadened their minds, and after the girls came out they had dined frequently at The Grove with the Clarendons, where the conversation, according to Theresa's *Memoirs*, was the most brilliant she had ever known in her life, and she had moved in many brilliant circles.

Edith was fair and very tall, taller than Robert, and, from all accounts, beautiful. She was also sweet-tempered, gentle, gracious and tactful, and she had a lovely speaking voice. Robert, who, at thirty-three, was longing to get married, fell deeply in love with her almost at first sight, a feeling she returned with her whole heart. Although birth, family and character were everything Bulwer-Lytton could have desired, he was at first opposed to the marriage, not so much because of Edith's lack of fortune as because Lord Clarendon was his political opponent living in the same county.

Robert did not feel he had enough to marry on without his father's increased support, but wrote to Lady Blomfield that he would rather wait twenty years to marry Edith Villiers than any woman in the world.[13] When Bulwer-Lytton realised how much Robert's heart was set on this marriage he gave it his blessing. He was not willing to increase Robert's allowance but he agreed to pay the premiums on a life insurance for him which would secure Edith £600 a year. As well as this, Edith had expectations of £6,000 from an old family friend, a legacy she came into the following year.

The marriage took place in London on October 4, 1864. At the end of six months in Athens Robert was promoted to First Secretary at the Legation in Lisbon. Edith was expecting a baby in August 1865 and it was thought wise for her to return to London for her confinement. It was while she was away that the twenty-four-year-old Wilfred Scawen Blunt arrived at Sintra where Robert was living. Blunt had got into a scrape in Paris, where he had been an attaché at the Embassy, over his passion for the courtesan 'Skittles' (Catherine Waters), and had been sent by the Foreign Office to Lisbon in disgrace. (Blunt was to become well known as a poet, traveller in the Middle East, vociferous opponent of imperialism, and, principally, for introducing the Arab horse into England.)

Disraeli's Offer

Blunt described arriving at Sintra in a state of profound depression and how Robert came out to meet him as soon as he was announced 'and with that prodigality of affectionate kindness which was so great a charm in him' welcomed him in. 'I had hardly been half an hour with him,' Blunt wrote, 'before I felt that, like the pilgrim in the Delectable Mountains, the burden of my sins was fallen from my back, and I had found a guide and friend to show me a way out of my misfortunes.... We spent three months together almost alone in those Portugese hills, and every day my admiration for him and love grew greater. On diplomatic business I do not remember that we wasted a single word or a single thought.' 'These delightful days' were for Blunt the first he had ever enjoyed 'with an intellect of the highest order—a kind of intellectual honeymoon'.[14] These months were equally delightful for Robert except that he was missing Edith badly; he was enchanted to find that Blunt was a poet.

After Edith's return to Lisbon with their son, Rowland, Robert began writing poems and articles for several English periodicals. It was through contributing to the *Fortnightly Review* that he formed a close friendship with its editor, John Morley.

In 1866 Bulwer-Lytton was made a peer, and perhaps under the softening influence of this honour he at last gave Robert permission to publish a book under his own name. *Chronicles and Characters* came out the following summer at about the same time as the birth of his second child, Betty, and only very gradually attracted notice. Its initial failure produced in Robert a great despondency and self-doubt. Edith loved him too uncritically to be of any intellectual stimulus to him. Robert relied on her advice in practical matters (throughout life he mismanaged his financial affairs) and accepted her moral judgments, but she had no originality of mind, no intellectual sparkle.*

Robert's next appointment, in 1869, was to the First Secretary-ship of Embassy at Vienna. Soon after their arrival a second

---

* An instance of the kind of advice she gave him was over three little notebooks of Leonardo da Vinci's which he had picked up for next to nothing in Florence and given to Forster. While she was in England for the birth of Rowland, Robert was told by an art dealer in Lisbon that the notebooks, if genuine, would be worth about £300. Robert asked Edith whether she thought he could ask Forster to give them back. Edith replied, 'A present once given *can't* be taken back because of more value than you thought, you dear, darling, funny

daughter, Constance, was born, but in the summer of 1871 they had the agony of losing Rowland, not yet six, and a particularly beautiful and promising little boy. He died after a long, painful illness from complications following whooping cough, and his parents could only watch helplessly as he choked to death. Eight months later Edith gave birth to another son, Teddy.

The Lyttons left Vienna in the autumn of 1872, but before taking up his new post of First Secretary at the Paris Embassy, Robert spent a few weeks alone with his father at Torquay. They really discovered each other for the first time, all wounds were healed and perfect confidence established between them. It was the last time they met. In January 1873 Bulwer-Lytton died suddenly. Robert's grief could not have been more heart-felt if Bulwer-Lytton had always been a model father. Robert now turned more than ever to Forster for sympathy and advice. He intended to retire from his profession, but when he discovered that his inheritance was not so large as he had expected he decided to stay on until a higher post earned him a retirement pension.

Robert enjoyed the social life in Paris now that he was married. He had a charming house in the Faubourg St Germain, entertained well and could afford to keep a carriage. He loved good food and wine and the company of talented men and lively, pretty women. He was a great flirt, a propensity which Edith wisely treated as a joke, however much it may have secretly distressed her. Of Parisian society he wrote: 'I think this is the only city in which social intercourse is studied as one of the arts of life. . . . Most clever Englishmen are chary of spending their wits. They hoard up their cleverness for great occasions—the book they are going to write or the speech they are going to speak. But the cleverest Frenchmen have all their cleverness in small change, and spend it lavishly on little things.'[15]

There was soon to be another tragedy. Little Teddy, not yet two, died in March 1874 of congestion of the lungs. 'We are all broken, worn out, stunned,' Robert told Forster. As an antidote to sorrow Robert began a long narrative poem, *King Poppy*, which was to be, on and off, his imaginative companion for the next twenty years.

In November 1874 came the promotion Robert had been waiting

---

chap.' (Lutyens, p. 207.) These priceless little notebooks are now in the Forster Collection in the Victoria and Albert Museum.

for, to Minister of Legation at Lisbon. 'The salary is £4400,' he wrote to Forster, 'the climate excellent, the work nil, the distance—ah!'[16] It was a five-day voyage from England. He was determined that this should be his last diplomatic or official post. He had been married for ten years and was still very much in love with Edith. A long pleasant stretch of life lay ahead of him. What he so much looked forward to on retirement was the stimulus of other literary minds and the company of kindred spirits as well as the opportunity to write. Edith too was longing to live in England again. Although she carried out her official duties perfectly she was of a retiring nature, had no social ambition and found complete fulfilment in her devotion to Robert and their children. Before they left Paris at the end of 1874 a third daughter, Emily, was born.

The Lyttons had been at Lisbon only seven months when Disraeli's offer arrived to disrupt all their dreams of the future. Robert did not keep it a secret from Forster: 'After the most torturing self-examination' he felt he could not 'refuse to undertake the arduous duties of that great office' once he had placed before the Cabinet all his reservations. 'But, oh, the heavy change—the *awful* change! ... how my heart is bleeding and aching. What thoughts of *you*, what thoughts of all that is cherished, beautiful, and pleasant in this life I had laid out for myself.'[17] To Morley he put his feelings more succinctly: 'I have not courted or willingly accepted the crushing gift of such a white elephant.'[18]

On January 27, 1876, came a telegram from Lord Salisbury, Secretary of State for India: 'Announcement of your appointment has been officially made and well received. Very important that you should come home soon, as many preparations to be made and much business to be transacted.'[19] Edith made a note that day in her diary: 'All now know the great change in our happy lives. Certainly happiness is not allowed for long in this world, and the appointment terrifies me.'

Robert decided to return to England immediately, leaving Edith to pack up, sell their effects at the Legation and follow him with the children as soon as she could. The girls, Betty, Constance and Emily were now aged eight, six and just a year. Should these children be taken to India? To add to the Lyttons' uncertainties it was

11

now known that Edith was 'expecting' again in August. Naturally they longed for a boy; a birth in India would add to the risk of Edith's confinement; nevertheless, it was never contemplated for a moment that Robert should go to India without her.

Don Fernando, ex-King of Portugal and a first cousin of Queen Victoria, wept when he heard Robert was leaving, so greatly attached to him had he become. There is no doubt that Robert exercised a compelling charm over anyone who gained his affection and sympathy. He was so warm, uncensorious and understanding, and he must have had the most seductive voice (I assume this from the voices of his sons which I well recall). But he was also completely un-British. He had not lived in England except for short periods of leave since he went to Bonn at seventeen. He was indifferent to all sport and actively disliked shooting. Although vaguely theistic he never went to church; he was unconventional in dress and foreign in manner (for instance, he could never break himself in England of the Continental habit of kissing the hand of a married woman on introduction); moreover, he was extremely demonstrative in his affections. John Morley said of him that he 'was born a Parisian with a pleasant touch of Bohemian added, and the Puritan and Philistine graces of Simla were repugnant to him'.[20] Equally, Robert's Parisian graces were to prove repugnant to the philistines of Simla and Calcutta.

2

Preparations for India

Robert Lytton arrived at Buckland's Hotel, Brook Street, London, on January 19, 1876, to such a confusion of activity that he had not a moment to write to Edith until the 23rd, by which time he had been assured by his doctor, Prescott Hewett, that it was quite safe to take the girls to India and that in Simla or Calcutta Edith would receive the best attendance for her confinement. Robert had also heard of an excellent English governess of thirty-five to take to India with them. All his friends and the members of the Government had been 'most generous, considerate and encouraging', and J. T. Delane, editor of *The Times*, had written assuring him that if he would give him private information of any measures he took in India likely to excite hostile criticism he would support them if he could. He was finding his work 'overwhelming and most puzzling and strange, but intensely interesting'. He had the appointment of a surgeon and had accepted an applicant who had been highly recommended to him who was already in India. As to other appointments, the only ones he had to make before leaving England were a Private Secretary, a Military Secretary and five aides-de-camp.

'A Private Secretary', he wrote in this same letter, 'is a post of paramount importance and I feel already that my success will entirely depend on securing a first rate man.' He hoped to obtain the services of Colonel Burne—'a man of rare ability and experience now high in the India Office'—who had been Private Secretary to the Viceroy, Lord Mayo, who had been murdered in 1872. Robert went on: 'The chief function of the Military Secretary is to arrange one's levees and Drawing rooms, and receive on one's behalf. The social popularity of the Viceroy mainly depends on that of the Military Secretary and it is essential that he should be a man of the world, with perfect tact, *savoir-faire*, and engaging manners.' Lytton had already had '56 applications for A.D.C.ships'. One half of his staff had to be chosen from officers who had passed the examination in Hindustani; a certain proportion had to be chosen from the Indian Civil Service, and it was etiquette for the new Viceroy to take on 'the household ADC of the old Viceroy'. The only aide-de-camp on whom he had privately decided was George Villiers, but the post would have to be kept open for him till December when he would have finished with the Staff College. (Villiers was a first cousin of Edith's on her father's side.)

This long letter was interrupted by the arrival of Cabinet boxes from the India Office. In continuing, Robert told Edith that the Queen had asked him to Osborne on the 25th and that Millais was painting his portrait for Forster. Forster was seriously ill at this time at his house in Kensington where Robert made time to visit him as often as possible.

Theresa Earle, Edith's sister, who had accompanied Robert to Millais's studio for two of the sittings, pronounced the portrait to be an excellent likeness. The portrait was exhibited at the Royal Academy that year. It is now in the Victoria and Albert Museum as part of the Forster Collection. Two full-size copies were made, one for Knebworth and one to be sent out to Calcutta.

The visit to Osborne was evidently a success, for the Queen recorded in her journal on January 25 that Lord Lytton spoke both briefly and sensibly, adding 'He is a man full of feeling'.[1] She presented him with the first two volumes of Theodore Martin's *Life of the Prince Consort*. When writing to thank her for these, his first letter to her, he wrote in the first person in ignorance of protocol. Not only did she forgive him this lapse but accorded him the unique privilege of writing to her in the first person in all his subsequent letters.[2] Her frequent letters to him while he was in India were written in the third person but always in her own handwriting.

The Queen, like Lytton himself, was blessedly free from colour prejudice. The Prince of Wales, who at this time was nearing the end of a five months' tour of India, was indignant with the British officials for their discourtesy to the native princes and their arrogance to the Indian population; he was outraged too that British officers habitually spoke of the natives as 'niggers'. He told all this to the Queen in his letters which she showed to Lytton during his

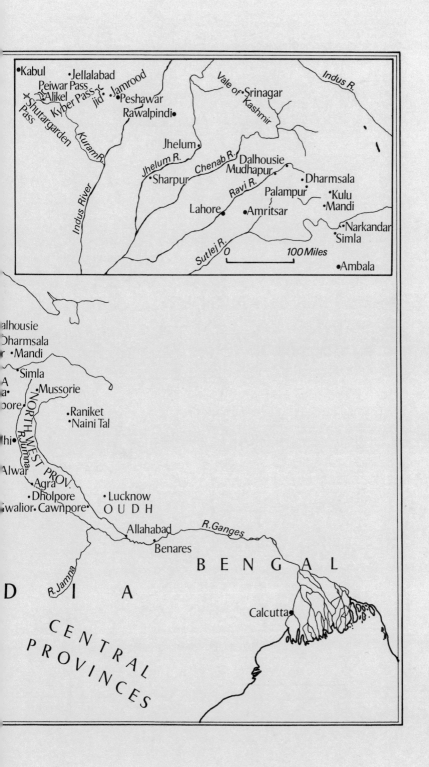

visit, asking him to do all in his power to change this attitude of the Anglo-Indians which she so much deplored.[3]

The day after seeing the Queen, Robert met James Fitzjames Stephen at a dinner party in London. It was a case of immediate mutual attraction leading to a close, lifelong friendship. This distinguished barrister and writer (called by his second name to distinguish him from his father, Sir James) was an elder brother of Sir Leslie Stephens, Virginia Woolf's father. He had been the legal member of the Viceroy's Council in India from 1869 to 1873. He and Robert naturally talked of India; they left the party together and spent half the night walking each other home, utterly absorbed in their conversation.

The next day Stephen wrote to Robert strongly advising him not to take the children to India and also warning him against the nuisance of English servants in India.[4] This advice was not taken, probably because Edith refused to be parted from her little girls and loyal servants, but it was decided that she and the children should go straight up to the hill station of Simla when they arrived in India while Robert went to Calcutta to be received by Lord Northbrook. It was etiquette for the outgoing Viceroy to stay and greet his successor and introduce him to members of his Council.

Forster died on February 2, a blow for which Robert, strangely enough, was totally unprepared. 'I feel quite crushed and bewildered', he wrote to Theresa Earle. 'All my little courage is gone. He was father, brother, and more, much more, to me. No man ever *had* such a friend as I had in him. I am an executor of his will, and I must do all I can to help and comfort his poor little wife, who seems to me so forlorn.'[5]

When Edith arrived at Southampton on February 6 Robert could not go to meet her because it was the day of Forster's funeral. Instead he sent a letter to greet her. It began, 'My darling, no words can say how I am longing for a sight of your dear, dear face,' and ended, 'never in my life have I loved as I love you. Never was woman dearer to man than you are to your devoted Robsy.' Edith was just as much in love with him as he was with her. Her chief regret in going to India was in knowing that she would see so much less of him.

Stephen had now written for Lytton a dissertation on the Indian

administrative system which, Robert declared, had given him 'the
master key to that magnificent mystery'.[6] It must indeed have
seemed a mystery to anyone as unfamiliar with its development as
Lytton. The Government of India had been taken over by the
Crown from the East India Company at the end of the Mutiny in
1858, and it was then that the alternative title of Viceroy had been
given to the occupant of the post of Governor-General. As com-
munications improved, so it became easier for London to control
its representative in Calcutta, then the capital (it was not until 1911
that Delhi was chosen as the new capital). This erosion of the
Viceroy's independence had begun with the opening of the electric
telegraph between England and India in 1865, at first overland,
via Teheran, then, after 1870, by cable to Bombay via the Suez
Canal.

The Secretary of State for India, to whom the Viceroy was
directly responsible, was a member of the Cabinet and had his own
advisory Council of fifteen members, most of whom had served on
the Viceroy's Executive Council in India. This Executive, or
Supreme, Council was the Viceroy's instrument of government and
consisted of six members, each the head of a department. He also
had a larger Legislative Council which included the Executive
Council.

British India then comprised nine provinces—Madras, Bombay,
Bengal, the North-West Provinces, the Punjab, Oudh, the Central
Provinces, British Burma and Assam. (Ceylon, though British, was
a Crown Colony administered by the Colonial office.) Only Madras
and Bombay were ruled by Governors, each with his own Executive
and Legislative Councils, whose degree of autonomy was limited.
The other provinces were either under Lieutenant-Governors or
Commissioners, though all the local Governments were financially
controlled by the Viceroy's Supreme Council.

The provinces were divided into districts, each about the size of
an English county, administered by District Officers who came most
in contact with the people of India. But the old type of District
Officer was dying out—men who had loved their districts and had
never wanted to leave them and who had once been looked up to
'as a supreme incarnation of power, wisdom and goodness'. With
a few invaluable exceptions, the object now of most of the officials
was to earn as much money as would enable them to retire as soon

as possible; few of them really had their heart and hope in India itself.[7]

The appointments of high officials in India were theoretically made from London, but, since it was very rare for the Secretary of State to disregard the Viceroy's recommendations, the power of making appointments virtually rested with him, always with the exception of the Governors of the chief provinces.

In theory it was only British India that London controlled through the Viceroy and this complex organisation. The vast tracts of the Indian continent which still belonged to the native States were nominally self-governing under the jurisdiction of their princes, with their own armies and revenues. Varying greatly in size and importance, these included the whole of Rajputana, comprising twenty-one States, Hyderabad, Mysore, Kashmir, Baroda, Nepal and many other States in Central India and even in the Punjab and other British provinces. In fact all these States were controlled by the Crown. A British political officer (called a Resident) and a military Commissioner resided in each one of them, ostensibly to offer help and advice but also empowered to interfere in instances of misrule or suspected treachery to the British, or even to depose a ruler or refuse to recognise his heir. In exchange, the British entered into treaties with the native rulers which secured their rights and protected them from attack, external and internal.

As well as Stephen's 'master key' to all this, Lytton had the benefit of several interviews with Disraeli, Lord Derby and Lord Salisbury and met the members of the Indian Council in London. A former Viceroy of India, the great Lord Lawrence, who still had considerable influence, was strongly opposed to Disraeli's new policy for Afghanistan, the wild, mountainous, independent, Moslem country to the north of India.

Since the end of the first Afghan War in 1842, when the British had been shamefully defeated by the troops of the then Amir of Afghanistan, Dost Mohomed, British policy for Afghanistan had been one of *laisser-faire*, what was sarcastically called by its opponents 'masterly inactivity'. It was also referred to as 'the Lawrencian policy'. Disraeli was now intent on what he termed a 'forward policy' in view of the alarming encroachments of Russia in recent years on territory north of Afghanistan. Russia was playing

17

a game of 'grandmother's steps', creeping towards the Afghan border when England's eyes were not on her, then stopping short when challenged and innocently protesting that she had no designs on Afghanistan. Since the days of Alexander the Great the conquest of India had been the dream of every Empire-builder, and the Tsar Alexander II was as great an expansionist as Queen Victoria. Disraeli did not trust Russia's assurance in 1873 that she would continue to regard Afghanistan as wholly beyond her sphere of influence.

And it was Russian influence more than the force of her arms that was feared. Should hostilities break out between England and Russia in some other sphere, the threat of an Afghan rising against India, encouraged by Russia and armed with Russian guns, could be disastrous to England in keeping British troops in India which were needed elsewhere. There were already few enough British troops to protect the frontier.

This frontier, known as the North-West Frontier, very wide and ill-defined, was occupied by independent Moslem tribes, Pathans and Afridis, who, although they owed only a loose allegiance to Afghanistan, could be counted on to join the Amir if he declared a religious war. The two main gateways between India and Afghanistan—the Kuram Valley, leading to the Peiwar Pass, and the terrible thirty-mile long Khyber Pass, the scene of so many massacres—were controlled by the tribes to the south and the Afghans to the north. No white man could enter tribal territory when Lytton first went to India without fear of being shot, yet the tribes made constant raids into British territory, murdering and plundering, and then melting away into their mountain fastnesses.

After the death of Dost Mahomed in 1863 and a bloody struggle for succession, one of his sons, Sher Ali, with no help from the British, had won for himself an uneasy throne as Amir at Kabul, the capital of Afghanistan. The Afghans were proud, independent people, and Sher Ali did not want to have anything to do with either Russia or England, but as the Russians crept ever closer to his northern border he realised that, sandwiched as he was between two great powers, he would be wise to place himself under the protection of one or other of them. Fearing the British less than the Russians, he had sent a special envoy to Lord Northbrook in 1873 with the offer of a treaty by the terms of which, in return for his allegiance, the British would guarantee him an annual subsidy, recognise his favourite youngest son, Abdulla Jan, as his heir and come to his aid in the event of a Russian invasion. Lord Northbrook was instructed by Gladstone's Government from London not only to turn down this offer but to castigate Sher Ali over the imprisonment at Kabul of his eldest, rebellious son, Yakub Khan.

After such a rebuff it is not suprising that the Amir turned to Russia, his contact being General Kaufmann, the Governor of Russian Turkestan at Tashkent. Although Sher Ali had not actually signed a treaty with Russia, it was known through native spies in the pay of the British that he was receiving at Kabul native agents from General Kaufmann who were fomenting his grievances against the British Government. Lytton was to maintain that it was this snub from Lord Northbrook that was responsible for all the conflict with Afghanistan which was to follow during his own Viceroyalty.

Disraeli's instructions to Lytton in London were for him to establish friendly relations with Sher Ali as soon as possible, then offer him the treaty he had previously asked for, with the important proviso that he must allow a permanent British envoy to reside either at Kabul or at Herat, further north. Disraeli entrusted Lytton with a written dispatch to this effect but left him to choose his own moment for revealing it to his Council. [8]

It was also Disraeli's intention that Lytton should proclaim Queen Victoria Empress of India, though for this it would be necessary to introduce what was called the Royal Titles Bill when Parliament assembled in March. This was a step which the Queen and Disraeli considered long overdue. Their reason for wanting this title was that it would put the Queen on a par with the Emperor of Russia. After all, a queen was no higher than a maharaja of whom there were dozens in India. In view of the political climate of the time Disraeli would have postponed the introduction of the Bill if the Queen had not insisted on having her new title as soon as possible. She did not even wait to consult the Prince of Wales who was most indignant on his return from India to find that such a step had been taken without his knowledge. Disraeli had the greatest difficulty in getting the Bill passed. Gladstone opposed it on the grounds that other colonies had equal rights to separate titles, that there was no proof that India desired the title and that, anyway, the Crown did not possess the whole of India. The Queen pronounced the opposition 'factious and unpatriotic'.[9]

Lytton was not really interested in politics and had no party affiliations. He was a liberal at heart although a great upholder of aristocracy. Nevertheless, he grasped Disraeli's new forward policy immediately, adopted it whole-heartedly and foresaw no difficulty in carrying it out, in spite of being warned that his Council in Calcutta would be against it; at least half of them were followers of Lord Lawrence. As for declaring the Queen Empress of India, that was something which appealed greatly to his imagination.

Lytton's suspicions of Russia were aroused by an extraordinary interview he had, a few days before leaving England, with Count Shouvalov, the Russian Ambassador in London. Shouvalov divulged to him a plan, emanating from General Kaufmann, and approved by Prince Gorchakov, the Russian Chancellor, whereby Russia and England should join in disarming Afghanistan and all the States with a Mahometan population between Afghanistan and Russia's possessions in Central Asia, and divide these territories between themselves. Shouvalov pointed out to Lytton the advantage to British India of having a powerful, friendly Christian Empire on her North-West Frontier. Lytton's deep distrust of Russia after this interview, which he reported to Salisbury, is understandable, and it coloured all his future dealings with Afghanistan. There was all the difference between having the frontier covered by loose groups of barbarous States whose power, compared to that of the British, was insignificant, and having it surrounded by a great civilised military Empire.[10]

Lytton went to India fully determined to bring justice to the people of that continent. As he was to discover, the treatment of the Indians by their conquerors was at best paternal. Most of the British had managed to convince themselves that they were ruling in a spirit of pure altruism. One might imagine from their attitude of superiority that poor India was being kept by her wealthy white patron. In truth, not only had the conquest of India brought enormous riches and prestige to England, but the Indian tax-payer was supporting the whole of the administration imposed on him, while his commercial interests were subordinated to those of the British.

Preparations for India

One grievance among Indians which continued to rankle was that they had been made to pay the whole cost of Sir Gilbert Scott's India Office building in Whitehall, completed in 1867. Even more unjust, when a lavish ball was held there for 2,500 guests for the Sultan of Turkey, for no reason other than it was a convenient place and before the new building had even been taken over by the India Office, the full cost of it had been drawn from the Calcutta treasury.[11] It was unfairnesses such as these which were resented in India almost as much as the greater injustices. As one newspaper in India summed up the situation: 'India is the one possession of the Crown concerning which the boast has been that "It was acquired without the expenditure of a shilling". And as if this were not enough, it is that one possession that has been remorselessly made the milch cow of the Empire.'[12]

But after the popular visit of the Prince of Wales, who had shown many signs of sympathy for the people of India and an understanding of her problems and grievances, the Indians had taken new heart. Before Lytton's arrival, the Bombay *Times* stated with satisfaction that the Queen had shown him the Prince of Wales's letter expostulating over the racial prejudice he had witnessed, and had asked him to right this wrong. The Indians were now as much prepared to welcome their new Viceroy as he was to serve them.

3

Voyage to India

The Lyttons with their daughters, servants and staff set out for India on Wednesday, March 1, 1876, via Paris and Naples. For his Private Secretary Lytton had obtained the man he wanted, Lieutenant-Colonel Owen Burne, who was 'lent' to him for two years by the India Office. This forty-year-old soldier had been all through the Indian Mutiny, showing exceptional gallantry. He was, moreover, a very good-looking man. For his Military Secretary Lytton had made the choice of Colonel George Pomeroy Colley, five years younger than Burne, strongly recommended by Lord Carnarvon, the Colonial Secretary. Irish by birth, Colley had served in the Ashanti War of 1872–4 and had just returned from Africa to take up the appointment of Assistant-Quartermaster-General at Aldershot when on February 4 he had received a note from Lytton offering him, with the permission of the Duke of Cambridge, the Commander-in-Chief, the Military Secretaryship. On the voyage out to India with the Lyttons, Colley wrote about the Viceroy as 'a man who keeps all parts of one's brain active, a poet and a statesman'.[1]

Lytton took only one aide-de-camp with him, Lieutenant Frederick Liddell of the Royal Artillery. Fred Liddell was another of Edith's first cousins, this time on her mother's side. Many friends and all Edith's family came to see them off. Edith's two sisters were also 'expecting' at this time. Edith felt particularly sad at parting with her beloved twin, Lizey Loch.

The others travelling with the Lyttons to India were the new governess, Miss Partridge; the Swiss governess, Mademoiselle Feez, who had been with them in Lisbon; Edith's personal maid, Robert's valet, a nanny, a nursery-maid, a groom, a footman and a French chef. Colonel Burne's wife, Evelyne, a sister of Lord Kilmaine, her two boys, nurse, maid and man-servant were also of the party.

Voyage to India

They stayed a week in Paris at the Embassy with Lord Lyons, Robert's old Chief. During their stay Edith ordered clothes from Worth, then the best known of the Paris dressmakers, to be sent out to India, and several smart little Paris hats. She had started dressing at Worth when they had lived in Paris in 1873–4, and having her hair done by August Petit. She had, as she said herself, learnt to be smart in Paris. Lady Mayo had told her that she would need to spend £1,000 on clothes for India. She felt sure this would be ample for herself and the girls, especially as Worth's things wore so well. Besides, Worth made a special price for her, having been saved from despair, so he told her, at the darkest moment of his career by reading Bulwer-Lytton's *Night and Morning*.

The Lytton party left Paris on March 7 (a *coupé lit* for Robert and Edith) and reached Bologna the following evening. There they met Sir Louis Mallet, permanent Under-Secretary of State at the India Office, who was on his way home after a visit to India. Robert had two long talks with him and was depressed to hear that all his Council in Calcutta would be opposed to the new Afghan policy. Edith wrote in her diary next day:

Sir Louis told me after luncheon that he was quite *astonished* at the way R. had mastered all the difficult and detailed subjects, and that he would have all at his finger ends if he could learn so much about India in a month, and he really seemed genuinely to admire R's powers—which pleased me *very* much, as I think when R. knows nothing of a subject he studies more, and then knows it better than others who have been long at it.

The Lyttons' next stop was Rome where they stayed very comfortably at the Hotel Constanzi and lunched and dined with the Ambassador, Sir Augustus Paget, who had been Lytton's Chief in Copenhagen, and his German wife, Walburga. The next day, March 11, they went on to Naples where the Pagets promised to join them. They stayed there five nights at the Hotel Russie. Naples was a disappointment in spite of a visit to Pompeii and dinner with an old friend of Robert's, Lady Holland, the sixty-four-year-old widow of the last Lord Holland, who lived there. The smells were terrible, even in Lady Holland's house.

On the 14th Robert, with Colonel Colley and Fred Liddell, went to Sorrento and did not return until the following evening. 'I missed dear R. so much as I always do,' Edith wrote, 'and others have such different manners, different conversation. Everyone is so dull compared to him. Colonel Burne is rather cross to his wife, I think.'

But their next evening, their last, made up for the previous one; they had 'a jolly party' of eleven for dinner. The Pagets had arrived as promised and also Colonel Sir Lewis Pelly who was going to travel with them to India. Sir Lewis had entered the East India Company's service in 1840, since when he had served in India in many capacities. In 1860 he had been sent on a special mission to Eastern Persia, Afghanistan and Baluchistan. He was now Commissioner of the native State of Baroda. With his experience of frontier affairs and a personal knowledge of the Amir of Afghanistan, Sher Ali, it struck Lytton that he would be the ideal person to negotiate a treaty with the Amir. During the voyage to India it was settled that he should undertake this mission.

The next evening, March 16, the Lytton party embarked on the troopship *Orontes* which had been put at the disposal of the Viceroy. Edith was sad to say good-bye to the Pagets. 'Wally was so cheery and pretty and I'm sure she's the last nice woman I shall see for many a long day.'

Unfortunately Edith found no companionship in Mrs Burne, who was cheerless and unresponsive. Edith thought at first that her reserve was the result of shyness, but it did not wear off the whole time she was in India although she and Edith were thrown continually together. Even more unfortunately it was found that she too was expecting and at the very same time as Edith.

After four days of rough weather and consequent seasickness, alleviated for Edith by cayenne pepper with brandy and Apollinaris water, they reached Alexandria on March 21. After a day of sightseeing they went, in four hours, by special train to Cairo. On the 23rd they all went to the Pyramids in a char-à-banc lent by the Khedive, Ismail Pasha, with six horses and two French postillions. Robert went inside one of the Pyramids with the other gentlemen which exhausted him, 'but Colonel Burne kindly got him a nip of brandy and takes such care of him', Edith recorded. 'This act quite touched me, but all are most devoted and spare no amount of labour for our comfort. I never travelled so luxuriously before and shall I fear become very helpless and spoilt.'

Voyage to India

On the 24th the Viceregal party went off early by train to Suez to meet the *Serapis* bringing the Prince of Wales home from India. Ferdinand de Lesseps joined the train at Ismailia. 'It was very interesting seeing the old gentleman [he was seventy-one] who like most Frenchmen never ceased talking and I need hardly say mostly about himself and the canal works of which he may be justly proud.' The Suez Canal had been opened in 1869.

At Suez they returned to the *Orontes*. The *Serapis* did not arrive until early next morning. The Lyttons with Colonel Colley and the Burnes were invited on board for breakfast at nine. Edith 'drest smart'. The Prince was looking very well and was 'most civil and cordial'. He told Edith that she would have to do as much as her husband in India to improve society, for 'he seemed to have found some curious types among the ladies'. After luncheon the Prince had some talk with Lytton with whom he had become well acquainted during visits to Paris, and then passing him over to Sir Bartle Frere (former Governor of Bombay and a member of the Indian Council in London), who had accompanied him to India, himself showed Edith and Mrs Burne over the ship, his own cabins and the menagerie of wild animals he was taking home with him. 'The gentlemen of the staff,' Edith commented, 'seemed very numerous but not overburdened with brains.'

The *Orontes* sailed that evening. The next morning Edith caught sight of some boys being caned which upset her for the rest of the day. Robert wrote a long letter to the Queen from the Red Sea telling her about the meeting with the Prince of Wales, and describing the sea as being 'as smooth as a speech by Mr Gladstone'.[2]

After leaving Aden, where they had spent the day of March 31, Edith made Robert sit at her end of the table at meals 'though the discussions at the other end between Col. Burne and Col. Colley amuse and prevent him from having indigestion'. There was whist every evening on deck at which Sir Lewis Pelly usually revoked, 'a great joke with him'. Robert was extremely fond of whist, though he did not take it seriously and told anecdotes between deals.

The day before they landed at Bombay, thirteen days after leaving Suez, Colonel Colley and Fred Liddell made out the cost of the journey so far; it came to about £700. The Viceroy's salary was £25,000 a year, but he was not expected to be able to save much out of this; indeed, he sometimes had to supplement it from his private income.

The Lyttons were received at Bombay on the morning of Friday, April 7, with Royal Salutes from the Arsenal, and a guard of honour. Lord Napier, the Commander-in-Chief in India who had just retired, Sir Charles Staveley, Commander-in-Chief in Bombay, and the Governor's Military Secretary met them at the dock. They landed through an arch of palms, beyond which was a large red-carpeted area where 'all the rank and fashion of Bombay' were assembled. Cheers from the thronged streets greeted their slow passage in a procession of carriages to Government House at Parell, then a countrified district north of the city. Sir Philip Wodehouse, Governor since 1872 and a widower, was waiting to greet them at the door.

That evening there was a dinner party of sixty, including Lord Napier and Sir Frederick Haines, the new Commander-in-Chief. Lytton stayed up very late talking to Lord Napier who was on his way back to England, and who assured him that the opposition of his Council in Calcutta would not be as great as he feared. Napier was in agreement with the 'forward policy' for Afghanistan and wrote a letter to that effect for the new Viceroy to show to his Council. Sir Frederick Haines, who had only just arrived in India, changed his plan of going straight to Simla in order to accompany Lytton to Calcutta and give him support. The Commander-in-Chief was an *ex officio* member of the Supreme Council.

After two nights in Bombay the Viceroy's party set off in a special train which had been fitted up for the Prince of Wales. Edith had 'a delicious bath which is such a luxury in a train as one never imagined such happiness possible'. She and Robert had 'many little talks during the night and morning'. In spite of the *tatties* on the windows (screens made of grass roots frequently soaked in water) the thermometer went up to 104° the first day. They were informed that there were always coffins on the trains for those who 'expired from heat apoplexy'. Since there were no corridors or restaurant cars, long stops were made at the principal stations where food could be obtained. For the Lyttons, large repasts were provided and the stations red-carpeted and decorated with flags and bunting.

At Jubblepore, where they stopped to have breakfast on the

second day, the Lyttons met Captain William Loch, a nephew of Edith's brother-in-law, Henry Loch, who was stationed there. Robert took a great liking to him, and appointed him to his staff as an extra aide-de-camp.

On the evening of April 10 the special train reached Allahabad, the capital of the North-West Provinces and a place of pilgrimage for the Hindus where the Ganges and Jumna meet. It was an important railway junction. The Viceroy and his party were met by Sir John Strachey, the Lieutenant-Governor of the province, and his wife, with whom they stayed the night. Between Robert and John Strachey there arose the same kind of immediate mutual attraction as had sprung up between Robert and Fitzjames Stephen, who was, as it happened, a great friend of Strachey's. Robert decided straightaway that Strachey was the man he wanted to fill the place on his Council of Sir William Muir, the financial member, who was soon to retire. Strachey had held that post before his promotion in 1873 to the Lieutenant-Governorship.

The most urgent matter the new Viceroy had to deal with in India was a financial crisis, and it was essential to procure a first rate man for his Finance Minister. The value of silver on which the rupee was based had dropped 25% so that the rupee was now worth only 1s. 6d. instead of 2s. in relation to the £. Although it would mean a considerable pecuniary sacrifice on Strachey's part, as well as a drop in status, he agreed to return to the Council, though he could not do so until the end of the year. Years afterwards he told Edith that Robert had so captivated him at their first interview that when he left Allahabad, after only a day's acquaintance, he felt he could refuse him nothing.[3]

The next evening came the sad parting between Robert and Edith. As had been arranged in England, Edith was to go up to Simla while Robert went to Calcutta. He would be joining her in a fortnight's time. In the hot weather the Viceroy and his Councils always moved up to Simla, from where, for five months, the Government of India was conducted. (The local Governors went up to hill stations in their own provinces during the hot weather.)

Dear R. and I said good-bye in his room [Edith wrote in her diary] and then drove alone to the station which was very nice. We settled on a cypher for him to telegraph if he spoke to the Council after being sworn

27

in, and how it went off and he told me he should probably speak and that Sir John Strachey was in favour of it. A little trouble at the station with our two special trains back to back, then I shook hands all round and was bundled into the saloon with the children, bitterly regretting my decision not to have gone to Calcutta which has haunted me ever since and will I fear all my life, but no one would allow it.

4

The New Viceroy

Fred Liddell, Mrs Burne, the children and all the servants, except the coachman and valet who had gone with Robert, went with Edith to Simla. They arrived late the next afternoon at Ambala, a military station in the Punjab where the railway ended. (The railway did not reach Simla until 1903.) The General in command of the station met them; also Captain Jackson, the aide-de-camp taken over from Lord Northbrook. They were lodged in three separate bungalows and were unable to get on with their journey because of torrential rain. Early next morning came a telegram from Robert from Calcutta: 'Rose planted and in full bloom' which meant that he had spoken successfully to his Council. But Edith could think only that this was probably the most important day of her husband's life, and she was not with him.

Edith and her party left Ambala at 2 p.m. on Good Friday, April 14, in three carriages and a char-à-banc, and arrived in four hours at Kalka, thirty-nine miles away at the foot of the hills. Here they found a good *dak* bungalow. These *dak* bungalows were situated all over India for the convenience of travellers where there was no railway. Minimally furnished—the traveller supplied his own bedding and cooking utensils—they varied very much in size and cleanliness. Dr Oliver Barnett, the personal physician whom Robert had appointed, came to Kalka from Simla to escort Edith on the last stages of her journey. He was an army surgeon with the rank of Major. Mrs Burne already knew him and his wife, for he had been Lord Mayo's doctor.

The next morning they set off on the next stage of their journey, climbing all the way to Dharmpur, twenty miles from Kalka. Edith and Mrs Burne went in two *tongas*, small two-wheeled, covered carts drawn by two ponies. Edith sat in front with the driver while Dr Barnett, little Emily and Wellham, the nanny, sat in the back. Mrs

Burne, her elder boy and her manservant went in the second *tonga*.
The other children with the governesses and servants went in
doolies—'exactly like the covered stretchers in which people are
taken to hospital', as Edith described them. Each *doolie* was carried
by four coolies. The occupants could sit up in them but it was more
comfortable lying down. Fred Liddell and Captain Jackson rode
on ponies. The *tonga* drivers blew 'a picturesque horn' as they
wound round the narrow hill road, and the thin little ponies 'got
on capitally'.

At Dharmpur, 4,500 feet above sea level, they spent the morning
of Easter Sunday reading prayers. Here the deodar trees began, and
Edith, to her great delight, heard a cuckoo. The next stop was Solon,
only eight miles from Dharmpur. Edith was very irked at having
to spend another night on the road to Simla after coming such a
short distance and climbing only another four hundred feet. She
was determined to reach Simla next day, though it would be a tiring
stage. They had come only twenty-eight miles from Kalka, and the
total distance between Kalka and Simla was sixty miles. Edith complained that Captain Jackson, who had made all the arrangements,
was very slow. No doubt he was afraid of tiring the two ladies in
their delicate condition. The *dak* bungalow at Solon was full of bugs
(Margy, the nursery-maid, found twelve on her pillow) 'though they
don't bite anything like European gentlemen of the same species',
Edith commented.

But there was compensation at Solon in the arrival of the first
letters from Calcutta. (The post, which came from Ambala in a *tonga*
by *dak* stages, was referred to as the *dak*.) Robert had written on
April 13, having arrived in good health and spirits at six o'clock
the evening before. 'There were not many people in the streets and
no cheering on our way to Government House. The members of
Council to whom I was there introduced were not a very lively crew
and looked I thought as if they would have eaten me without salt.'
They all then went into a small, dark room to which the public were
admitted and Lytton, after being sworn in, delivered his little speech
'to an appallingly frigid audience'.

The new Viceroy had broken all precedents in addressing his
Council immediately on arrival and had thus at once made his
mark for eccentricity. As far as the press was concerned the experi-
ment was highly successful. He merely said in his speech that he

expected co-operation and unflinching firmness for the safety of the Empire, for the progress of the millions of people committed to 'our fostering care' and for the undisturbed enjoyment by native princes and allies beyond the border of 'their just rights and hereditary possessions'.[1]

Robert went on to tell Edith that he had sat up till two talking to Lord Northbrook: 'My impressions of him are much pleasanter than I expected. I don't notice any unusual coldness of manner about him and he has I think received me frankly and kindly.' (Lord Northbrook, a widower, left Calcutta on April 15 with his daughter, Emma Baring, who had acted as his hostess.) 'Government House is magnificent for reception purposes, but I doubt if it be a very comfortable house to live in.' In a subsequent letter he told her that the house was full of cockroaches the size of elephants.

At Solon Edith also received letters from Colonels Burne and Colley. Colley confessed to her that he had not wanted the Viceroy to speak on arrival but was very glad now that he had done so: 'I had not realised either the power or the modulation of his voice before; nor, though I was prepared for beautiful language, was I *quite* prepared for such perfect and easy command.'

The new Viceroy, who felt he was 'treading on eggs at every step', held his first Council meeting on April 20, which went off on the whole satisfactorily. As a first step towards dealing with the financial crisis it was decided to cut down all but essential Government spending, appeal to all the local Governments to make drastic economies, and try to arrange a loan of four million pounds from England.

In a letter to Lord Salisbury, written on the evening of the meeting, Lytton reported that he had obtained the consent of his 'six duennas' to the general policy for Afghanistan. (He did not disclose to them the details of Disraeli's instructions until June.) The co-operation of Sir Frederick Haines had been a great help, as had also Lord Napier's letter in which he had expressed the opinion that the present position in Afghanistan was 'unsafe and humiliating'. Lytton had, therefore, telegraphed to General Sir Richard Pollock, Commander at Peshawar near the North-West Frontier, to meet him at Ambala on his way to Simla. There he would instruct him to write a letter to the Amir, Sher Ali, requesting him to receive Sir Lewis Pelly as head of a mission to Kabul, and inviting him on behalf of the Viceroy to the great Durbar at Delhi at which the Queen was to be proclaimed Empress of India. 'Burne is the greatest comfort and help to me,' he added. 'My gratitude for so kindly sparing me his quite invaluable assistance increases hourly. Colonel Colley too is a great success. He is a decidedly able man, and personally a very pleasant fellow.'[2]

Five days later, Lytton, on his way to Simla, was writing to Salisbury again: 'I am told I have already shocked all the social proprieties at Calcutta, by writing private notes to members of Council, calling on their wives, holding levees by night instead of by day, and other similar heresies against the laws of these Medes and Persians. But I fear I shall have to shock all the official proprieties more severely before long.'[3]

Lytton complained in a letter to Lady Holland that he could never be alone. If he looked through the window of the privatest corner of his private room there were sentinels standing guard over him. If he opened the door there were ten *jemadars* (superior footmen) in red and gold livery crouching on the threshold. If he went up or down stairs an aide-de-camp and 'three unpronounceable beings in white and red nightgowns' rushed after him. If he stole out of the house by the back door he looked round to find himself 'stealthily followed by a tail of fifteen persons'.[4]

Although so protected, the Viceroy was aware of the feeling in the country through the newspapers. In the eighteen years since the Crown had taken over the government of India, two of its most cherished democratic institutions had been introduced into the country—education and a free press. A network of schools and colleges, for the most part financially supported and controlled by the Indian Government and with English principals, was slowly spreading through India, promoting European literature, history and science at the expense of Indian culture. The natives were avidly reading about the *Risorgimento*. More and more newspapers were being started. There were papers in English with English editors, in English with Indian editors, and dozens in vernacular languages. In consequence there had grown up in India for the first time an educated middle class whose voice could be heard in editorials and letters to the various newspapers, and who had become sensitively aware of the racial discrimination practised against them by the British. They felt they were being treated like the natives of Africa, quite unmindful of their glorious civilisations, great rulers, artistic heritage and ancient religious cultures.

The growing number of young men with degrees from Indian universities could never hope to rise above the lowest rungs in the administration of their own country, as tax collectors, magistrates and judges in the lower courts dealing in cases involving only other Indians, for no European would have tolerated a 'nigger' sitting in judgment over him. It was the same in the army; the higher ranks were reserved for the white man. As one newspaper put it: 'If that fine soldier the Emperor Babur, were alive, we should make him a subadur in an infantry regiment, and put over him a public school boy. If the Emperor Akbar offered his services, we should think him abundantly provided for by a writership in one of our offices.'[5]

It is true that by the East India Company Charter Act of 1833, the Covenanted Civil Service,* which virtually ruled India, had been theoretically thrown open to Indians, and the Act had been confirmed in 1858, the year the Government of India was transferred to the Crown, by the Queen's proclamation that 'no native of India by reason only of religion, place of birth, descent, colour, or any of them, would be disabled from holding any office or employment'; but it was almost impossible for Indians to take advantage of this opening. The candidate had to pass an examination and sit for it in England; the papers were geared to an English public school education. If Indians could raise the money to go to England and stay there for the necessary period of coaching before sitting for the examination, they were deterred by the fact that in crossing the ocean they would lose caste and become disgraced in the eyes of their families. Nevertheless, in spite of all the difficulties, seven natives did manage in thirty years to get to England and pass the examination; whereupon the authorities stopped this loophole by reducing the age for passing the examination from twenty-one to nineteen. The truth was that the Covenanted Civil Service (called simply the Indian Civil Service), consisting then of 914 members including the seven natives, which had become the highest paid Civil Service in the world, had no intention of allowing Indians into

---

* So called because in the early days of the East India Company the Civil Servants had been so badly paid that they had had to augment their incomes by trading; Lord Cornwallis had introduced a reform whereby they were adequately paid but had to enter into a covenant on joining the Service not to engage in trade or accept presents.

their jealously guarded preserves any more than into their social clubs. They had difficulty enough in getting into the Service themselves. In 1870 there had been 325 candidates for forty vacancies.

Another grievance among Indians was that in the much larger uncovenanted or subordinate Civil Service to which they did have entrance they were not given the same pay as Europeans for doing the same job. The British Government argued that Europeans needed higher salaries to tempt them to go and live in a faraway unhealthy country with an atrocious climate. The Indians countered this by demanding why, in that case, employ Europeans? Why not employ more natives and thereby save Indian revenue?

The Liberal Press in England was also at this time stressing the right of the natives to take a larger share in the administration of their country. Lord Northbrook had tried, unsuccessfully, to introduce more Indians into the Covenanted Service. Many of the articles in the Indian papers were but copies of the English ones. The vernacular press was, of course, particularly vociferous in its demands for equality, and through these local papers in translation the Government of India was able to gauge native feeling in the country—a very valuable source of information for them.

The new Viceroy had come to India hoping to succeed above all where Lord Northbrook had failed, in opening the Covenanted Service to more Indians, either by dispensing in their case with the examination in England in favour of selection by the local Governments with the approval of the Governor-General in Council, or by holding the examination in India, but he soon realised the utter impossibility of getting Europeans to serve willingly under Indians. Nevertheless, the Government had made promises to the people of India which must be fulfilled, so some solution would have to be found.

Soon after Lytton's arrival in Calcutta an instance of grave injustice to a native came to his notice. A Mr Fuller, a barrister at Agra, setting out for church with his family on October 31, 1875, had found that his *syce* (native coachman) was absent, having deputed another man to drive in his place. Mr Fuller sent for the *syce*, and without waiting to find out the cause of his absence, struck him with his open hand on the head and face and pulled his hair, causing him to fall down. The man managed to crawl to a nearby compound where he immediately collapsed and died. The postmortem examination revealed that he had died of a ruptured spleen. Mr Fuller was brought before the Joint Magistrate of Agra, a Mr Leeds, convicted of 'voluntarily causing what distinctly amounts to a hurt' and fined thirty rupees, about fifty shillings, or fifteen days' imprisonment. The fine was, of course, paid and made over to the *syce's* widow in full compensation for her loss. Upon this, a native journal commented that, in the eyes of British justice in India, the life of a native was apparently valued at Rs.30. When this remark came to the notice of the Home Department of the Government, it asked the local Government of the North-West Provinces, in which Agra was situated, to institute an enquiry into the matter. The local Government merely turned it over to the High Court at Allahabad which ruled that although the sentence was perhaps a little too light it did not call for further notice.

It was this ruling that was brought to Lytton's attention and it seemed to him that if the matter were allowed to drop, the honour and credit of British rule would drop with it. In consequence, after consulting his legal department and with the consent of his Council, he published in the Government Gazette a severe minute censuring Mr Leeds for his want of judgment and judicial capacity in summarily dealing with the case, and desiring that he would not be employed in any higher office for at least a year. Lytton also censured the Government of the North-West Provinces (although Sir John Strachey was Lieutenant-Governor of that province) for originally allowing the case to pass without notice, and the High Court for deeming their duties and responsibilities adequately discharged by the expression of an opinion and for not asking for a full investigation.[6] Part of the minute read: 'The Governor-General in Council expresses his abhorrence of the practice, instances of which occasionally come to light, of European masters treating their servants in a manner in which they would not treat men of their own race.'[7] Such a round of reproofs had never before been issued by any Governor-General to the Indian Civil Service.

Lytton wrote to the Queen that his minute had 'provoked the anger of nearly all the English journals in India, who attribute it to a sentimental impulse of maudlin philanthropy, and denounce it as a libel on the English in India. On the other hand it is hailed with satisfaction by the whole of the native press.'[8] In replying to this letter on behalf of the Queen, General Ponsonby, her Private

Secretary, wrote that her Majesty 'rejoiced' that the Viceroy had 'thus put a check on the conduct of the rough Anglo-Indians towards the natives'. General Ponsonby went on, 'From those I have spoken to I find the impression exists that you were acting in excess of your powers in censuring the High Court but they are uncommonly glad you have done so.'[9]

The Allahabad High Court sent a letter of protest to the Viceroy, pointing out that he could not legally interfere with the exercise of the Court's judicial discretion, and asking for the whole matter to be referred to the Secretary of State's arbitrament. Lord Salisbury supported Lytton's views on the grounds that Indian judges held office 'during Her Majesty's pleasure, instead of, as in England, during good behaviour'.[10] Feeling in England was, for the most part, sympathetic to Lytton. *The Times* went so far as to announce: 'We are glad to hear that the Secretary of State supports Lord Lytton's famous minute on the Fuller Case.'[11] The Indian Civil Service, however, never forgave him for his interference with the judiciary, and the whole of Anglo-Indian society considered that he had let the side down. He received several letters from Fitzjames Stephen criticising his minute and advising him to try to conciliate the Civil Service. It was no doubt Stephen's influence that induced Lytton to remove the restriction on Mr Leeds's promotion.

An American in India three years later, travelling with General Grant, ex-President of the United States, wrote about the case:

I cannot exaggerate the feeling which the incident caused. I heard about it in every part of India we visited. Even from the case as presented by critics of the Viceroy, it seemed a noble thing to do.... When you read the history of India, its sorrow, its shame, its oppression, its wrong, it is grateful to see a Viceroy resolved to do justice to the humblest at the expense of his popularity with the ruling class.[12]

5

Simla

The hill station of Simla in the Punjab was a small British enclave surrounded by native States. 7,000 to 8,000 feet above sea level it runs west to east along a narrow, crescent-shaped ridge five miles long, bounded to the west by Observatory Hill and to the east by the higher Jacko Hill. Along the ridge are smaller hills—'bunched up into little tops like hills on a map' as Edith described them—among which, at that time, nearly four hundred European houses were situated, clinging to the hillsides wherever a ledge could be found safe enough to withstand a landslide or tropical storm.* The town itself, stretching for about a mile along the saddle of the ridge, consisted of one main street, the Mall, ending at the church (Christchurch, consecrated in 1857), and, on a lower level, a native bazaar. After Simla had become the summer capital of the Supreme Government in 1863, good shops had appeared on the Mall. There were also a couple of hotels, a club, a library, a bank, a town hall, a post office, assembly rooms for concerts, a theatre for amateur theatricals and a hall for the new popular sport of 'rinking' (roller skating).

The widest part of the saddle was in front of the church, and here parades were held. Most of the Mall was, however, so narrow that there was room for only two horses abreast, and no carriages were allowed in the Mall except those of the Viceroy, the Commander-in-Chief and the Lieutenant-Governor of the Punjab. The rest of the inhabitants walked, rode on ponies or went in *jampans*, boat-shaped sedan chairs fitted with curtains and carried on poles

---

* When Edwin Lutyens, the architect of New Delhi, went to Simla in 1912, he wrote, 'The hills and depths below are heroic, the building and conception of the place by the Public Works Department is beyond the beyond and if one was told the monkeys had built it all, one could only say, "What wonderful monkeys—they must be shot in case they do it again." ' (Hussey, p. 254.)

by four coolies (*jampanees*), and reported to be miserably un-comfortable.

The hillsides were thickly wooded with deodars and rhododen-dron trees as large as oaks, in bloom when Edith Lytton arrived. To the north were vistas of the Himalayan ranges, while to the south one looked down the precipitous mountain-side to the plains. The climate was not very good; fires and furs were needed in April; it became very hot in May when a particularly unpleasant kind of bit-ing fly appeared, and so dry and dusty before the rains came at the end of June that zero humidity had been recorded. The rains, lasting until the end of September, were not continuous but so heavy that there were few houses which did not leak, and always a few were swept away each year in a landslide. Twelve hundred feet below the ridge on the north side was a wide valley called Allandale where there was a racecourse and cricket and archery grounds, and where gymkhanas and fêtes were held.

Government House was then an ordinary country house called Peterhof, rented from the Maharaja of Simur, on a little hill-top to the west of the town near the beginning of the *tonga* road. Edith and her party arrived there from Solon on April 17, nine days before Robert joined her. From the *tonga* stop, Edith and the other occu-pants of the *tongas* had to be carried up to Peterhof in *jampans* since the road to the house had collapsed. Edith was delighted with the house which she described as like an old English rectory except for the wide verandahs. The furniture was 'hideous stuff but still old English shapes'. She was most appreciative too of the beautiful views. There was just enough level ground for a lawn in front of the house. Bungalows for the staff were dotted about close by on the hillside. The elder girls would have to be carried each day in a *doolie* to their lessons, for there were only five bedrooms and the governesses were in a separate bungalow.

Edith was tried on first arriving by having to make all the arrange-ments for the house through Captain Jackson, the Household aide-de-camp, whom she found 'rather indifferent how things are done, though good natured and anxious'. When she discovered that he could not speak French she succeeded to her joy in being allowed to discuss the meals herself with Lemercier, the chef they had brought with them. The roses were over by the time she arrived and there were only a few geraniums; the gardeners, however, arranged the wild flowers so beautifully in saucers for the dinner table that all she had to do was to approve.

In her first letter home to Lizey Loch, her twin, Edith confessed how dreadfully disappointed she was with Miss Partridge. The governess had been encouraged to sing on the voyage out although 'her style was very disagreeable' and had become 'so forward, cocky and tiresome'. She was so selfish too with the children, thinking more of her own pleasure than of theirs. She spoke to the gentlemen as though they ought to wait on her as they did on Edith and Mrs Burne. Fred Liddell 'felt it very much', and none of the staff could bear her except for 'good kind little Mademoiselle' who got on with everyone. Edith was getting on rather better with Mrs Burne since they had parted from their husbands—'Colonel Burne sits on her and squashes her'—but the improvement was to be short-lived. The Burnes were to occupy the house they had had in Lord Mayo's time—Beatsonia, a little distance away—but were to have their meals at Peterhof. Unfortunately Betty and Conny did not like the Burne boys who were of the same ages—they were 'so spoilt and muffy'.

Edith described Fred Liddell to Lizey as 'very nice in lots of ways, but rather loungey, dull and Liddelly and selfish'. When Colonel Colley arrived Fred was going to share a house with him called Inverarm on a little hill just above Peterhof. Edith hoped that the 'conversation of a cultivated well read man' (Colley was also an excellent amateur artist) would 'bring Fred out'. She wrote in a joint letter home:

The ladies are like that of any garrison town, Folkestone or Dover. The native servants *try* me very much, they smell so very strong when hot—like squashed bugs—but our own here have more on (red tunics with gold braid) and smell less strong. The other trial is that there is no such thing as a W.C. in India so that at Calcutta and everywhere we shall only have horrid night tables—there are always little bathrooms for them, but still it is horrid. Otherwise the ways are far more English than I have been used to.

The 'night tables', or commodes, were, of course, emptied by the 'sweepers' (the untouchables) or else by native Christians.

In her next letter Edith told Lizey that she received from two to three o'clock which was very unpopular, for the usual hour was from one to two, but everyone came, and by receiving in the afternoon she could be sure of getting some gentlemen who seemed to be a better type than the ladies. She complained that the present fashion in dress, with the tunics made so tight and fitted to the skirts, was not at all good for ladies over twenty, certainly not for those 'in the family way'. She was getting to like Dr Barnett 'rather better' but wished she did not have to have him for her confinement. A doctor in Calcutta had engaged a very good nurse for her. She ended this letter by saying that she was flattered to hear that Fred Liddell had praised her: 'I am afraid I am very open to a little butter. I can't fancy being at all popular here, the ladies are not at all my style, either so dowdy or fast.'

At last the happy day came, April 26, when Robert arrived at Simla. At eleven Edith was told not to go out of the house before he had been received by Sir Henry Davies, Lieutenant-Governor of the Punjab; then it was suddenly announced that he was *coming*. She had heard the horn of the *tonga* driver, but before she could get her hat from her bedroom he was with her, for he had walked up to the house with Colonel Colley by a short cut, avoiding, to his great delight, all the ceremonial of his official reception. This could not have endeared him to Sir Henry Davies. 'Oh, what happiness it was to have my darling again,' Edith wrote, 'and to get some good talks.'

Robert had been suffering from incessant nausea for the last week in Calcutta and during the journey, and he was still feeling far from well. Nevertheless, he had achieved his object at Ambala by sending off by a native agent a gracious, tactful and friendly letter to the Amir asking him to receive a mission headed by Sir Lewis Pelly with the object of entering into negotiations that it was hoped would end in a satisfactory treaty. Nothing was said at this stage about the establishment of a permanent British Resident in Afghanistan. The letter was ostensibly written by Sir Richard Pollock.

On his way up to Simla, Lytton had visited Patiala, one of the Sikh States close to Ambala. He felt very strongly the need to win the confidence and loyalty of the Indian princes, and this he hoped to do, not only by visiting their States and receiving them at the Viceregal Court, but by inviting them to the great assemblage at Delhi at which he was to proclaim Queen Victoria Empress of India.

Simla

'I have personally called it an Imperial Assemblage instead of a Durbar,' he wrote to the Prince of Wales, 'because it will materially and essentially differ from all previous Durbars, besides being on a much vaster scale.'[1] Not only would he treat the princes magnificently but impress them with the might of the Empress. Memories of the Mutiny were still raw after only eighteen years. The self-confidence of the British in India had been badly shaken; they were aware of an undercurrent of intense hatred among Indians for British rule. The British army in India, although half as large again as the army in England, was a tiny force compared to the vast population. The princes all had private armies, and if their loyalty could be counted on, the *Raj* would feel far more secure. 'Here is a great feudal aristocracy,' Lytton told Disraeli, 'which we cannot get rid of, which we are avowedly anxious to conciliate, but which we have as yet done nothing to rally round the British crown as its feudal head.'[2] He wrote to the Queen that he was all the more anxious to hold the Delhi Assemblage since the opposition to the Royal Titles Bill, and had fixed the day for January 1, 1877. He had found that the opposition to the Bill had had a rather mischievous effect in India which he hoped to be able to counteract.[3]

The dry climate of Simla did not agree with Robert and he felt as ill there as he had felt in the steamy heat of Calcutta, and was unable to eat any solid food for several weeks after his arrival. Moreover, he was disgusted with Peterhof. He described it to Salisbury as 'a hideous little bungalow, horribly out of repair and wretchedly uncomfortable', as well as being ten times too small for its purpose. The minor Raja from whom it was rented was not prepared to spend a penny on it, yet the rent was £2,000 a year. In addition, £400 had to be spent regularly every year on repairs, although the rain continued to come through the roof and the kitchen was 'a cow stable'. However, when Salisbury authorised him to spend £100,000 on improvements at Simla, he declared it would be impossible in the present state of Indian finances to spend anything like such a sum when the Supreme Government was preaching retrenchment to all the local Governments. Besides, he was convinced that every sixpence spent on Simla beyond what was absolutely necessary was a waste; nothing would do but a new summer capital. The roads in Simla had to be mended every week in the

41

rainy season; the ladies had to choose between being shaken to a jelly in a horrible palanquin or risk being pitched over a precipice by a pony. And to crown it all Simla was not even on British territory: 'The whole Government of India is the tenant of its smallest feudatories.'[4]

Lytton had taken on in Calcutta another of Lord Northbrook's aides-de-camp, this time one recommended by the Prince of Wales—Lord William Beresford, brother of the Marquess of Waterford, a Captain in the 9th Lancers, who loved everything to do with horses. Colonel Colley had described him in a letter to Edith as 'full of fun and full of go, and immensely delighted at being placed in charge of the stables'. He had already procured two capital ponies for the girls, and almost the first thing he did on arriving at Simla was to teach them to ride. He became a great favourite with all the Lytton family and was so delightful to the children, as was also Colonel Colley, that Edith feared they would be spoilt.

Disraeli had asked Lytton before he left England whether he would, as a personal favour, take on to his staff young Harcourt Rose, son of Sir Philip Rose, who had been a member of Lord Napier's staff. On arriving in Calcutta Lytton reported to the Prince of Wales:

Captain Rose has returned to England invalided and is not likely to resume service in consequence of an extraordinary accident: the bite of a donkey had reduced him to a condition that would be a very appropriate and appreciated qualification for employment in any other Oriental Court, but which is discouraged by the British Government of India. The story is a strange one and I am quite unable to understand how the donkey could have perpetrated such an assault on the Captain.[5]

In spite of this accident it was not long before Captain Rose returned to India and joined the Viceregal Court at Simla. Edith described him as 'such a muff but a very good whist player'. Captain William Loch from Jubblepore also soon joined the staff and to Edith's joy was put in charge of the Household instead of Captain Jackson and 'managed everything to perfection'. Lytton treated his staff without any formality, as part of his family, and welcomed them to have all their meals at Peterhof. They would play 'Consequences' with the children to peals of laughter. Apart from Captain Jackson who remained Lord Northbrook's man (Robert called him 'a Trojan horse'), Lytton's staff all became personally devoted to him and to Edith.

*   *   *   *   *

The members of the Viceroy's Executive and Legislative Councils were now at Simla with their wives and families, and the first Executive Council meeting at Peterhof was held on May 10. The Commander-in-Chief, Sir Frederick Haines, who had his own staff and grand establishment at Woodville, east of the town, also attended as an *ex-officio* member. Work went on at Simla just the same as in Calcutta. The Private and Military Secretaries had their own staff and offices at the bottom of the Peterhof hill; Colonel Burne ran a small printing press, and Edith was astonished how the native clerks managed to read any hand-writing, however difficult, without understanding a word of the language, and print the words with perfect correctness.

The great excitement of the week was the arrival of the English mail, though it took Robert the whole day and most of the night to read and answer letters. He normally worked from nine to six and again from after dinner until the small hours. Sometimes he had as many as forty Government boxes a day to deal with. He described the Government of India as 'a despotism of office-boxes tempered by the occasional loss of keys'.[6]

Samuel Butler wrote that life is like playing a violin solo in public and learning the instrument as one goes on. Likewise, a Viceroy as ignorant of Indian affairs and Indian history as Lytton, had to learn about that vast continent at the same time as governing it. British Prime Ministers have an ingrained background knowledge of their own history and people; those people have the same religion, speak the same language and share the same customs and ways of thought as themselves. India, on the other hand, was an amalgam of different races, religions, cultures and languages, all totally alien to the new Viceroy, and, in spite of the local Governments, he was ultimately responsible for all that went on under his rule, not only in British India but in the native States, in one or other of which there was always some trouble. At the same time he had to fill the ceremonial role of a monarch. It is true that the Viceroy was not a political appointment so that he was not responsible to Parliament, but he was responsible to the Secretary of State for India; therefore every step he took had to be approved not only by his own Council but by the Indian Council in London. This entailed the writing of long detailed weekly dispatches to the India Office on an extraordinary variety of subjects. (Fitzjames Stephen told Lytton that his minutes were as carefully written as an article in the *Fortnightly Review*.) On top of this there were long private letters to be written in longhand for every mail to Lord Salisbury and the Queen as well as to friends. The pressure on the Viceroy and the amount of work he had to get through were unending.

Lytton received less help from his advisers than he had hoped for. After he had been in India less than a month he told John Morley that he thought the 'general ability' of the Civil Service was 'overrated'. 'They look at everything from a small local point of view.'[7] He had already formed two strong impressions of Indian affairs which he communicated to Stephen—'first, that the whole administrative system is too much centralised in every department, and secondly, that the provincial jealousies and rivalries of our Civil Service here are lamentable'. He described the members of his own Council as 'a rummy lot as the Devil said of the Ten Commandments'.[8]

If I had only health I should feel a great and quite unexpected confidence in myself, proportional perhaps to my great disappointment in the intellectual calibre not only of my immediate councillors, but also of almost every representative of the official class in India, with whom I have yet come in contact. I came here with the most profound respect, which is rapidly changing into the lowest estimate of the ability of these men. Our politicians must, I fancy, have greatly deteriorated of late years. I find myself obliged to correct almost every draft written by my Political Department [part of the Foreign Department], and many of the drafts written in the Financial Department [this was before Strachey had become Finance Minister], and as to our frontier officers, they seem to me to be worthless.[9]

Stephen agreed that the number of first-rate or even second-rate men in India was lamentably small. 'I think I told you, you would have to do some first-rate work with fourth-rate tools. You must never forget that nineteen civilians in twenty are the most commonplace and the least dignified of Englishmen. They are in India ten times more fidgety and peppery about their dignity and independence than they are in England.'[10]

Towards the end of May the Lyttons took a cottage for the season called The Gables at the village of Mashroba, five miles from the eastern extremity of the Simla ridge. Robert felt much better there where the air was not so dry; they could take Betty and Conny with them and get away from Friday to Sunday from the dreary social life of Simla. As Robert wrote to Lady Salisbury:

I do miss the pleasant scamps and scampesses of pleasant France. I don't agree with Schiller that if virtue were a woman all the world would fall in love with her. Of course we are nearer heaven up here than you down there at the bottom of Arlington Street; but being of the earth earthy, I envy you the pleasure of living among so many naughty people. Our own social surroundings here are so grievously good. Members of Council and heads of departments hold prayer meetings at each other's houses thrice a week, and spend the rest of their time in writing spiteful minutes against each other. The young ladies are not allowed to dance lest they dance to perdition; and I believe moonlight picnics were forbidden last year by order of the Governor-General in Council lest they should lead to immorality. I wish I could report that our Empire was as well guarded as our piety.[11]

A large open-sided, flat-roofed tent called a *shemiana* had now been erected on the lawn outside Peterhof in which to hold receptions. On May 26 the Viceroy received in state (or in Durbar as state receptions were called) the Maharaja of Jaipur from Rajputana, one of the richest, most important and westernised of the Hindu princes, and a Grand Commander of the Order of the Star of India. Lytton returned the visit next day, and the Maharaja came again to Peterhof on two other evenings. On the 27th a levee (attended only by gentlemen) was held and a dinner party given, both in honour of the Queen's birthday. They went off satisfactorily although Robert was again suffering from such nausea that it was feared his health might break down altogether. 'There is nothing organic in his illness,' Edith told Lizey, 'and it all seems chiefly irritation of the mucous membrane which makes him retch at all food and before meals also. I do hope he will give up smoking altogether.'

On May 30 the Lyttons gave their first Viceregal ball, also in honour of the Queen's birthday. The day before, Colonel Colley and Edith had planned how to make the rooms look more cheerful. They decided to have white calico curtains made, edged with bands of red silk, and to cover the existing dirty Japanese wallpaper with panels of yellow calico. In each panel was hung a looking-glass and 'branches of candles' they had borrowed, and the cornices were decorated with large bows of red silk in festoons. Edith's maid, Oswald (Ozzie), the nanny, Wellham, as well as twelve tailors and Edith herself worked at the wall coverings and curtains all day; Colonel Colley and Captain Rose hung the calico, and everything was just finished by eight o'clock on the evening of the ball.

But the day had been more agitating in another way. In the morning there had been a consultation with Dr Barnett and another military surgeon, Dr Bellow, who were firm in their opinion that if the Viceroy did not give up cigarettes and wine and go on a strict diet he would be seriously ill when the rains came; his heart was becoming weak from continual retching. This made Edith miserable all day, especially as she herself was suffering from bad neuralgia. She described the ball in a letter home:

We dined upstairs. The people were asked for half-past nine, and soon after ten the whole staff came to fetch us and walked before us which was very grand and made me rather shy, at the same time inclined to giggle. We went straight to the Ballroom where R. danced the first Quadrille and I had a chair to look on as I was not going to wriggle across a Quadrille and look ridiculous. I wore my Worth red Ball gown as being rather old fashioned it didn't expose one's figure so. The verandah was covered and not much light for the flirting couples to go and sit. We went to supper at half-past twelve [served in the *shemiana*]. One big centre table held 18—then there were 16 little round tables and it looked very well as there must have been 150 there at once. There were 300 asked to the Ball but I don't think more than 250 came in all and there were not more than 200 at the supper time. *Private* What spoilt all to me though were the people—Oh what a contrast to the foreign societies we have been in—so vulgar, so badly drest, so cold, so flat, and dancing so badly, it made me feel so low after as it will be *so difficult* to congregate them often.

It was only the unmarried girls for whom there were fears of dancing 'to perdition'. The married women had almost complete freedom. Edith was evidently writing about the women, rather than the men, whom she had previously described as being either dowdy or fast. It was the great age of the 'Memsahib' which lasted until the end of British rule in India. Since the opening of the Suez Canal in 1869, which had cut 4,500 miles off the voyage to India, more and more British women were coming to share their husbands' lives in this alien land, bringing with them their prejudices and inappropriate customs. The Memsahib did far more than her husband to create social barriers between the British and the people of India— or, as they were usually referred to in those days, the Europeans and the natives. (A half-caste was then called an Eurasian. Anglo-Indians were the British who lived in India.) As Lytton was to find out for himself, the gap was rapidly widening between the natives and their British rulers. 'The moral prejudice and middle class propriety of the later Indian administrators,' he was to write, 'have practically put an end to the illicit connection between the British officials and native women which was formerly almost universal, and have thus destroyed one of the few, and, at the same time one of the strongest channels of social intercourse, and sympathy, left open to a conquering race.'[12] The moral prejudice and middle-class propriety had been brought to India by these British wives whom Edith described as 'so vulgar, so cold, so flat'.

Perhaps the reason why all the people invited did not turn up at the ball was because an order had gone out from the Lord Chamberlain's Office in London to the effect that ladies at Viceregal evening parties were in future to wear trains. This order was strongly criticised by the Calcutta *Statesman* in an editorial which regarded it as most inconsiderate on the part of Lord and Lady Lytton since it would involve an outlay of Rs. 1,000 for a man with a wife and two daughters. 'Lord Lytton is no popularity-hunter,' the article went on. 'The charm of his manner springs from the heart of the man, and captivates all who have any intercourse with him, and it is most unwise of those about the Viceregal Court to do anything to create an impression that it is all manner, and that there is no real consideration for others therein.' The order was soon modified and the wearing of trains became voluntary. The Lyttons had not instigated the order but they were in favour of it.

Poor Robert, who had had to get through the ball without a cigarette or a glass of champagne, went off next day to Mashroba without Edith to try to carry out the regime ordered by the doctors. On his return he and Edith started giving theatrical parties at Peterhof, and a band played at dinner which helped conversation; moreover, Edith introduced the innovation of having several small tables at dinner parties instead of one large one which 'worked much better'. The Lyttons were the first Viceregal couple to bring some style and glamour to Simla.

By the middle of June they had made a lawn tennis court at Peterhof which also helped their social life. It amused Edith to see at the various dinners they gave and parties they attended how English people flirted in comparison with 'the foreigners who never dared speak for five minutes for fear of being noticed in public, but here all the Verandahs are filled with *couples*, and the quietest married ladies sit out dances as a matter of course, and it is all quite innocent I should think'. She ended this letter with the surprising comment: 'They dance 3 *temps* valse here, is that not very funny? I am sure in England that is not done.'

Edith regularly attended the Popular Monday concerts at the Assembly Rooms. She did all she could while she was in India to raise the tone of music among Anglo-Indians. She had brought out from England 'a good new Broadwood piano', but since it was difficult to keep it out of a draught it was seldom in tune. Nevertheless, she found a lady to play duets with her and would accompany anyone willing to sing. Colonel Burne and Fred Liddell both had good voices, but Miss Partridge, who was more willing than anyone, seems to have been more often out of tune than the piano.

Robert encouraged the theatricals, both at Peterhof and at the Gaiety Theatre where the amateur Dramatic Society of Simla performed, and opened the Fine Art Exhibition, the most important annual event at Simla, which was held at Peterhof that year. Although he did not shoot or indulge in any other form of sport—he did not even play tennis—there was one outdoor activity he had always enjoyed immensely—the sending up of fire balloons. The first one he tried at Simla was a failure; the second, made by him and Fred Liddell and sent up from Inverarm, Colonel Colley's house, was such a success that it could be seen for twenty minutes. One *jemadar* became so expert at making them that he was given the title of Balloon Jemadar. Edith noted in after years that 'R. used to be quite superstitious about the balloons sent up while in India,

thinking, if they started off well, the official work would be successful, and cheerful or depressed according to the ascent'.

*   *   *   *   *

On June 5 the Amir's reply to the Viceroy's letter eventually reached
Simla. It was a rejection of all Lytton's friendly advances. Sher Ali
asserted that he could not receive a British mission without receiving
a Russian one, and that, moreover, he could not guarantee the safety
of any British officer through his territory. The invitation to the
Delhi Assemblage was ignored. This snub, wholly unexpected,
brought home to Lytton the extent to which relations between the
Amir and the Government of India had deteriorated since Sher Ali
had attended the durbar at Ambala in 1869 when Lord Mayo was
Viceroy.

At his next Council meeting the Viceroy disclosed the details of
the instructions he had received from Disraeli, the most important
of which being the insistence on the Amir's reception of a permanent
British mission either at Kabul or Herat, though this was not as
yet to be revealed to Sher Ali. Three members of the Council (Sir
William Muir, the financial member who was soon to retire, and
two others who, like Muir, were disciples of Lord Lawrence) dissented from this policy on the grounds that Sher Ali was acting
within his rights in refusing to receive even a temporary British mission; but the Commander-in-Chief together with the other three
members made up a majority in favour of it, and Pollock was instructed to send another letter to the Amir. It was a long flowery
letter, written by Lytton, the punch coming only at the end: 'It
will . . . cause the Viceroy sincere regret if your Highness, by hastily
rejecting the hand of friendship now frankly held out to you, should
render nugatory the friendly intention of His Excellency and oblige
him to regard Afghanistan as a State which has voluntarily isolated
itself from the alliance and support of the British Government.'[13]

The three dissenters on the Council disapproved of this passage
in the letter, considering it to be almost a declaration of war, which
was probably the reason why it was not dispatched until July 8.
At the same time instructions were sent to the native British agent
at Kabul to notify the Amir that the Viceroy would be willing to
meet him in person in November at Peshawar, the British station
in the Punjab close to the Khyber Pass; and the invitation to the

Imperial Assemblage was repeated. Lytton wrote about the situation:

The Ameer, and his whole durbar, having apparently come to the conviction that there is nothing more to be got, and nothing more to be feared, from us, are, at this moment, to all appearances, completely under Russian influence—not from love, but from fear; and Afghanistan has slipped out of our sleepy hands. Whether we can recover, and consolidate, our influence at Cabul is now the question. My great difficulty in working that question has been my own Council: a heavy impediment to my policy; for I found them in a state of abject, and to me unaccountable, terror of doing or saying anything that might offend Shere Ali,—their only notion of a policy being to conceal, as long as possible, the thorough rottenness of the whole situation.[14]

Lytton received three more native princes at Peterhof in July, each time with great state, a guard of honour and the band playing. One of them, the Raja of Nabha, whose Sikh State was to the west of Patiala, a handsome man of thirty-three, with beard and upturned moustaches and beautiful great emeralds in his turban, had a house at Simla where he gave a lavish ball. Another, the Maharaja of Bhurtpore, a Rajput, with a poetical turn of mind, arrived soaking wet from an unexpected downpour. Lytton lent him his father's purple velvet dressing-gown, which was very precious to him, to wear while his own clothes were drying; assuming it to be a gift the Maharaja was too polite to take it off and went away in it. It had to be recovered next day at aide-de-camp level.

Edith and Mrs Burne, who were both expecting their babies about August 20, were getting very large by this time. 'It is absurd both of us being such a size,' Edith wrote, 'and I'm afraid the gents among themselves must joke a great deal.' She complained that Mrs Burne did not have much life or pluck; she was so dull, never getting beyond the question and answer stage; she did not talk to Robert at meals or draw him out.

There were only two women at Simla attractive enough for Robert to enjoy flirting with—Mrs Batten and Mrs Plowden (see pp. 98 and 155). Edith wrote home about the latter when describing the last ball they gave that season at Peterhof on July 27: 'Mrs Plowden's dress was very outré with a lovely water lily stuck just where she ought to sit, but it was pretty though she and a few others had great difficulty curtseying in the Lancers, and I can understand the story from England of the dress splitting and nothing being found underneath but a pair of *tights*.'

Since Robert now had lumbago added to his other ailments, it was arranged that after a few days at Mashroba with Edith and the children, he should set off on a little tour into the hills to Narkanda, 9,000 feet above sea level and seventy-five miles north-east of Mashroba. Edith was feeling exceptionally well, and he expected to be back in plenty of time for her confinement. Conny and Emily were also well but Betty looked like 'bad seakale' and all the English servants were indisposed in one way or another. Edith loved being at Mashroba because she saw more of Robert there. 'My talks with R. are my greatest joy,' she wrote, 'and I get a good many over everything and always try and cheer him—but he has foolish longings and yearnings for Knebworth.' They were both enjoying Emily Eden's letters at this time, and Robert was following the Bravo Case in England with intense interest. (This was one of the most intriguing poisoning mysteries of all times about which several books have been written.)

Robert set off for Narkanda on August 2 in torrential rain with Colonels Burne and Colley and two aides-de-camp while Edith returned sadly to Simla with the children. She was thankful that Lord William Beresford, 'always so cheery', had been left behind to look after her. Robert wrote to her every day. He was having no meat or wine and was doing his best to give up smoking. (He did not succeed in giving it up nor did he give up wine for more than a week.)

On Sunday, August 6, Edith received a telegram with the news that Lizey Loch had been safely delivered of a daughter. Edith was tearful with joy and went to church with her heart full. Perhaps it was the proverbial empathy between identical twins that brought on the birth of her baby almost a fortnight before it was expected and while Robert was still absent, though on his way back. As Edith's nurse, Mrs West, had not yet arrived from Calcutta she had the help of the nurse engaged for Mrs Burne. The pains came on badly on the evening of August 8, and at half past two in the afternoon of the 9th she was screaming for chloroform which was given to her by Dr Barnett, rather too much at first and not enough at the end, but it was 'a great help', and at 3.15 '*Master* baby came yelling into the world with only one long last pain'.

Lord William galloped twenty-six miles to take the news to Robert at Fagu and was sent galloping back again with a note: 'Oh, my darling, I am so rejoiced by the good news. God be thanked! God bless you both my dear wife and my dear son. Your happy and loving R.'

Robert arrived back at Peterhof the next afternoon, and he and Edith talked for over an hour, discussing everything, even the Bravo Case. This was the first baby that Edith was not to nurse herself; her official engagements made it impossible. She had an abundance of milk which was very painful, and she was dreadfully upset when Robert told her that the native *dai* (wet-nurse) was outside, 'a horrid dirty woman with a baby'.

Everything seemed to go wrong after that. A week before the baby was born Margy, the nursery-maid, had gone down with fever which was diagnosed as typhoid; a week later Wellham, the nanny, also went down with it, and then Robert's valet, Henry Green, though he did not have it so severely. Margy in particular was desperately ill for several weeks. Her temperature went up to over 106° and she was often 'raving'. The children, looked after by Edith's maid, Ozzie, and an ayah, moved up to Inverarm, Colonel Colley's house. Dr Barnett's kindness at this time and care of the invalids whom he visited twice a day, completely reconciled Edith to him and thereafter she became very fond of him.

Then Miss Partridge fell ill, though not seriously. Edith considered this very selfish of her, for she had brought it on herself by staying out late at night. But far worse, Captain Loch, suffering from an enlarged liver, had to go home. Captain Jackson became Household aide-de-camp again.

Edith remained in bed for the customary month, her convalescence overshadowed by deep anxiety. At one moment it was feared that Conny too had caught the fever. Robert also went to live at Inverarm which was considered a much healthier situation. Peterhof had been built on the site of an old graveyard and there may have been something in the rumour that it had been a plague spot. Robert felt much better at Inverarm as well as finding it easier to work there. His trip to Narkanda seems to have done him good in every way and to have cured his nausea. He visited Edith for only half an hour a day and she felt sad and isolated without him and without her baby whom she scarcely saw, and with the continuing anxiety over Margy and Wellham. Moreover, Mrs West was a failure—she was fat, slow and untidy. And then the rains went on and on, and Simla was as dreary as any other mountain resort enveloped in cloud. The Peterhof roof leaked and great chunks of plaster fell off the bedroom ceiling. No wonder Edith wrote to Lizey, 'Everything seems so joyless this time.'

Colonel Colley had been sent to the hill station of Raniket to see whether it would make a suitable summer capital for the Government instead of Simla. When he returned on August 20 to find his house full of Lyttons he slept in a damp tent as a result of which he too fell ill and Robert was obliged to move back to Peterhof. Colley reported that the water supply at Raniket was inadequate. Lytton decided that he would have to make do with Simla, but that a new Government House must be built with proper sanitary arrangements.

Mrs Burne's baby had been born on August 14. It too was a boy but she had wanted a girl. The two babies were christened together by Archbishop Bayly of Calcutta at the Simla church. Robert was godfather to the Burne baby who was called Edward Robert. The Lytton baby was given the names of Victor Alexander George Robert—Victor after the Queen who had asked to be godmother (and who sent a great gilt cup of elaborate workmanship), Alexander, a name suggested by the Queen (her own second name), George after Edith's Uncle Clarendon who had died in 1870, and Robert after Lord Salisbury. Victor was not a pretty baby. His mother described him as a mixture of an owl and a monkey, but he was to grow up to be extremely good looking.

6

The Russian Menace

Preparations for the Imperial Assemblage had been going on all the summer. Various committees, sanitary, decorative and military, had been sitting every day. Colonels Burne and Colley had been entrusted with the invitations and all the arrangements. The Punjab Government was collecting sufficient quantities of food stuffs at Delhi for the fortnight it was to last. The date of the Proclamation of the Queen's new title, January 1, 1877, had been announced in a special Gazette on September 11, and by the end of the month seventy-nine principal chiefs as well as smaller feudatories had already accepted the invitation, although they were to come to Delhi at their own expense. Only on the day of the Proclamation itself were they to be guests of the Government. So great was the response by the princes to the invitation that it became necessary to limit the number of attendants on each chief to 500, not including servants—a revealing glimpse of the splendour with which the princes reigned.

At the end of July Lytton had outlined his plans for the Assemblage to Lord Salisbury. First, the title of Kaiser-i-Hind had been chosen in the vernacular for the new Empress, after much discussion. It had the advantage of meaning the same in Sanscrit and Arabic and of being familiar to the oriental mind. Then the system of exchanging presents between the Viceroy and the princes was to be abolished. Instead, gold commemorative medals were to be given in the Queen's name to all the chief dignitaries present, both European and native. These medals were to be struck in England. They were to cost no more than £20 each and 100 of them would be sufficient. A greater number of silver medals would also be struck for lesser chiefs and officials. In addition, the most important princes were to receive banners with their coats of arms emblazoned on them. The Viceroy wished to establish a College of Heralds in

54

Calcutta for the registration and organisation of the native peerage of the Indian Empire, to make out their armorial bearings and register their pedigrees. He believed that such an institution would not only pay for itself but soon become a source of revenue, so great an importance did the princes attach to such matters. A few of the most important princes would also have the number of guns increased in their salutes.

Above all Lytton planned to constitute a native Privy Council to include, as *ex-officio* members, all British Governors and members of the Supreme Council. This native Privy Council would have no legislative, judicial or executive powers and could be assembled only by a summons from the Viceroy; all the same, Lytton was convinced that nothing would please the princes more or bind them more closely to the Crown than the creation of such a body.[1] He obtained the sanction of the Queen, Disraeli (as he was still usually referred to although he had been created Earl of Beaconsfield in August) and Salisbury for all these measures. The Queen indeed was so enthusiastic that she insisted on designing the medals herself, to be worn on a red ribbon round the neck on all ceremonial occasions. The Prince of Wales too was delighted with the arrangements, though he had not been at all pleased on returning from India to hear that Disraeli had decided to proclaim his mother Empress of India without consulting him.

All these preparations took a great deal of the Viceroy's time. He was also working hard that summer on some other projects—among them, army reform, the amalgamation of Oudh with the North-West Provinces, a scheme for giving the natives a Civil Service of their own and the reduction and equalisation of the Salt Tax.

Lytton felt it was quite wrong that salt should be taxed at all in a country like India where it was a necessity of life. However, as the tax brought in a considerable revenue he had no hope of abolishing it altogether in the present state of Indian finances, but he did hope to be able to reduce it and see that it was fairly levied. At present the tax was much lower in those parts of India where salt was produced. In some of the native States of Rajputana, where there were great salt lakes and salt mines, salt was plentiful, and in order to prevent its being smuggled out of these States, the British had had to put up a customs barrier consisting of a thick, high hedge of prickly pear, stretching for 1,500 miles across the continent and manned by 12,000 inspectors and tax collectors. All the same, a great deal of smuggling went on.

Lytton believed that the only way to dispense with this customs line was to get the supply of salt in the Rajput States into British hands. This was one of the reasons why he had invited the Maharajas of Jaipur and Bhurtpore to Simla where he had managed to persuade them to give up to the British their salt mines and the manufacture of salt in their States in return for monetary compensation. Prolonged negotiations with the other Rajput States were eventually successful. By saving on the inspectors and tax collectors at the customs barrier, Lytton was able to reduce the tax on salt and equalise it throughout British India within two years. This he achieved in spite of his advisers who had told him it was impossible, and that if he 'touched a stone of the temple of the fiscal Solomons of the past' he would be 'buried alive under the ruins'.[2]

On September 2 a reply was received from the Amir in answer to the Viceroy's second letter sent on July 8. Sher Ali was evidently employing stalling tactics. He suggested that the native British agent at Kabul, Atta Mahomed Khan, should go to India to explain to the Viceroy the Amir's difficulties. Again Sher Ali made no mention of the invitation to Delhi nor did he reply to the Viceroy's offer to meet him personally at Peshawar.

The native agent was immediately summoned to Simla but did not arrive for another month. In the meantime Lytton was more successful in carrying out another of Disraeli's instructions—the negotiation of a treaty with the Khan of Khelat. The Khan was the ruler of Baluchistan, with its capital at Khelat, another wild, mountainous, Muslim country, bordered by Afghanistan on the north, India on the east, Persia on the west and the Arabian sea on the south. The Khan, like the Amir, had gained a shaky throne after a fierce war of succession, but the animosity between the Khan and the rebellious chiefs (Sirdars as they were called) had not subsided, and three days before Lytton arrived in India Major Robert Sandeman, with a strong military escort, had been sent by Lord Northbrook to Khelat to try to restore peace. This he had done so successfully that the Khan now seemed ready to enter into a treaty with the British who, in exchange for granting him an annual subsidy and maintaining him on the throne, would be allowed to control the

Bolan Pass and occupy Quetta, close to the Baluch-Afghan frontier and the Kojak Pass, the third main gateway into Afghanistan.

On October 2 Colonel Colley was sent off from Simla on a secret mission to the Khan of Khelat, with the draft of a treaty to present to him. That same day a telegram arrived from London expressing fears of a possible war with Russia. The recent Turkish atrocities in Bulgaria would be an excuse, the British Government believed, for an invasion of Turkey by Russia in the name of Christendom. Disraeli feared that such an invasion would lead to the conquest of Constantinople and the seizure of Suez. This the British could never allow.

The news stirred up all Lytton's indignation against the former policy of 'masterly inactivity' which had driven Sher Ali into the arms of Russia. As he had written to General Ponsonby, 'Any foreign power, possessing a dominant influence over Afghanistan, especially ... Russia ... would command all the passes into India in time of war, together with the support of a very warlike turbulent population, easily excited to plunder, and having many of their clansmen enlisted in our army, to which, in that case, the disaffection would probably spread.'[3] Since the Mutiny the danger of a rebellion in the north was a very real one.

The native agent, Atta Mahomed Khan, arrived at Simla from Kabul on October 6. He reported that the Amir was greatly embarrassed by the relay of native agents sent to him by General Kaufmann, the Russian Governor at Tashkent, but that he did not know how to stop them. Recent history had shown that the British were equally impotent to arrest Russian aggression. He reiterated that if he, the Amir, accepted a British mission it would be impossible for him to refuse a Russian one, and that he could not guarantee the safety of British officers in his kingdom. The Amir was aware, the agent went on, that sooner or later Russia would attack Afghanistan, but in that event the British would defend him in their own interests; nevertheless, he was willing to enter into a treaty on virtually the same terms as those he had offered Lord Northbrook— viz., that no Englishman should reside in Afghanistan, that the British should recognise and support his favourite youngest son, Abdulla Jan, and have no dealings with his rebellious imprisoned son, Yakub Khan; that the British should refrain from all interference in Afghan affairs, should grant him an annual subsidy and agree to support him with troops and money against foreign aggression, and allow him a place of refuge in British territory where he could send his family and property when the expected Russian attack took place.[4]

Lytton was prepared to agree to these terms except for the most important one—that no Englishman should reside in Afghanistan: now that the Amir himself had brought up the point, Lytton felt free to make it a condition that in exchange for granting the Amir his wishes a British envoy should be allowed to reside there and that the Amir should cease to have any communication with Russia. If these provisos were accepted, Sher Ali should send his chief minister, Syud Mohomed Noor, to meet Sir Lewis Pelly at Peshawar to discuss details of the treaty, but there would be no point in his sending his envoy unless he agreed to the establishment of a British Resident somewhere inside his territory.

Sir Lewis Pelly, who had been at Simla all the summer, regretted this condition which he was sure the Amir would never accept. Lytton was quite firm on the point, however, as Disraeli had instructed him to be; he was convinced that Russian influence could never be countered without a British envoy on the spot. A third letter, therefore, in which the invitation to Delhi was again repeated, was dispatched to Kabul by the hand of the native agent.

What Lytton does not seem to have understood was the fierceness of the hatred that the people of Afghanistan still felt for the British as a result of the first Afghan War, which had also been started out of fear of Russia; nor does he seem to have realised what a very loose hold Sher Ali had on the tribes over which he was supposed to rule, in spite of a trained, well-equipped army of over 70,000 troops. He was personally hated for his cruelty and rapaciousness; his treasury was almost empty and his army so badly paid that there was constant fear of insurrection. The tribes, headed by their Sirdars, were only really united in their intolerance of all interference from the foreign infidels. (Afghanistan was self-supporting except for sugar and tea. A pastoral country, its chief source of revenue was the export of lambskins. It also exported wool, cotton, dried fruit and carpets.)

For the time being Lytton felt he had done all he could to win the Amir's friendship while at the same time carrying out Disraeli's instructions. He must now look to the Indian princes. If he could secure their loyalty and co-operation at the Delhi Assemblage it would be possible to withdraw troops from the interior to protect the North-West Frontier should war between England and Russia lead to a clash in Central Asia.[5] The success of the Assemblage had now become vitally important to him.

*   *   *   *   *

It was customary for the Viceroy to take an autumn tour in the hills when the rains ceased. The Lyttons had planned a nine weeks' tour which would eventually take them to Delhi for the Assemblage after visiting the North-West Frontier town of Peshawar, and Jacobabad, near the border of Baluchistan, where Lytton hoped to sign the treaty with the Khan. The children were to be left at Simla until they joined their parents at Delhi. Dr Barnett had offered to stay behind to look after them while another doctor, Dr Hervey, went on the tour. Wellham and Margy had now recovered, and Miss Partridge was being sent home, Edith no longer being able to bear her 'cold selfishness' and disinterest in the children. (How one would love to hear Miss Partridge's own account of those six months at Simla!) The girls' education was being left to Mademoiselle, who seems to have been a treasure.

Lytton had been put in good heart by the tremendous enthusiasm with which the Indian princes, from the greatest chiefs to the smallest hill rajas, had responded to the invitation to Delhi. Even the Nizam of Hyderabad, a Mahometan and the premier prince of India with an annual revenue of £3,000,000, who had never before been induced to attend a Viceregal Durbar, had eagerly accepted the invitation. Lytton's indignation, therefore, was understandable when it was published in the London *Times* that many of the princes were far from pleased because the expense of attending the Durbar in full state, coming so soon after the Prince of Wales's visit, would be a heavy drain on them. It was also reported in *The Times* that the Assemblage was to cost half a million pounds. Lytton, who had estimated that it would cost no more than half that sum, immediately took steps to correct these misstatements. *The Times* published an apology, but a good deal of harm had been done.

Before setting out on the tour Lytton had heard that there was a scarcity of food in the Bombay Presidency due to the failure of the monsoon, and that there was a danger of its spreading to Madras and Mysore. Sir Philip Wodehouse had telegraphed for permission to begin an important line of railway in order to provide employment and thereby enable the workers to buy food when, as seemed inevitable, the price of grain went up. Lytton felt unable to sanction this proposal, the cost of which would have to be borne by the Supreme Government. He was not convinced that this was the best way of dealing with the shortage nor even that there was as yet any real threat of widespread famine. When he set out on the tour he left the Council under the presidency of the senior member, General Sir Henry Norman, who was one of the dissenters over the new policy for Afghanistan.

The Lyttons left Simla for Mashroba on October 16, and on the 19th started out for Narkanda in beautiful weather. Their party consisted of Dr and Mrs Hervey, Thomas Thornton (the acting Secretary of the Foreign Department: the Foreign Secretary always accompanied the Viceroy on his tours), the Burnes and other members of the staff (with the exception of Colley who was at Khelat), the English servants and 1,500 native servants and coolies. Colonel Burne was in unusually good spirits (he was apt to be glum), though Mrs Burne looked 'gloomy as usual, poor little woman', Edith tells us, and was 'certainly no addition to the party'.

The first week of the tour was probably the happiest time Robert and Edith spent in India. The scenery was wild and beautiful, the air laden with autumnal nutty smells; Robert was 'like a boy let out of school'. They alternately rode on ponies and walked. There were fearful precipices on the outer side (the *khud*) of the narrow mountain path, which was unprotected.

The second day Edith recorded that she tied up her habit and 'walked along with R. about five miles, and we tripped along at the head of our train so gaily—and it is so nice to be with dear R. and have him in such good spirits'. She owned to being better in health than she had been for years, and Robert too was wonderfully recovered. They had the choice of sleeping in tents or in *dak* bungalows. They loved the life, the packing and unpacking, the cooking out of doors at which the native servants were so expert, just like a gypsy encampment. It was hot in the day but bitterly cold at night; many of the native servants had fever and Dr Hervey 'doled out the quinine in great quantities'. In the evenings they played whist.

The Russian Menace

Robert wrote to Wilfred Blunt: 'I am writing to you at the door of my tent, like Abraham, surrounded by my tribe, behind me a tiny city of canvas with gaily bannered domes, in front a grassy plateau swarming with mules, horses, ponies, and naked dusty figures who squat round huge wood fires. Beneath me, a mountain torrent ... and above and beyond three pinnacles of sunlit snow.'[6]

Runners came after them with telegrams and letters so Lytton was not left in peace for long. On October 24 he received a telegram from Lord Salisbury to say that war against Russia might be declared in three weeks' time; in that event what could be done to strike 'a rapid and effective blow' at Russia in Central Asia and raise the population of those regions against her? It was, of course, impossible for Lytton to give an adequate reply to this question, especially while on tour, and it seems an extraordinary question for Salisbury to have asked, knowing as he did that a hostile Afghanistan lay between India and Russian territory in Central Asia.*

On the same day Lytton heard that the Government of Bombay, without the sanction of the Governor-General in Council, had published its proposals for starting major works in the Bombay Presidency, and that Sir Philip Wodehouse, without any reference to the Viceroy, had announced in the Bombay Gazette that in consequence of the anticipated severe food shortage, and the inability of the Supreme Government to assist the local one, he would be unable to attend the Imperial Assemblage. Lytton immediately wrote a stern letter to Wodehouse saying that 'the failure of the Assemblage would be more disastrous to the permanent interests of the Empire than twenty famines' and 'requiring' his presence at Delhi on January 1.[7]

In a letter to Sir Henry Norman, Lytton called Wodehouse's behaviour 'abominable' and 'disloyal', adding, 'It is not for him to decide whether or not he will obey the orders of the Governor-General in Council.'[8] The announcement certainly caused the Government great embarrassment. The Bombay newspapers began an active agitation against the Assemblage which was taken up by the rest of the Anglo-Indian press and then spread to the native

*When the information in Salisbury's telegram was passed on to Colley at Khelat, he worked out a detailed plan for military action on the Oxus. If the Amir remained unfriendly, the plan would involve British troops forcing their way through Afghanistan. Colley dreaded any such military operations, and fortunately circumstances changed to make it unnecessary to put the plan into action. (Butler, pp. 172 & 174.)

journals. The false statement as to what the Assemblage would cost was repeated, and the press 'fulminated against the heartless expenditure on mere display,' as Lytton told the Queen, 'while a portion of the population is starving. The newspapers teemed with articles, and caricatures, representing the Viceroy as Nero fiddling while Rome burns.'[9] In the end Lytton managed to suppress this agitation so successfully, by issuing statements to the press and the local Governments, that there was a reaction of public opinion in India in favour of the Assemblage.

The Viceregal party went in slow stages, averaging about twelve miles a day, through small native States towards the Kashmir border. (The Lyttons had wanted to go on to Kashmir but this had been forbidden because of an outbreak of cholera at Srinagar, the capital.) From Narkanda their route descended to cross the Sutlej River and then north to Sultampur, the principal village of Kulu, ruled by the Raj of Rupi, who came out to meet them with musicians and presents of food. Edith was shocked at the disgraceful way the servants fell on the food until she was told it was their prerogative. Then on to Spitti. The Nono of Spitti entertained them with native dances and gave more presents of food and yaks' tails for brushing away flies.

The next prince to entertain them and bring food and skins was the ruler of Mandi who would not allow them to pay for anything in his territory. Being more important than the other two rulers he was received next morning by the Viceroy in Durbar (they had brought the *shemiana* with them as a Durbar tent) and given a gold watch and chain, whereas the other two had been given only opera glasses and silver watches.

They reached Palanpur in the Kungra valley, the centre of 10,000 acres of tea plantations, on November 8, Robert's forty-fifth birthday. Here they were met by fifteen English tea planters and three Rajas, and slept in a comfortable bungalow decorated with flags, in a red-carpeted room with a double bed. Lytton received the Rajas in Durbar and delivered an address to the tea planters, after which there was a dinner party of twenty. The next morning the Lyttons visited a tea plantation. Edith was distressed to see how much of the tea was touched by dirty hands. The Assistant-Commissioner of the district was a native 'but such a nice man, so gentlemanlike and civil'. This seems to have been the first Indian Edith had met who was not either a prince or a servant. The Kungra Valley was so beautiful that it consoled them for not seeing the Vale of Kashmir.

The next day at Dhamsarla, a military station in British territory, two disturbing telegrams reached the Viceroy; the Amir and his chief minister were both ill and unable to receive the native British agent bearing Lytton's third letter (more stalling tactics?), and Lord Salisbury was going to Constantinople at the end of November for a conference of the Great Powers to consider the future of Turkey and the whole Eastern Question. Although the conference would probably avert war, it was a great worry for Lytton to have Salisbury out of the country just when negotiations with the Amir had come to a standstill. Lytton's relations with Salisbury were at this time 'delightful'. 'It is impossible to do business with him and not love him,' Robert had written to John Morley. 'I can't conceive how he ever acquired the reputation for being overbearing. I find him singularly considerate, most sympathetic, and most loyal in supporting me through my difficulties.'[10]

The Lyttons were met at their next stop, Sharpur, by the Commissioner of the Chumba district, Colonel Reid and his wife— 'a regular grim old Anglo-Indian and she looks as if she had said "prunes and prisms" all her life. R. in good spirits would play his game [flirting?] naughty boy. I made him laugh as we said good night by telling him it was so nice his only getting ladies like "prunes and prisms" to *look* at. He will be a worse flirt than ever when he gets home after these ladies.' At Sharpur the English mail brought news that Edith's elder sister, Theresa Earle, had had a boy after great suffering. The little Raja of Chumba, whom they met next day, was only ten, a very pretty boy and ruler of one of the most ancient Rajput houses in India. Colonel Reid was in political charge of him and partly responsible for his education.

From Dalhousie, a British military station near the Kashmir border, where they spent the night of November 14, Lytton wrote a very long letter to the Queen. He apologised for not having written to her for three weeks and then went on to tell her about the unbounded enthusiasm of the native princes for the Assemblage, and enclosed several of their letters to prove it. At the same time, he continued, he could not disguise from her the fact that all this enthusiasm was to a large extent inspired by the princes' expectations that it would be the occasion to recognise their political importance and status by associating them more closely with the Government of the Indian Empire. The creation of a native Privy Council, for which he had obtained approval nearly four months ago, although he had not publicly announced it, was the act, he believed, most calculated to fulfil their highest expectations. It was with the greatest disappointment, therefore, that he had just learnt by telegraph from Lord Salisbury that the measure had met with a wholly unforeseen and quite inexplicable opposition from the members of the Indian Council in London which Salisbury did not feel he could override. This would leave a gap in the Delhi programme which Lytton would do all in his power to 'cover and conceal', though he now had nothing at all equivalent to offer the princes and was afraid they would go away dissatisfied.

Lytton ended his letter by informing the Queen that he had heard from Colonel Colley from Khelat that the Khan was willing to sign the treaty Colley had presented to him on October 18. This would put an end to civil war in Baluchistan, and was regarded by the tribes and Sirdars with satisfaction. It secured for ever for the British Government the right to place troops at any time in any part of the Khanate, and, in view of the uncertain nature of present relations with Russia, the Viceroy had already, with the Khan's consent, thrown a small British force into Quetta, a post of great strategic importance in the event of war; at the same time the trade routes had been reopened so that commerce had been peacefully resumed after months of chaos and disruption.[11]

From Dalhousie the Lytton party descended to the banks of the Ravi River, which formed the border of Kashmir, and went down the river next day. Robert wrote to Lady Holland a few days later:

The most original part of our march was our descent of the river Ravi on beds placed across buffalo-skins inflated with air, and here called mussacks. These mussacks are guided down the rapids by men who swim alongside of them the whole way. It is a mode of locomotion which really transports one into remotest antiquity, for I remember to have seen an exact representation of it on the Assyrian sculptures in the British Museum. [Three reliefs, now on the west wall of the Nimrud Gallery, representing King Ashurnasirpal II (883–59 B.C.) crossing a river.] In this wonderfully conservative East custom seems immortal, and in some shape or other the past is always present. At Sultampore the village gods came out to meet us; twelve hundred silver images on arks, or sacred cars, and preceded by minstrels, whose instruments probably differed in no important particulars from those which David played before the Ark of the Hebrews.[12]

Edith tells us that it took six hours to get down the Ravi. Six times they had to get off the rafts and walk when the water became too shallow. Each bed lay on two separate skins and was guided by two men. Descending the first rapid, when the raft shook a good deal, turned Edith rather sick and giddy but after that she enjoyed it very much as did all the rest of the party with the exception of Mrs Burne who was frightened. Poor Mrs Burne seems never to have enjoyed anything although she was only thirty-five. She was carried in a *jampan* the whole tour because she was too nervous to ride, whereas Ozzie, Edith's maid, got on very well on a quiet pony. But then Ozzie was 'quite perfect' in Edith's words, though she, like Edith, was too tall to stand upright in the tents.

The Lyttons were met when they left the river by a grand carriage which the Prince of Wales had given to the Maharaja of Kashmir* and in which they drove to Mudhapur where the Maharaja had arranged a splendid camp for them on the border of his territory. The Lyttons each had two tents, besides a large drawing-room and dining-room tent. The furniture in Edith's tents was all covered in 'cashmere shawl material' which Ozzie wanted to take away with them. Edith was thankful to have a halt for three days at Mudhapur, yet sad that their free gypsy life was over.

The next morning the Maharaja came to visit the Viceroy with his three sons and attendants on eleven elephants. He was dressed all in yellow while the Viceroy's staff were in scarlet and gold. The Viceroy returned the visit at one o'clock and received the Maharaja again at four when matters to do with his northern frontier were discussed. A group of British explorers, employed by the Indian Government during Lord Northbrook's Viceroyalty, had discovered that the passes through the Pamir Mountains, east of Afghanistan, which had been considered impenetrable except by the

---

* Ranbir Singh, Maharaja of Jamu and Kashmir, K.C.S.I., was a Rajput, forty-five years old and had in 1857 succeeded his father, Gulab Singh, founder of the family whom the British had made Maharaja. Although an important prince he was not rich compared to other Indian princes, with an annual revenue of only £825,000.

mountain people, were in fact accessible even to troops. This meant that a Russian army could descend on India from Russian-occupied Khokand, south-east of Tashkent, without going near Afghanistan. These Pamir passes could easily be held on the southern side, but it would be a very expensive business to maintain a British garrison up there. Kashmir's territory extended as far north as Gilgit. What better plan, therefore, than to get the Maharaja, with his well-trained private army, to guard these passes for the British? Lytton seems to have had little difficulty in persuading him to accept the assignment in exchange for guns, rifles, ammunition and permission to extend his northern frontier. Kashmir did, however, jib at the Viceroy's insistence on establishing a British agent at Gilgit, and only gave way on this point when the agent named was John Biddulph, the chief explorer employed by Northbrook, who had reported favourably on the Maharaja's rule in his northern territory. Lytton felt reassured as to the Maharaja's loyalty, something which had previously been in question, and an agreement was concluded that afternoon.

After dinner on the same day the Maharaja came again to the Viceroy's camp with his sons. Edith described him as a very handsome man with very distinguished manners. The heir-apparent was quite different—'very vulgar with large eyes and speaking groom's English'. The younger sons were good-looking boys, and it was arranged that the middle one should be one of the Viceroy's pages at the Delhi Assemblage. The Maharaja and his party stayed while the Scotch regiment, which had come to meet the Viceroy, played the bagpipes, 'but seven at once in a tent was too much of a good thing'. The Maharaja then sent for his own musicians from his camp who played 'for a tedious hour'; one man then sang and danced in imitation of a nautch girl which was 'very horrid' to Edith.

The following morning the Maharaja gave them a picnic in Kashmir territory, four miles the other side of the River Ravi. The ladies went in *jampans* and Robert on an elephant for the first time. 'After luncheon we watched an elephant fight, and some horrid sports of a cheetah and lynx going for a poor hare and deer, and some hawking which made one feel to be living in the time of William the Conqueror.'

Before dinner that day the Maharaja's Prime Minister brought them shawls, cloaks, jackets and 'gold things' which, to Edith's great joy, they were allowed to keep. No Government servant was as a rule allowed to keep any presents; they had to be turned over to the the Calcutta treasury. It is not recorded who decreed that the Lyttons might keep these presents from the Maharaja.

7

The Khan of Khelat

Leaving Mudhapur on Sunday, November 19, the Viceroy's party drove fifty miles to Amritsar and then took the train to Jhelum. From Jhelum the Lyttons had their own barouche which had been sent by train from Calcutta, and four artillery horses which, according to Edith, took them at full gallop in five hours to Rawalpindi, one of the largest military stations in India, a distance of seventy miles. The next day they went on to Attock, the site of Alexander's first battle in India. The Commander-in-Chief, Sir Frederick Haines, met them there and accompanied them next day to Peshawar; they were escorted by a regiment of the Probyn Horse in their splendid uniforms. Tents had been pitched at the last stage before the town. Here the gentlemen put on uniform for a state entry. They were met there by Colonel Colley whom they were delighted to see again, and by General Roberts, V.C. (who was later to become the famous Field Marshal, Lord Roberts), Military Commander at Peshawar. He was soon to win fame in Afghanistan.

During the three days they spent at Peshawar, the Viceroy was fully occupied with problems to do with the North-West Frontier. The Afridi border tribes had become so bold that they were frequently raiding Peshawar itself. Lytton found that the frontier officials were 'men over-burdened with judicial and administrative work, who sat at their desks all day, and had no personal intercourse with the frontier tribes'. Their relations with these tribes were conducted by native middlemen 'all more or less corrupt, self-seeking and untrustworthy'.[1] The Viceroy was not allowed to go to the Khyber Pass, less than ten miles away, for fear of being shot. He realised that there must be a complete reorganisation of frontier policy, that direct intercourse between the frontier officials and the tribes should be established, and friendly relations encouraged. In this he met with strong opposition from the die-hard officials.

68

The Khan of Khelat

Among the younger frontier officers, however, was one who possessed, Lytton believed, the necessary qualifications for dealing with the situation as well as being in full sympathy with the Viceroy's policy. This was Major Louis Cavagnari, the son of a native of Genoa, General Adolph Cavagnari, who had been Napoleon's secretary during his Italian campaign, and his Irish wife. Louis had entered the East India Company as a cadet in 1858 having been naturalised British in 1857. He had travelled in Afghanistan, spoke several native languages fluently and had a great knowledge of the Frontier tribes. In 1871 he had married an Irish girl, Emma Greaves. Before leaving Peshawar, the Viceroy appointed Cavagnari Deputy Commissioner of the district. He was to play a very important part in events which followed.

Returning by Rawalpindi and Jhelum, the Lytton party, which now included Colley, reached Lahore by train on the afternoon of November 28. Robert had a cold on the chest and Edith bad neuralgia. They had found Peshawar very unhealthy. At Lahore, the capital of the Punjab, they stayed for three nights with the Lieutenant-Governor, Sir Henry Davies, and his wife, whom they had known at Simla, in a charming old house that had been a tomb. There was a ball the first evening, but, as Edith wrote, 'I always feel one's position at a ball, no one speaks to one or asks one to dance unless through an official quadrille, and I stay most of the evening alone in a recess. Dear R. was very brave and cheery, though seedy also.' Lady Davies fascinated Edith; she was the only woman whose looks she had admired at Simla; but she found something hard and cold about her. Sir Henry was soon to retire, and when Edith told Lady Davies how sorry she was that they were leaving India she got no response from her and felt very snubbed. Edith, in spite of her hasty judgments of people, which were usually reversed on further acquaintance, was really very humble. She responded immediately to warmth which she had not yet found in any of the Anglo-Indian ladies. She realised that they were for the most part overawed by her position; all the same, she was hurt by their coldness for she had always managed to make friends very easily in Europe.

From Lahore the Viceroy and his party went to Multan, then down to the Sutlej River for three days by steamer to Sukkor where they arrived on December 6 and were met by Sir William

69

Mereweather, the Commissioner of Sindh. Sukkor was a very beautiful place with the old town on one side of the broad river (the Sutlej had now flowed into the Indus) and the new town on the other, with islands in between. The next morning they set out in a wagonette on the long drive to Jacobabad, the chief military station in Sindh, close to the border of Baluchistan, where the Viceroy was to meet the Khan for the signing of the treaty. Colonel Colley, Mr Thornton (Foreign Secretary) and Lord William went on camels. They received an official reception and were dead tired by the time they arrived at Jacob's Castle, as the Residency was called. It had been built by General Jacob who had founded the town and who was buried there under a massive tomb.

At 11.30 next morning the Viceroy received the Khan 'in a beautiful big room decorated with flags belonging to one of the Sindh horse regiments'. From a gallery in this room Edith and some of the other ladies were able to peep at the ceremony.

The Khan is a small man [Edith wrote] with long hair and such a savage rolling eye. He wore a gold helmet and was handed a series of yellow green handkerchiefs for he takes snuff even in Durbar. There were about 40 people who came with him—very wild ill mannered creatures but who grouped themselves round on the ground with much effect. The Khan looked in a mortal funk as he came up the room with R. but the latter has such a graceful easy manner with the chiefs that the Khan soon became more at ease, and even broke into a fiendish grin now and then. The usual compliments were exchanged, the Sirdars and other people introduced, then the Khan went away and R. a quarter of an hour afterwards returned the visit at his camp. Directly after luncheon there was a levee and then at half past three the Khan returned on business, and I can't describe how very interesting this was, I alone was allowed to peep. The Khan this time was dressed in red velvet with a dark turban and looked better. After a few words exchanged the Treaty was signed, Robert signing with pen and ink the two copies and the Khan spitting on and then stamping his seal on them. The treaty is a very satisfactory one and has secured peace with the Khanate without any bloodshed, and we are now on the best of terms with the Khan and he with the chiefs round him. Robert through the interpretation of Major Sandeman gave the Khan a little lecture about his treatment of the chiefs round Khelat and then the ceremony ended after about an hour most amicably. As I was coming away from my listening gallery, I saw the Khan and his people just outside go through the most curious prayers; clothes were

The Khan of Khelat

laid down and then a priest laid down a sheathed sword, and they all
bowed down to this about three times very solemnly. I was told afterwards they were giving thanks for the terms of the arrangements that
had been concluded, which the sunset hour obliged them to do at once.

Lytton described the Khan in a letter to Sir Henry Norman as
having 'the furtive face and restless eye of a little hunted wild beast
which has long lived in daily danger of its life'. He trembled violently while the Viceroy was leading him up to his seat. All the
Sirdars had been present, and they and the Khan had accepted the
invitation to Delhi. Lytton added that the treaty was signed quite
privately since he thought it best not to publish it immediately.[2]
He must have known that it would be very disquieting to the Amir.
Quetta was the base from which the British had invaded Afghanistan in the first Afghan War.

Colley took leave of the Lyttons that night after a dinner party
given by Sir William Mereweather. He was leaving at two in the
morning to ride a hundred miles to meet the railway which would
take him to Delhi where there were many preparations for the
Assemblage still to be completed. The rest of the party returned to
Sukkor next day and went aboard another steamer which took them
down the Indus to Kotree—'a far more luxurious one—such nice
cabins for us both, real W.C. and splendid saloon all painted white
and gold—it is really nicer than any room we have had in India'. But
when Robert woke up coughing in the night and struck a light, Edith
to her horror saw an enormous cockroach on the bed beside her.
She jumped up screaming. Green, Robert's valet, caught it very
cleverly, but as soon as she had settled down again, though keeping
the light on, she saw another on the mosquito curtain. 'I really cried
from sheer terror and fatigue.'

During the two days on board, Robert finished his speech for
the Delhi Proclamation which he had started on the boat to Sukkor.
He had taken great pains over it, for, as Salisbury had pointed out
to him:

You must remember you have two audiences: one in India, oriental, fond
of the warm colours of oratory, and pardoning exaggeration more easily
than coldness; the other partly in India, mainly in England, frigid, cap-
tious, Quakerish, Philistine, only considering a composition faultless

when it has been divested of all richness and all force. It would be very agreeable to speak for the benefit of one audience only: a task of appalling difficulty is to please both. Yet it must be attempted.[3]

From Kotree the Viceregal party went by train to Karachi and thence by sea to Bombay where they arrived on December 16 and spent five nights with Sir Philip Wodehouse at Parell. The famine was no longer a threat but a reality. Lytton was able to see conditions for himself and entirely came round to Wodehouse's way of dealing with the emergency by starting large public works so that those employed on them might be able to meet the cost of rising food prices. Lytton made his peace with Sir Philip who travelled with them to Delhi.

At Bombay the Viceroy heard that at last the Amir had agreed to send his two chief ministers to Peshawar to confer with Sir Lewis Pelly. But Sher Ali still ignored the invitation to Delhi, a discourtesy that infuriated Lytton almost as much as his dilatoriness.

The dresses Edith had ordered in Paris from Worth arrived just in time at Bombay though she did not have a chance to unpack them. She heard that all the children had arrived safely in Delhi, and that Colonel Colley on his own initiative was going to bring Betty and Conny to meet them at Gazeeabad, half an hour away from the city. Their own carriage and coachman had also arrived in Delhi.

Lytton had invited all the members of his Council with their wives and families, and some other officials to be his guests at Delhi; also some friends from England. The closest of these friends were Lord and Lady Downe. (Lady Downe had been Lady Cecilia Molyneux, daughter of the Earl of Sefton. She had married in 1869 Hugh Dawnay, Viscount Downe, a Captain in the Yorkshire Hussars. He acted as an extra aide-de-camp to the Viceroy while he was in Delhi.) The other friends were Mrs Burne's brother, Lord Kilmaine, Sir Robert Abercrombie, Bart., and Lord Brooke, son of the Earl of Warwick—three eligible bachelors to flutter maiden hopes.

The departure from Bombay for Delhi on the morning of December 21 would have been very exciting if Robert, Edith and Lord William had not all been violently sick. They believed that they had been poisoned with some bad food. Fortunately Dr Hervey was there to give them 'soothing draughts' and they had two nights in the train in which to recover. The temperature dropped 30° during the journey, and it was difficult to keep warm even with furs and hot water bottles.

8

The Imperial Assemblage

Delhi had been chosen as the place of the Imperial Assemblage because it had been the principal city of the Mogul Empire. The last Mogul King of Delhi had been deposed for disloyalty to the British during the Mutiny. The site of the camp was on a great plain four miles north-west of the city, running beside the ridge from which the British troops had besieged the rebels in 1857. The Viceroy's camp for his family, staff and fifty-nine guests consisted of a double row of plain tents forming a wide street laid out with turf and flowers. At the end of the street was a big Durbar tent with the Viceroy's throne at one end with a life-size copy of Angeli's portrait of Queen Victoria hanging behind it. The camp was lit with gas made from castor oil supplied by the Maharaja of Jaipur at his own expense; he had lit his own camp in the same way. In the 'street', parterres of artificial flowers burst out with hundreds of jets of gas, while in the Durbar tent there were triple cast-iron lamps clustered on one standard, designed by Rudyard Kipling's father, Lockwood Kipling, Principal of the Mayo School of Art at Lahore. (The ten-year-old Rudyard was at school in England.) Thomas Cook & Co. of Calcutta had sent up to Delhi forty carriages and eighty horses for the Viceroy's guests.

The Governor of Bombay, the Governor of Madras (the Duke of Buckingham), the Lieutenant-Governor of Bengal (Sir Richard Temple) and the Commander-in-Chief all had their own camps. But the camps of the native princes were far more gorgeous and elaborate—blue, yellow and scarlet, with gold knobs to the tent poles—and with hundreds of attendants to look after their elephants and camels. Each ruler had brought his own troops and his own band. Only the Khan of Khelat, who was too poor to come in state, had asked Colley to provide him with tents, elephants and camels for a hundred men. He and his Sirdars had been terrified of going by train for the first time and had insisted on having all the doors locked. The day they arrived, Major Bradford, who had been put in charge of them, sent a ready-cooked dinner into their camp. They appropriated all the cutlery, ate the cakes of Pear's soap provided for them, threw out the beds and used the washing basins and jugs for the purpose of eating and drinking.[1]

The place of Assemblage, where the Queen was to be proclaimed Empress, was a grassy plain about two miles north of the Viceroy's camp. Two thousand coolies had been employed for weeks levelling the ground. Three structures of painted iron had been put up there—a red and gold hexagonal pavilion for the Viceroy, like a glorified bandstand, raised ten feet from the ground, its conical roof capped with an imperial gold crown; for the princes, representatives of foreign governments and chief British officials a semi-circular pavilion in blue, white and gold, 800 feet long, facing the throne pavilion; and, behind the throne pavilion, a stand for guests, staff and lesser British officials.

In October Lytton had commissioned Val Prinsep on behalf of the Indian Government to come to Delhi and paint the Imperial Assemblage as a present for the Queen. Prinsep's connections with India made him an ideal choice; his father, Henry Thoby Prinsep, had been a distinguished Indian administrator; his elder brother was in the Indian army and another relation was a High Court judge in Calcutta; moreover, Val's mother was one of the Pattle sisters (Julia Cameron, the photographer, was another) whose father had been in the East India Company. Val himself had been intended for the Indian Civil Service until he decided to take up art professionally. Now thirty-nine years old, he had been exhibiting at the Royal Academy since 1862. He had known Edith Lytton before her marriage through G. F. Watts, who for many years had lived at Little Holland House with the Thoby Prinseps, and who was a great friend of Edith's mother.

Prinsep was to receive £5,000 for the picture, plus his return fare and expenses while in India. This money was to be raised from the princes who had expressed a wish to give a present to the Queen. Those who contributed were to have their portraits recognisably painted into the picture and to receive a lithograph of it.

Prinsep arrived in Delhi on December 16 and stayed with his brother who, as Deputy-Assistant-Quartermaster-General, with a certain number of Rajas to look after, had a camp of his own. 'Oh, horror! what do I have to paint?' Val wrote in his journal after his first sight of the place of proclamation. 'A kind of thing that outdoes the Crystal Palace in "hideousity". It has been designed by an engineer, and is all iron, gold, red, blue and white. The dais for the chiefs is 200 yards across, and the Viceroy's dais is right in the middle, and is a kind of scarlet temple 80 feet high. Never was there such Brummagen ornament or such atrocious taste.'[2] To modern eyes the buildings have all the charm of 'pier' architecture with the addition of circus colouring.

Everyone, with the exception of the Lyttons' guests from England, had assembled in Delhi before the Viceroy arrived—sixty-three rulers of native States with their retinues, including one woman, the Begum of Bhopal; about 800 titular princes and nobles; the Khan of Khelat and all his Sirdars, the Prince of Arcot, the Princess of Tanjore, the Imam of Muscat; ambassadors from Burma, Siam and Nepal; deputations from Yarkand, Chitral, Yasin, and Kashgar; the Governors-General of Goa and Pondi-cherry; all the foreign consuls and senior British officials; 15,000 troops; the editors and correspondents of fourteen European newspapers published in India and twenty-four native papers; a special Reuter correspondent and representatives and artists from the *Graphic* and the *Illustrated London News*. Altogether there were some 100,000 people camped on the plain as well as hundreds of horses, elephants and camels. The sanitary and police arrangements were admirable. The sun warmed up the air in the daytime, though there was frost at night and the red dust was so thick that it had to be laid with rushes. The correspondent of the Calcutta *Statesman* thus wrote about the day of the Viceroy's arrival:

Lord Lytton has certainly added to the history of India an event which up to this time would have been pronounced an impossibility. Even in the golden days of the Delhi Emperors, can anyone say that a Nizam of the Deccan ever met his brother potentate of Mysore on the same footing as these two young chiefs met to-day? Can anyone tell of a Gaekwar of Baroda, and a Scindiah of Gwalior meeting on terms of friendship and equality? The success of to-day's ceremony is doubtless the beginning of great good for India.

The Viceregal train arrived at Gazeeabad at 1 p.m. on December

23. Betty, Conny, Mademoiselle and Colonel Colley were waiting on the platform. 'I jumped out as the train stopped a little,' Edith wrote, 'and was so enchanted to see the pets. We did so cling to each other.' After a cold luncheon at the station Robert put on diplomatic uniform and Edith changed into a grey and brown silk dress from Worth which she had worn only once before, to go on board the *Serapis* at Suez to breakfast with the Prince of Wales. They reached Delhi at exactly 2 p.m., the time arranged three months ago. Edith described their welcome:

The station was crowded with Indian chiefs and European officials, the former Robert addressed by a few words which Mr Thornton interpreted, welcoming them for coming to Delhi, then R. shook hands with all the Chiefs and moved slowly on. The dear Commander-in-Chief [Haines] took charge of me so kindly. R. and I then got on our elephant and the two girls followed us on a small one. Four A.D.C.s headed the procession, then trumpeters etc. We were about $2\frac{1}{2}$ hours getting over six miles, and in spite of a gold umbrella and a parasol, the sun was so hot getting to our camp, but R. kept in very good spirits and we had great fun talking about all the different things we saw. The reception was a very hearty one, and the troops so excellent and such good tunes. The native troops were so ludicrous dressed in their type of Highland dress but it was a good idea of R.'s having them with our troops along the sides of the road. At last we reached the Flag Staff which heads our main street of camp, and in the Tower [famous in the Mutiny] besides many Simla people I recognised dear Emily and saw baby held up at the back. Our camp is certainly quite perfect, not only in size but from its excessive neatness and order, there is grass on each side of the road and then 25 tents each side. Several Governors and Sir F. Haines came afterwards to welcome us at the entrance, and soon our dear babies came up. I am sorry to say I felt much more at seeing dear Emily than poor little baby, but Oh how little one knows of a baby one does not nurse. Emily was intensely fascinating, clinging to me as poor Teddy [the second son who had died] used and not shy with anyone. I spent the rest of the afternoon with the dear children, and dined in my sitting room with Melle, not wanting to bother to dress. R. dined with one or two of the gentlemen as all our guests have a different mess.

The reason why it had taken so long to reach the camp was because the procession had wound through Delhi, traversing the whole length of the Chandni Chowk, the chief shopping street, before leaving the city by the Lahore Gate, and then continuing along the ridge to Flagstaff Tower; also the Lyttons' elephant, evidently of an inquisitive disposition, had kept stopping to look around and this had held up the whole procession. Three detachments of cavalry and twelve trumpeters had headed the procession before the aides-de-camp on elephants, two abreast. Edith had been insufficiently impressed by the native troops and did not seem to have noticed the war elephants in chain-mail, their mahouts also dressed in armour, nor the Gaekwar of Baroda's real gold and silver cannon on carriages with gold and silver wheels, drawn by bullocks with their horns dipped in gold.

Prinsep, who had watched the procession from the crowded stand on the steps of the Jumma Musjid (the principal mosque, backing on the old palace-fort), sitting squashed between the Ambassador from Siam and the envoy from Kashgar, described the Lyttons' splendid elephant with 'an abominable silver *howdah* made for the Prince of Wales. . . . Nothing I ever saw or have dreamed of could equal the rush of native chiefs' elephants that closed the procession. The chiefs themselves were not there [they had gone to the station] but their courtiers and retinue were, and they all jostled and pushed together in a most glorious confusion of dress, drapery and umbrella.' Prinsep stayed at the Musjid to make sketches after the procession had passed, and then hurried off to the camp to catch up with it on the Ridge:

A double line of elephants lined the way, swaying backwards and for-wards, for the elephant, like some huge men I know of, never keeps a moment quiet [Prinsep himself weighed twenty stone]. On their backs magnificent *howdahs*, and in the *howdahs* a motley crew,—men in armour, men with shields and large swords, men with trumpets 8 feet long, all sorts of wild men, shouting and scuffling; and behind all the golden sun-set.

The next day, the 24th, Robert was feeling ill. Fortunately it was a day of rest except for the English mail which came in. On Christ-mas morning he was busy conferring with Sir Philip Wodehouse, the Duke of Buckingham and Sir Richard Temple about the famine which had now spread to Madras. Temple, who was to become Governor of Bombay when Wodehouse retired the following year, had had a great deal of famine experience in Bihar in 1874. Lytton decided to send him to Madras as soon as the Assemblage broke up to advise the Duke of Buckingham. The Duke was dealing with the famine in his Presidency in a very unsatisfactory way by setting up refugee camps which were costing a frightening amount of money.

Although Lytton told the Queen that Divine Service was held on Christmas morning in the Viceroy's camp, he did not mention that he himself had not attended it. In the afternoon he rode to the place of Assemblage with Edith and Val Prinsep. 'It is all in rather bad taste,' Edith wrote. 'Poor Mr Prinsep was in despair.' Prinsep complained on this occasion, 'They have been heaping ornament on ornament, colour on colour, on the central or viceregal dais, till the whole is like a Twelfth cake. They have stuck pieces of needle-work into stone panels, and tin shields and battleaxes all over the place.' He felt it was impossible to paint the scene because of the size, and was relieved to find that Lytton himself was anxious that he should make rather a fanciful picture of it with the Jumma Musjid in the background.

The Lyttons rode back to their camp past the polo ground where a game was going on and where they saw Captain Clayton, a great friend of Lord William's, take a fall, without realising how serious it was. That evening there was a dinner party of forty-five. Prinsep wrote, 'All our party dined with the Viceroy on Christmas Day. Lady Lytton is as charming as ever, and very popular, and the entertainment good.' He added that she had the same sort of charm as the Princess of Wales.

The children acted some scenes from *Alice in Wonderland* after dinner with the Burnes' little girl who had just come out from England. Edith missed Lord William and Colonel Colley but suspected nothing until she heard someone say, 'Oh, I am so sorry for poor Captain Clayton'. After the party was over she sat up in her tent till 1 a.m. when Robert came to tell her that Captain Clayton had died at midnight as a result of his fall, without regaining consciousness. Edith was miserable for Lord William; they were in the same regiment and had been 'like devoted brothers'.

The next day, the 26th, was entirely taken up for the Viceroy with receiving visits from the ruling princes. He told Queen Victoria that the order of the chiefs' visits 'had been carefully arranged on a new principle, which completely obviated all difficulties and heartburnings about precedence'.[3] We are not told what this principle was; it was certainly not based on the size or prosperity of the State, nor on the antiquity of the ruler's lineage, for the first prince to be received was the Maharaja of Alwar whose State was not among the richest and had been founded only in 1771; nor was the order of precedence alphabetical.

Each ruler with his suite was received at the entrance to the camp 'street' by mounted officers, and as he advanced towards the Durbar tent the salute was fired to which he was entitled. He was then conducted into the tent by Mr Thornton and introduced to the Viceroy who placed him on a seat before taking his own place on the throne under the Queen's portrait. After some conversation the prince was presented with one of the gold medals and a coloured satin banner fastened to an elaborately worked brass pole, embroidered in coloured silks with his titles on one side and his armorial bearings on the other. (Rudyard Kipling's mother, Alice Macdonald, had been one of the ladies at Simla to help embroider these banners.) The brass poles, made in England, had, by some oversight of design or construction, turned out to be so heavy that it needed two Highlanders to carry them, and the princes had to hoist them on to elephants when bearing them in procession. Lytton wrote to the Queen that the Khan of Khelat had asked to have a banner given to him: 'It was explained to His Highness that the banners were only given to your Majesty's feudatories, and that he, being an independent Prince, could not receive one without compromising his independence. He replied—"But I *am* a feudatory of the Empress, a feudatory quite as loyal and obedient as any other. I don't want to be an independent Prince, and I do want to have my banner like all the rest." '[4] He did not get his banner in spite of this plea.

The Viceroy received twenty-one ruling chiefs in this manner on the 26th from 10 a.m. till past 7 p.m. without intermission, and the next day he received sixteen and returned fifteen visits to those princes who were entitled by their rank to a visit from the Viceroy. And so it went on until the 29th. There was only one hitch in the presentations. The forty-three-year-old Maharaja Sindhia of Gwalior, one of the richest and most important of the Hindu princes, who had shown great courage and loyalty in the Mutiny, had most unfortunately, through a mistake on the part of the British officer in charge of him, been kept waiting for two hours outside the Durbar tent. He had greatly resented this and had been very sulky through-out the audience. Eventually all was put right by a brainwave on the part of the Viceroy: he telegraphed to the Queen and obtained her permission to create Sindhia a Grand Commander of the Order of the Bath and inform him immediately of this honour.[5] (He was already a G.C.S.I.)

It had been an imaginative idea of Lytton's to increase the number of guns in the salutes of some of the most important princes. Soon after arriving in India he had written to Disraeli, 'I believe that at the present moment an Indian Maharaja would pay anything to obtain an additional gun to his salute; and were we not such puritans, we might ere this have made all our railways with the resources thus obtained.'[6] During the Assemblage, three princes had the Salutes of their States raised to twenty-one guns—the Nizam of Hyderabad (a Muslem), the Gaekwar of Baroda (a Mahratta) and the Maharaja of Mysore (a Rajput). These were the three richest States in India and it so happened that their rulers were all boys, of ten, thirteen and fifteen respectively. Seven others, including Sindhia of Gwalior, and the Maharajas of Jaipur and Kashmir, had their personal salutes raised to twenty-one guns. These princes were delighted, for it put them on a par with the Viceroy, until they discovered from the Government Gazette that the Viceroy's salute had been increased to thirty-one guns. That of the Queen Empress was raised to 101. To those princes whom the Viceroy had intended to make Privy Councillors he gave the dignity of Councillors of the Empress.

Edith received each afternoon from three to five, and there were great state dinners every evening. Sir Richard Temple recorded that after each one of these the Viceroy 'made a notable speech to the company. He was highly gifted as an after-dinner speaker, and was a master of splendid language; indeed the assemblies were aglow with his speeches'.[7]

On the morning of the 27th Captain Clayton was buried in the old cemetery just behind the Viceroy's camp. Lord William was 'wild with grief', according to Edith, 'and could not be left alone for a moment in case he went off his head'. That afternoon little Emily, who had celebrated her second birthday on the 26th, and baby Victor were sent off to Calcutta because they had caught cold in the tents. On the 28th the Viceroy held a levée after dinner which went on till 1 a.m. and was attended by 2,500 gentlemen, European and native. As Lytton wrote to the Queen, there was inevitably a crush and many Europeans who had come to Delhi determined to find fault complained that proper arrangements had not been made for their comfort. It seems, though, that there really was a danger at one moment of the Durbar tent collapsing from over-crowding. Prinsep was a witness to the behaviour of the British subalterns at this levee:

They made loud remarks about the rajas there present, and expressed a wish to cut their ears off to get their jewels—quite forgetting that many of the rajas understood English. This was, no doubt, the mere silly chaff of a lot of young fellows who were hot and uncomfortable, who kept up their spirits by a running fire of *badinage*. But I doubt whether rajas understand chaff. One cannot be surprised if they, like the worm, wish sometimes to turn.... To see the great rajas at a party is pitiable. Their dignity is offended. The small fry take to receptions and champagne, but the big ones look awfully bored and do not understand waiting in the cold for their carriages.

The Lyttons' guests from England arrived on the morning of the 30th. Edith's first cousin, George Villiers, whose place as aide-de-camp, it may be remembered, Lytton, had been keeping open, arrived on the same day. (Villiers, a son of Lord Clarendon, was a bachelor of twenty-nine and a Captain in the Grenadier Guards.) Edith was delighted to see him and also to see Lord and Lady Downe. Lady Downe was with Edith at mid-day when the Begum of Bhopal, who had been received in Durbar by the Viceroy on the 27th, came to call. The Begum was a Moslem and the only female ruler of a State. The consort she had chosen had been a schoolmaster and she was, according to Prinsep, terrified of him. She was not staying in camp but had taken a house in Delhi for a week. (She had had a state coach built in London for the occasion which had been on show in Long Acre for some weeks.) Edith described her as 'a scruffy little woman with a wretched lolling husband who only allows her to unveil as a great favour. She wears little shoes like goloshes.'* The ladies Grenville, 'the three plain daughters of the

* Nawab Shah Jehan, Begum of Bhopal, G.C.S.I., was thirty-seven. Her first husband had died. The British Government had recognised her second as her official consort under the title of Nawab. She had succeeded her father in 1844 but had resigned her claim to the

The Imperial Assemblage

Duke of Buckingham with a dull miss to look after them' also came that morning to return a visit of Edith's and were 'so stiff'.* Edith was particularly glad to have Cecilia Downe there to help her, for she complained that Mrs Burne 'got out of everything she could and was never any help with general entertaining'.

On the last day of the year, a Sunday, Robert managed to accompany his family for a picnic to the Kutub Minar, the most famous sight in Delhi, about eleven miles south of the city. That evening, after a small dinner party, Robert sat up late in his tent talking to Sir John Strachey. Edith, after kissing her two little girls goodnight, waited up for him in her own tent until 12.30, expecting him to come and say good-night and wish her a happy New Year. But he did not come, and not liking to pass the guards in undress she did not dare go to him. She went to bed feeling very low, and found the band playing Auld Lang Syne in the distance most melancholy.

*   *   *   *   *

January 1, 1877, had been declared a public holiday; every soldier in the Indian army received an extra day's pay; nearly 16,000 prisoners were released and an amnesty extended to all those exiled after the Mutiny with the exception of Feroz Shah, a Mogul prince related to the late King of Delhi. (An uprising under his leadership was still feared.) As well as an enlargement of the Order of the Star of India, the Queen had instituted a new Order, the Order of the Indian Empire. Up till 1886 this new order consisted of one class only, that of Companion. It was not until 1878 that the Queen instituted the Order of the Crown of India, exclusively for ladies.

The great day, which has been planned and talked of for months, has come at last [Edith recorded in her diary] and the weather is perfect. Poor R. was so seedy from sitting up so late thinking over his speech for the Banquet. I had to dress about ten so as to let Ozzie go away. Worth

---

throne in favour of her mother who had ruled until her death in 1868. Bhopal was not a large or rich State but an important one with a long record of loyalty to the British.
* The 3rd Duke of Buckingham and Chandos (1823–89) was Governor of Madras from 1875–81. He had held office under Lord Derby and Disraeli 1866–8. His wife had died in 1874 and he remarried in 1885. At his death the Dukedom became extinct. His three daughters, Mary, Anne and Charlotte were 24, 23 and 20. In 1882 Anne married one of her father's A.D.C.s. Mary married Major L. F. Morgan in 1884 and inherited one of her father's titles as Baroness Kinloss. Charlotte never married.

sent me a lovely gown of purple blue silk and velvet stamped with blue velvet brocade—the bonnet was a sort of wreath of feathers with rim of pearls making it a Marie Stewart shape which was so becoming and I wore my pearl and diamond bracelet round my neck—the body and skirt fit quite beautifully and made me look so slim. It was handsome and picturesque without being too gaudy. The two dear girls had blue green velvets and very becoming hats and looked great pets. R. and I went into the hall [of the Durbar tent] when ready about 11.30. R's head was so bad but I was very jolly with children and gentlemen. We had to wait some time while the road was cleared, then started in two carriages and a char-à-banc. Captain Jackson came with us, the little girls followed in the second carriage, then the brake with the staff. The troops struck us so much as we approached the Assemblage place, though the plain is so vast it is very difficult for anything to make a show on it. Just outside the circle of the seats of the Assemblage there was a tent for R. to robe. The robe [of the Grand Master of the Star of India] was beautiful blue velvet embroidered with gold flowers and an ermine cape. He looked very well with uniform, Star of India Order and two pages holding his robe (son of the Maharaja of Kashmir, such a pretty boy, and Mr Grimstone, Midshipman, in a Charles II blue and white dress). I walked after him with a little girl on each side, and the staff, a very brilliant one, fell in after us, and so we walked solemnly up to the dais. Having never walked except in a funeral procession and being rather shy I am afraid I felt very serious but the whole thing was most properly solemn. R.'s chair was, of course, put rather forward and mine at his right and the childrens' at his left just behind. The Chiefs were all in front in a semi-circular covered stand, and their new banners, gold unbrellas and dress made it a splendid sight, but the British uniforms pervaded very much amongst these. [There had been a hundred elephant processions of the princes to reach the stand.] Our Governors, Lieutenant-Governors and Members of Council were all facing the throne also. The bands placed on the left all played the Tannhäuser march which was very effective. The Chief Herald, Major Barnes, an enormous man of, I am sure, seven feet, then read on the steps [of the dais], facing the Chiefs, the Queen's proclamation [announcing that she had assumed the title of Empress]. Then Mr Thornton, bowing as he passed the Viceroy, went forward to the steps and read out the same in Urdu. After this there were salvos, a *feu de joie* running up and down the lines and more music.* All this

* There were three salvos of thirty-one guns with a *feu de joie* in between each, making a salute of 101 guns for the new Empress and lasting twenty minutes in all. The *feu de joie* 'was splendidly executed and with excellent effect, for it made the rajas jump and raised quite a stampede among the elephants who "skedaddled" in all directions, and killed a few natives'. (Prinsep, p. 35.)

time one became calm and could contemplate the splendours around. Mr Prinsep never stopped sketching different effects. At last the Viceroy went forward and delivered *his* address. His voice was not in its best condition but very telling—and he got through it well with continual sips of water. He ended 'God save Victoria, Queen of the United Kingdom and Empress of India', then the whole assembly rose and joined the troops in cheers. After this we marched away in the same order as we arrived. We waited [back at the camp] to shake hands with the staff on the success of the whole thing for it is indeed a matter of congratulation all round, and how the staff have worked. R. says if offered any order or other mark of approval for what he has done he could not accept without his secretaries receiving something as well. Poor R. was quite well after it was all over.

Lytton was not given any honour in recognition of his services on this occasion, but Burne, on the Viceroy's strong recommendation to the Queen, was made a Companion of the new Order of the Indian Empire.

Edith's afternoon was spent galloping round the racecourse with Lord Downe and Lord William who looked tired and miserable having been up all night making arrangements for the carriages. Robert meanwhile had a meeting about famine policy which lasted until dinner time. The banquet that evening began late and was attended only by gentlemen, native as well as European. The Viceroy displayed his own gold plate from Knebworth for the occasion. Edith, after dining in her own tent with the children, went behind a door to hear Robert's speech proposing the health of the Queen-Empress; then she went to change for the party which was to follow:

I wore a lovely white ball gown of Worth's. All the front was done with gold and pearl fringe. The natives thought the front was all real jewels I'm sure as I saw them looking at it. The party was very amusing—there were lots of Native Chiefs and all the swellest Europeans, and all mixed so well. I was presented to several Native Chiefs who seemed in excellent spirits. Nearly all asked to be presented to me which is a great change, but I have been more brought forward than any lady yet in India. Everyone was so cordial in congratulating on the success of the whole day and none more so than the dear Commander-in-Chief to whom I am devoted. R. and I jumped for joy when he came to my tent for a few minutes, and I'm sure he could go to bed thoroughly satisfied and happy, and so ended the greatest day in our lives and what a position for my dear husband!

1877

The Delhi Assemblage was, according to Lytton, the first time that any female member of a Viceroy's family had appeared at a public function or ceremony to which natives were admitted. It had hitherto been thought that the appearance of ladies would lower them in native eyes. Lytton's decision to allow his wife to attend the Proclamation and subsequent parties deeply shocked Anglo-Indian opinion. It was apparently, however, much appreciated by the princes who had all asked to be presented to her at the banquet. When they afterwards saw her at the races they 'rose, greeted, and conversed with her as respectfully and cordially as the most polished English gentleman could have done'. Lytton hoped that this course he had adopted would 'help to bridge over at least some portion of the inconvenient and deplorable gulf existing between English and native society'.[8]

The three days following the banquet were taken up with more receptions, visits, dinners and the distribution of medals and decorations. (Lytton lost his own gold medal while out riding: it was never recovered.) Then on January 5, the last day of the Assemblage, the Viceroy reviewed a march-past of native and British troops which lasted from eleven till four. One body of native infantry, dressed from head to foot in yellow, marched past with a band playing 'Home Sweet Home'. Robert was all that time on horseback in the full sun. Edith dreaded his falling off his horse with sunstroke. Lord William did actually faint in the saddle. At 6.30 the girls with Mademoiselle and Mrs Burne and her children left by train for Calcutta, and at 10.15 the Lyttons with their staff and Lord and Lady Downe took the Viceroy's special train to Patiala where Lytton was to instal as Raja the five-year-old prince who had not been at the Assemblage.

Soon after their departure there was a tremendous thunder storm and a downpour of rain that lasted all night, flooding the camp and turning it into a sea of red mud. One can imagine the resulting chaos if the rain had come sooner. As it was, Lytton was able to write to the Queen with justifiable pride that 'to bring together, lodge and feed, so vast a crowd without a single case of sickness, or a single accident due to defective arrangements, without a moment's confusion, or an hour's failure in the provision of supplies, and then to have sent them all away satisfied and loud in their expressions

1 Robert Lytton at Sintra at the time of his
appointment as Viceroy, 1875

2 Conny, Edith Lytton and Betty, Calcutta, 1879
'Lady Lytton was splendidly attired'

3 Simla

4 The Khan of Khelat
'He takes snuff even in Durbar' (note snuff-box)

5 The Viceroy in the robes of Grand Commander of the
Star of India, Delhi Assemblage, 1877

6 Prinsep's picture of the Delhi Assemblage

7 The Place of Assemblage, Delhi, 1 January 1877
'All iron, gold, red, blue and white'

8 Maharaja Sindhia of Gwalior. The richest and most important of the Hindu princes

9 The Maharaja of Kashmir. 'A very handsome man with very distinguished manners'

10 The Begum of Bhopal. 'She wears little shoes like goloshes'

11 The Maharaja of Jaipur, the most westernised of the Hindu princes

12 Outside Government House, Calcutta, January 1877

Standing from left to right: ?, Colonel Colley, Lord William Beresford, Captain Rose, Captain Villiers, Dr Barnett, Lieutenant Liddell, ?, Lord Downe, Lady Downe, Captain Jackson. *Seated from left to right*: Mrs Burne, Sir John Strachey, the Viceroy, Lady Lytton, ? Strachey, Lady Strachey, Fanny Strachey, Colonel Burne, Lord Kilmaine. *On floor*: Betty and Conny

13 The Viceroy on the Throne, Calcutta, 1877

14 Part of the Bala Hissar at Kabul, 1879

15 The Fort at Jamrood

16 Sher Ali with his favourite son and Sirdars at Lord Mayo's Durbar at Ambala in 1869

17 Mr Jenkyns, Sir Louis Cavagnari, Yakub Khan, Daud Shah, and ?, at Kabul, 1879, soon after Cavagnari's arrival

of gratitude for the munificent hospitality with which they had been entertained, (at an expenditure of public money scrupulously moderate), was an achievement highly creditable to all concerned in carrying it out.'[9]

Unfortunately everyone was not satisfied. Prinsep, who stayed on in Delhi for a fortnight, found 'discontent and dissatisfaction' in the European community. People talked of the 'Black Raj' where everything was sacrificed to the native. There had been no balls for the ladies who had come with trunks full of new dresses; indeed no parties at all without 'dark gentlemen' present.

Lytton was quite aware of this feeling in spite of what he had told the Queen, for he was to write to Lord George Hamilton a few days later: 'The fact is, the whole of Anglo-Indian society is mortally offended with the Prince of Wales for not having sufficiently appreciated its superiority to everything else in creation. His visit has left a deep rankling sore in the Anglo-Indian mind, which has got an idée fixe that I came out to India with secret instructions from his Royal Highness to snub and aggravate the whites, and pet and spoil the blacks.'[10]

There was certainly a preponderance of Indians in the New Year's Honours list. The four new Knight Grand Commanders of the Star of India were all Maharajas; of the new Knight Commanders four were Indian princes. (Among the new English Knights of the Order was Fitzjames Stephen.) Of the twenty-five new Companions of the Order ten were natives. Apart from this, Rajas were promoted to Maharajas (Kings to great Kings), lesser chiefs to Rajas, etc.—in all more than 200 Indians had native titles conferred on them. Even so, the Viceroy had not managed to satisfy the pro-Indian members of the press. The Calcutta *Statesman* which, although European-owned, was particularly sympathetic to the Indians, wrote on January 6:

We trust we have now seen the last of these ceremonials for a long while to come. The atmosphere of our relations both with the Princes and people of India should be less artificial. The policy of pattings and praises is an anachronism with the land full of High Schools, Colleges and Universities; and it is more than time that we abandoned finally this treating of the people as children. They long to be spoken to as men like ourselves, and there is a sickliness in the tinsel pageantry of all these proceedings, that makes us long for the simplicity of a strong, just, and manly word to the country, in its place. The Princes and people of India are not the children we persist in making them, and we would have given all these Beaconsfield 'fireworks' with the medals, and banners, and salutes, and embroidered arms, fifty times over, for a single strong and just word at the Assemblage. But it was not in Disraeli to speak it, or to conceive it. Lord Lytton was doomed by the ages to try what 'fireworks' would do, and no more unhappy destiny could well have been allotted to an able man.

Without anything of real value to offer the educated Indians, the Viceroy's speech had been a tissue of carefully and beautifully woven platitudes. If he could, he would have announced to them the opening of the Covenanted Civil Service without their having to go to England to sit for the examination. That he was not able to do so was due to the dead weight of Anglo-Indian opinion, crushing any measure for giving the natives real opportunities for taking a rightful share in the government of their own country. Even a Viceroy as racially unprejudiced as Lytton could do little to shift that weight; what he did eventually do was at best a compromise.

9

Calcutta

After visits to Agra and Benares, made particularly pleasant by the company of the Downes who remained cheerful in all circumstances, the Viceregal party arrived in Calcutta on January 13. Edith was delighted with Government House. This great white palace, as she called it, begun in Lord Wellesley's time and finished in 1803, had been partially copied from Robert Adam's Kedleston Hall in Derbyshire. The rooms were white and gold with marble floors and dark polished teak doors. 'The Ball room is a charming room for singing in,' Edith wrote. 'It quite gives one a voice. I feel so happy to have a piano and be with the dear children again. Dear baby is growing so nicely and I am getting quite fond of him, and in hopes that Wellham will soon be able to take charge of him when I shall like him much better.' (He did improve greatly after the *dai* weaned him. Edith believed that being a dull woman she had made him dull.) The elder girls were to have visiting masters for arithmetic and English history.

The Viceregal rooms looked on to a large garden and a park like Regent's Park; the mosquitoes were trying but not more so than in Southern Europe. (They became much more of a trial later in the season.) The rooms were kept cool by *punkahs*. The *punkah* was the only fan then available, a long piece of cloth on a wooden frame suspended from the ceiling and stretching the whole length of a room, attached to cords which went through holes in the wall. The *punkah-wallahs* sat outside pulling the cords with their big toes.

For Saturdays and Sundays, whenever possible, there was the Viceroy's house at Barrackpore, some twelve miles north of Calcutta on the west bank of the Hooghly River, which had enchanted all the Governor-Generals and their wives since it was built at the beginning of the century. While staying there they had their meals out under the arches of a great banyan tree. The house was situated

89

in a park, with a beautiful garden and a view of the river. In the grounds were separate bungalows for the staff. It could be reached either by carriage or by the Viceroy's launch. 'You have no idea what a lovely country place this is,' Edith wrote to Mrs Forster. 'The park is like England and the river like the Thames at Mortlake.' Any place in India that reminded a European of home always found special favour.

The Calcutta palace was so huge that Edith found it very tiring. 'I sometimes long for a cottage again,' she told her mother. 'There is too much work and duty to be made worldly or spoilt here.' When Lemercier found it impossible to manage the hundred native cooks (there were altogether three hundred indoor servants at Government House), Robert allowed him to go home and took on Lord Northbrook's French chef, Bonsard, who had remained in India. Although his wages were higher he was more economical. Among other special dishes, he invented 'Quenelle à la Lytton, a very refined paste filled with soubise, breadcrumbed over and served with a hot brown sauce'. Lytton also engaged an Italian pastry-cook.

Soon after the Lyttons' arrival they held a levee and a Drawing Room. 'The latter was a great success,' Edith recorded. 'There were about 300 ladies, the bows were some of them very funny, some snubbing me, others ignoring R., but there were a good many trains as we had wished, all very well got up. I had a bad headache. The whole thing made me nervous.' It was not until Lord Minto's Viceroyalty (1905–10) that curtseying to the Viceroy was introduced.

On January 25 the Lyttons gave their first big dinner party of the season with the gold plate on the sideboards. Edith had introduced a new system of receiving: 'We bow and go into dinner at once with one or two different people and then are presented to everyone after dinner and can talk to each other and get to know all a little. It was such an improvement. I am so glad I have carried it. Colonel Colley vows I have such a will.' Another innovation of Edith's was to have small tables of eight for dinner parties, as they had done at Simla, instead of one large one. Captain Jackson, who had become more assertive in Calcutta, would not present Edith at functions in the way she asked him to. 'He seems to dislike anything we do which was not done in Lord Northbrook's time,' she complained. It was a great relief to hear that he was soon going home. George Villiers, who was very popular, was to take his place in managing the Household until Captain Loch returned.

Edith really enjoyed herself in her official capacity during those first weeks in Calcutta. The Downes were still staying with them as were also Lord Kilmaine, Lord Brooke and Sir Robert Abercrombie. (These young gentlemen were soon to return to England without attaching themselves to any of the Anglo-Indian girls.) Sir John and Lady Strachey and their children were also the Lyttons' guests until they could find a house of their own. Sir John had now joined the Council as financial member and was helping the Viceroy with his first Budget. (On the day the Budget was presented Robert was given a black and white Japanese dog which he called Budget and became very devoted to.) Fortunately the price of silver had gone up slightly which eased the financial situation, and the demand for opium, which was highly taxed and a great source of revenue, had increased.

Ashley Eden, the new Lieutenant-Governor of Bengal, was a great addition to the social life of Calcutta.* He possessed Edith's favourite quality of cheerfulness, and Robert considered him the first man of the world he had met in India. All these people were present at the Lyttons' first ball in Calcutta. Edith wore the gown she had worn for the banquet on January 1, and in her hair an emerald and diamond necklace of Indian workmanship which their Delhi guests had given her, and her pearl and diamond bracelet round her neck. Robert admired her which pleased her very much. Everyone was very jolly and it went off admirably. Captain Jackson had gone home and George Villiers, not being able to speak Hindustani, had great trouble over the supper arrangements with the servants but made up for it by his kindness and willingness to please. He became a great favourite with everyone.

It was a sad day when the Downes left at the end of February. Edith wrote home that no one could have helped their season

---

*Ashley Eden (1831–87), 3rd son of the 3rd Baron Auckland and nephew of the Earl of Auckland (Governor-General of India), had been Chief Commissioner of British Burma before he was appointed to Bengal in succession to Sir Richard Temple, a position he held until 1882. (It was an anomaly, later rectified, that Bengal, the largest of the provinces, should be headed by a Lieutenant-Governor when Bombay and Madras were both under Governors.) Eden was a great gardener and made many improvements to the garden of his official house in Calcutta, Belvedere. In 1861 he had married Eva Money who had died in England on January 7. They had no children.

more—the whole staff had been at her feet and he was 'one of the nicest society men' Edith had ever met and 'so good looking'. They were devoted to each other, and so well suited.

Apart from riding, playing duets, entertaining and going to functions held by other 'swells', Edith's activities were restricted to visiting schools, hospitals and the wives and children of British soldiers stationed at Calcutta and Barrackpore. The education of native girls was her most genuine interest in India and she really seems to have enjoyed visiting Zenana schools. She was instrumental in opening schools for Eurasian children whose interests had been neglected up till then. Of Robert she saw very little. 'Poor R. works, works, works, all day and every day,' she told her mother, 'but keeps wonderfully well thank God, and he does very good work and is growing so to the occasion and events as they happen, though he *won't* get quite the self-confidence I should wish him to have, he is so humble and always fears not doing well enough.'

Lytton had a great deal on his mind at this time. Not only was the famine news increasingly worrying but Sir Lewis Pelly had failed to come to terms with the Amir's chief Minister, Syud Noor, at the conference at Peshawar which had been going on since the end of January. The Amir still refused to allow a British mission to enter Afghanistan, let alone reside there, and the Viceroy, who had stipulated that it was useless for Sher Ali to send his Minister to Peshawar unless he agreed to this condition, refused to yield the point. Since the situation had not changed, there was really no basis for discussion.

In the exchange of letters between Lytton and Pelly during the conference it could be seen that the Viceroy was becoming more and more impatient. He believed that the Russians were pressing rapidly towards Merv, an important town in Turkoman country not far from the Afghan border, with a view to occupying Herat in Afghanistan itself; he reasoned that if Sher Ali refused to accept the proffered friendship of a power so much greater than his own it could only be for sinister reasons: he must be prevaricating in order to give the Russians time to advance.

Lytton had won over the Khan of Khelat, he had won over the princes and the majority of his own Council, and he could not accept his powerlessness to win over the Amir. It was a tragedy that the two men never met. Half an hour of Lytton's charm might have done more than all the written pages of cogent arguments couched in language which it is doubtful the Amir understood even through his interpreter (his native language was Pushtu).

Fitzjames Stephen was fomenting Lytton's impatience by such words as 'Chiefs like the Amir ... must be dealt with on the understanding that they occupy a distinctly inferior position—that inferiority consisting mainly in this, that they are not to be permitted to follow a course of policy which exposes us to danger ... we are exceedingly powerful and highly civilised, and they are comparatively weak and half barbarous'.[1] That may have been so, but Syud Noor was stating a greater reality when he told Pelly, 'The British nation is great and powerful, and the Afghan people cannot resist its power, but the people are self-willed and independent and prize their honour above life.'[2]

Even while the Peshawar conference was going on, news reached Calcutta that Sher Ali was massing troops on his frontier and exhorting his subjects and the Frontier tribes to make preparations for a holy war against the British. His attempt failed but this naturally did not exonerate him from treachery in British eyes.

On March 26, Syud Noor, who had been ill throughout the talks at Peshawar, suddenly died, and the Viceroy closed the conference. The rumour that the Amir was sending another envoy was never officially confirmed, and, anyway, Lytton believed that his object was to prolong the conference while he went ahead with preparations for another holy war. Soon afterwards the native British agent at Kabul was withdrawn, Lytton and Colonel Burne both being convinced that he was a spy in the pay of the Amir. The Viceroy was now further away than ever from achieving the task entrusted to him by Disraeli. Nevertheless, the latter wrote to Salisbury at this time, '... we must, completely and unflinchingly, support Lytton. We chose him for this very kind of business. Had it been a routine age, we might have made, what might be called, a more prudent selection, but ... we wanted a man of ambition, imagination, some vanity and much will—and we have got him.'[3]

Lytton himself felt that his negotiations with the Amir had had one practical result:

They have dispelled the profound darkness in which the Government of India has, for years, been content to carry on, or not carry on, its relations with Cabul: the situation now revealed is certainly most un-satisfactory, not to say serious: for it shows that the Ameer has long ago slipped altogether out of our hands into those of Kauffmann; who has been wide awake while we were fast asleep in a fool's paradise.[4]

Two more members of the Viceroy's Executive Council had now retired, General Sir Henry Norman and Sir Arthur Hobhouse. These two, with Sir William Muir (who had been succeeded by Strachey) were the three members of the Council who had dissented the previous June from the Government policy with regard to Afghanistan. The two new members, General Sir Edwin Johnson (military) and Witley Stokes (legal) had been chosen by Lytton, so now all six members of his Council were in agreement with him. Norman and Hobhouse, however, who were to join the Indian Council in London the following year, continued to oppose Disraeli's forward policy. Norman in particular, who seems to have taken a personal dislike to Lytton, was to work against him in a very reprehensible way.

Towards the end of the Calcutta season farewell dinners had to be given for Norman and Hobhouse. Lytton worked all day on his speech for the dinner for Sir Henry and was unable to attend the garden party which Edith gave every Thursday afternoon. 'He did not get out until dark,' Edith recorded, 'and then was like a boy, jumped about and had a little dance with pretty Mrs Plowden whom Robert chaffs and is fond of.' Robert was so nervous over his speech that he 'almost fainted at dinner', but then 'spoke admirably. Dear R. was so cheered by my praise after we came to bed, he is so curi-ously susceptible to being appreciated even by me who always admire him so, and cares for what everyone says of him (though luckily he don't care much for what these papers say).'

It was not only Lytton's policy that was being attacked now in certain sections of the press in England, as well as in India, but his personal habits and characteristics. Two unpleasant articles about him had appeared in *Vanity Fair* in England on February 24 and March 10. The first reported that at a levee at Government House on January 23, the Viceroy had interrupted the proceedings, ordered the door of the Throne Room to be shut and then, while seated on the throne, had smoked a cigarette. The second article bit deeper:

Calcutta

Few Governor-Generals had ever left these shores for their new and responsible post under happier auspices than the present Viceroy ... Lord Lytton's arrival was hailed as the inauguration of a new and popular *régime* which would conciliate even adverse opinions, and enlist the sympathies of all. The English papers as well as private letters told the expectant Anglo-Indians of his polished manners, of his refined tastes, his transcendental culture and sparkling coversation, which would shortly transform English Society in India into something far superior to anything that had yet been known, and made Government House a mixture of a dignified Court and an agreeable Parisian *salon*.

It is not too much to say that these expectations have been utterly annihilated. Hardly had Lord Lytton been three months in this country when his mischievous indiscretion in the Fuller case raised a storm of just indignation against him throughout the length and breadth of the land ... it might be said that one mistake in judgment should not ruin a man's whole reputation. What, however, are the accounts we receive of Lord Lytton in India? We forbear to write what we are told of his vagaries in Simla, his strange indolence, love of personal ease, and petty egotism, his fanciful eccentricities of dress and bizarre love of finery. ... But what, we ask, can be said of one who, placed as he is, the direct representative of her gracious Majesty, went out of his way on an occasion like the last assemblage at Delhi to insult and disregard the feelings of his own countrymen while he earned the scarcely disguised contempt of the natives by cringing abjectly before them? ... We learn also from Calcutta of open affronts to the whole of the European Society, of Lord Lytton's neglect of the ordinary courtesies of social life, and of the undignified innovations, which are certainly not calculated to improve the habits or refine the talk of the younger generation of Anglo-Indians, or afford good examples of English manners to natives of rank. The story we told a fortnight ago of his stopping a Levee in order to refresh himself with a cigarette, which he smoked while sitting on the Queen's throne, speaks volumes. ...

Edith was quick to defend Robert in a letter home. She begged her family to take no notice of the 'horrid articles in *Vanity Fair*'. The story of the cigarette at the levee had been absurdly exaggerated: 'Between the entrée people and the general public there is always a little pause, and being so soon after dinner he took a puff or two'. She went on wisely, 'However, you can't be in such a position without having every word and act criticised, but please don't be distressed about such trifles.'

Robert does not seem to have minded the personal attacks on him. What he did resent were the attacks on his policy, for these, he felt, handicapped his 'faculty for good and efficient' action. To John Morley, who, as editor of the Liberal *Fortnightly Review*, had become a political enemy, though still a personal friend, he had written, 'Only one friend can justify my work in India, and that is the future.'[5]

Lytton told Salisbury and Stephen that the articles in *Vanity Fair* had been written by Colonel Malleson whom he had been obliged to remove from his post in Mysore where he was doing incalculable mischief and who had returned home vowing that he would 'write down Lord Lytton and get him recalled'.* In his letter to Salisbury, Lytton went on, 'So long as I remain in India, every energy and faculty I have will be devoted to the endeavour to justify your confidence in sending me here. But I am always ready to return to England at a moment's notice, without a moment's regret. The trappings of this great office have no charm for me, and it is only worth holding as long as I can hold it with your general approval.'[6]

Subsequently he was able to report to Salisbury that there had been a reaction in his favour in the Indian press as a result of the attacks on him in the English papers: 'The Anglo-Indians regard their Viceroy, whatever he be, as a *cosa nostra* to be blackguarded only by themselves. To admit that people in England can also see what a fool or a knave he is, would be to admit that anything connected with Indian affairs can be understood by anyone in England.'[7]

Wilfred Blunt, who later stayed with the Lyttons at Simla, gives the best idea of what it was that the Anglo-Indians objected of in their Viceroy:

It is quite certain that Lytton's demonstrative and unconventional manners in public lend themselves to misconstruction and it is probable that if he had erred more practically in act it would have involved him in less discredit. The Anglo-Indian world, though very immoral, is one which insists on decorum in high places, and Lytton was constantly violating their rules and conventions. He could not resist sitting, sometimes a whole evening through, with a pretty woman talking nonsense to her

*Mysore was at this time temporarily under British rule, but the Government had guaranteed to restore it to the young Maharaja when he obtained his majority (at eighteen in Indian law) in 1880. Colonel Malleson, who had been in political charge of him and his brother, had bullied them in various ways and insisted on living in the same house and eating with them in violation of caste rules.

on the sofa, to the neglect of his other guests, simply because it amused him to do so, and the tale of it was speedily spread abroad by those less favoured. It was only his wife's admirable talents as a hostess that saved the situation for him. He himself had no kind of dignity. He would address the members of his Council as 'my dearest fellow', and I have seen him walk up and down for a quarter of an hour together with Sir John Strachey, his finance Minister, his arm round the other's neck, a really amusing spectacle, for Sir John a bilious and elderly official in spectacles with his head habitually on one side was more like a sick raven than an object of such endearments of any kind and their talk was of figures and the revenue and how they were to arrange the budget. This lack of decorum stood constantly in Lytton's way all through his Indian reign. He never could learn how to mete out the exact degree of familiarity a Viceroy was allowed to indulge in with the native princes and Maharajas who attended his durbars, nor could he remember them one from the other. He told me himself that once, on his return late for an appointment with one of them at Government House in Calcutta, running up the steps of his palace he found himself confronted with a splendidly dressed personage whose face he knew and whom he thought he recognised as that of the Raja he was expecting, and in his desire to make amends for the delay embraced him with effusion, only to discover that the man in gold and lace and turban was his own head jemadar. Neither could Lytton ever be persuaded to forgo the cigarettes he smoked all day even at the most solemn viceregal functions—This was a terrible grievance against him, and hardly less so his refusal to be bound by etiquette which required the Queen's representative to attend divine service with his wife. All such obligations were hateful to Lytton's Bohemian nature.[8]

Talking to pretty women to the neglect of the wives of senior officials was a complaint that had also been levelled against the Prince of Wales when he was in India. Much of the personal criticism of Lytton seems to have been due to the resentment of those who felt unjustly neglected by him, though his habit of smoking, even during meals, and transacting business at night, was certainly most inconsiderate. And the Anglo-Indians were also outraged by his demonstrative affection for the natives—he would embrace them as warmly as he would any white man..Those who found favour with him, however, such as pretty Mrs Plowden, had no cause to complain. One can imagine the scandalised disapproval of the Anglo-Indians when he had a little dance with her at the tail-end of a garden party!

1877

Fitzjames Stephen felt it to be his 'miserable duty' to warn Robert of the slanderous gossip that was being circulated about him in England, though he assured him that he did not believe a word of it himself. Stephen had heard the same stories from several people and found that they boiled down to three main accusations:

(1) that one piece of patronage was given or offered to a man called Plowden because you have taken a fancy (it is not suggested that it is more than a fancy harmless in itself) to his wife (2) that on several occasions you have treated people with rudeness—e.g. by keeping a number of them waiting for an hour in the sun at Benares by stopping a levee in order to smoke a cigar (3) that you had made some speech to a Mrs Hatch [wife of a Calcutta lawyer] after dinner one day about kissing her. . . . You must never forget the sort of people with whom you have to deal. They have many splendid qualities but they have also the pettiness and narrowness and in particular the rigidity of second-rate English people. You may depend on it that any story with a woman in it ever so slightly will give indescribable offence to the Civilians and through them to all their English connections whose name is legion. . . . For God's sake be as careful as you possibly can.[9]

Robert replied, 'I don't think any man even yourself—could have done me a truer or more unselfish kindness than the one I gratefully recognise and value in that most considerate and helpful letter.'[10] He did not refute the charges specifically but attributed the gossip to disgruntled Anglo-Indians, and repeated the story about their believing that he had entered into a conspiracy with the Prince of Wales to snub them. The remark to Mrs Hatch was probably one of his flirting jokes, and he could not have kept people waiting in the sun because he always held his levees in the evening (the origin of that story was no doubt the one about the cigarette during the levee in Calcutta). But the accusation of giving patronage to Mr Plowden just because he had taken a fancy to his wife may have had some substance. Trevor Plowden had been Inspector General of Police in Assam until, in January, the Viceroy had offered him the Under-Secretaryship of the Foreign Department in Calcutta. But Lytton's motive for this may not have been only the wish to see Mrs Plowden's pretty face at his dull parties. He wanted to strengthen his Foreign Department and Trevor Plowden was a very able man. The Plowden family had been well known in India for years, and it so happened that Lady Strachey was not only a cousin of Trevor Plowden but a step-sister of Mrs Plowden.

Stephen wrote back that he had felt, when writing his letter of warning which had been 'the most hateful task' he had ever undertaken, 'that if you took it as I hoped you would and as you most assuredly have, I should be your unchanging friend to the day of my death, and should feel you were a man whose friendship was better worth having than most of the things of this world ... you are hated in India for the very qualities that make me feel that your friendship is so valuable and so delightful to me that I am ready to risk it by plainness of speech in order to help you.'[11]

After so much resounding criticism it is pleasant to hear a little praise from Calcutta. One man wrote home: 'Lord Lytton's geniality is a new feature in Government Administration where everything is as solemn, earnest, matter of fact, resolute, unsympathizing and dull as is well possible—as was said in a native paper "Lord Lytton can laugh". I'm not sure officials like this but non-officials certainly do.'[12]

Lytton's chief crime in India from a social point of view seems to have been that he remained himself. He was not in the least overawed by his own position and behaved as he would have done in any drawing-room in Europe. He was incapable of pomposity except on state occasions. He retained this naturalness all through life; it was one of the qualities that most endeared him to his staff as well as to his friends. When, in later years, he became Ambassador in Paris, where he was greatly beloved by the French, he had no hesitation in stopping the Embassy carriage, even when his wife and daughters were in it, directly outside a *pissoir* if he felt the need to use it.

It was said of him after his death that 'conventions to him were incomprehensible things. He could not understand them, nor learn them, nor, consequently, respect them, and up to the last moment of his life they were to him as meaningless as to a child of some savage race.'[13]

Why was it then that he cared so much that his Court should be dressed up? He even went so far as to complain to the Queen that the Viceroy had no power to prescribe the costume of those who attended his levees and Drawing Rooms;[14] he also wanted a uniform for the Indian Civil Service. This was all part of the flamboyant, theatrical side of his nature which revelled in investitures and other ceremonials and had found its most imaginative outlet in the 'fireworks' of Delhi. It was this side of his contradictory character that made him so proud of his lineage, which could be traced back on both the Bulwer and Lytton sides to the Conqueror, and wish to start a College of Heralds in Calcutta for the native aristocracy. (This scheme was never carried out due to lack of support from Salisbury.)

Lytton seemed incapable of reconciling the different sides of his nature. Towards the end of his life he was to write:

I think I am as variable as the wind, and I certainly don't know myself. All I know is that I have at least half-a-dozen different persons in me, each utterly unlike the other—all pulling different ways, and continually getting in each other's way—and I don't think anybody else knows all of them any better than I do myself.[15]

In spite of Stephen's warning Lytton did not change his behaviour in India. Throughout his time there he continued to outrage certain sections of the Anglo-Indian community while endearing himself to more and more individuals.

10

Famine

Alterations were being made to Peterhof, so the Lyttons could not go to Simla that year until May when it was hoped the workmen would be out of the house. However, the babies with Dr and Mrs Barnett and Mrs Burne and her children went off to Inverarm at Simla a few days before Easter, which fell on April 1 that year. The Lyttons meanwhile were to go on a little tour. The elder girls and Mademoiselle would go with them as far as Lucknow.

When the Lyttons reached Lucknow, the capital of Oudh, on April 3, the girls and Mademoiselle with Fred Liddell went on to Naini Tal, a hill station further north, where their parents were to join them for a holiday. The Lyttons spent two nights with the Chief Commissioner of Oudh, Sir George Couper and his wife, who had been all through the siege of Lucknow during the Mutiny. Edith was, of course, thrilled to visit the old Residency and other relics of the siege, not yet twenty years away. The Coupers had been in the Residency throughout the siege. Lady Couper had given birth to a baby, which died a month later, just as a mine was sprung close by. Sir George Couper had been standing beside Sir Henry Lawrence when he was killed by a shell. A shell had burst in the same room the day before and Sir Henry had said, 'This cannot happen again', and had refused to move his room.

From Lucknow the Lyttons went to Bareilly and from there drove sixty miles to Ranibagh. Edith arrived dead tired and 'tumbled' into her tent where she found her 'beloved Ozzie', 'who had been fifteen hours on the road in the sun, and alone, without a grumble, making the best of everything, unpacking, making beds, and only thinking of our comfort'.

The Lyttons' next stop was Naini Tal, some 7,000 feet above sea level and set by the side of a mile-long lake. They stayed there for three weeks with the girls, rowing on the lake and going for expeditions. It was a real holiday, and Robert was able to 'give himself up to naps and novels in a delightful way in the afternoon'. But on April 26, the day before they left Naini Tal, Lytton received a telegram announcing that Russia had declared war on Turkey. The Russian army assembled on the Pruth, the border of Rumania, then Turkish territory, and was to cross the Danube in June into Bulgaria, also part of the Ottoman Empire.

The Lyttons reached Simla on May 1 in an atmosphere of great uncertainty, not knowing how the war would develop. It looked at first as if England must come in, for the majority of the British people were pro-Turkish. It was not generally believed that Russia had embarked on a crusade to rescue the Christians in the Balkans; this was a mere cover, it was felt, for her own self-aggrandisement; her real aim was to add those Christian people to her own Empire.

As the alterations to Peterhof were not yet finished, in spite of 1,700 coolies working on them, the Lyttons as well as the children stayed at Inverarm where Colonel Colley was relegated to two small rooms at the top. William Loch, quite recovered from his liver complaint, had just returned from England and taken over the duties of Household aide-de-camp again. Edith 'jumped for joy' at the thought of not having to entertain until they could move back into Peterhof. She joined in all the activities that summer:

You will think us very larky when you hear about rinking, dancing and all our amusements, but India is an absurd mixture of this and serious official work. You tell me to tell you more about dear R., but I can only say that from the moment he gets up till about an hour before dinner he is always buried in papers or in Council. As for a thought of a poem or any private work he has never had a minute for such a thing since he heard of his appointment to India. He has been very low lately but I do my best to cheer him, though often when alone I feel low also.

The chief reason for Robert's depression was that his relations with Salisbury were no longer as harmonious as they had been. Since the Conference at Constantinople which, though averting war between Russia and England, had achieved no lasting settlement, Salisbury, according to Lytton in a letter to Stephen, had become 'so vehemently and unreasoningly anti-Turkish—and so contemptuously regardless of the fact that our Indian Empire is a great Mahometan power and can never be anything else, that his letters fill me with dismay and alarm'. Before leaving England Lytton had agreed with Salisbury and Disraeli every point of policy, and had been given 'emphatic assurances of their support in carrying them out'. 'That support,' Lytton continued, 'as far as concerns Lord Salisbury is now replaced by opposition. His notion is that the right policy now for England at this moment is to try and go shares with Russia in the plunder of Turkey; and that for the prosecution of this grand idée every Indian interest must be disregarded.'[1]

Lytton was greatly perturbed by the Cabinet's decision to remain neutral in the war, even though this neutrality was conditional on promises from Russia to respect British interests. Lytton believed that such a passive attitude would be regarded in India, and even more so in Afghanistan, as subservience to a stronger power. While England's attention was concentrated on the Russian advance in the Balkans, Russia was again pressing towards Merv. Lytton advocated some immediate military intervention to counteract this advance. Salisbury, who no longer saw any danger from Russia in Central Asia, refused to sanction any form of intervention. He conceded that 'the awkward result of the Lawrencian policy is that we may, at the moment it suits us least, have to deal with both the Amir and the Russians'.[2] Subsequently he wrote:

The Russians are not now moving from the Caspian—and therefore an enquiry as to what we should do if they ever come to Merv is not of immediate interest. We have told the Russian Government that, if they do, we must make a corresponding advance. It must be, I imagine, either to Candahar or to Herat. . . . If my view is correct, that you have time, you will probably by then have acquired sufficient influence in Afghanistan to enable us to take a step amicably as far as the Amir is concerned.[3]

This letter must have been particularly depressing to Lytton knowing as he did, and as Salisbury should have known, that there was no hope of ever winning the Amir's friendship since he had long ago gone over completely to Russia.

On June 11 Salisbury pronounced in the course of a speech in the House of Lords that the Russian danger in Central Asia was one 'which might possibly interest a future generation of statesmen'. The distances still to be covered by the Russian army and the obstacles to be overcome before it could reach the Afghan border were immense. 'I cannot help thinking,' he went on, 'that in discussions of this kind, a great deal of misapprehension arises from the popular use of maps on a small scale. As with such maps you are able to put a thumb on India and a finger on Russia, some persons immediately think that the political situation is alarming and that India must be looked to.'[4]

This public pooh-poohing of the Russian danger called forth a protest to Salisbury from the Governor-General in Council, and Lytton in his private letters to Salisbury stressed the grave reality of the situation as was unanimously understood by all expert opinion in India. Salisbury replied that policy in London differed entirely from that in Simla. England listened with 'profound deference' to opinions of retired Anglo-Indians of which the Indian Council in London was largely composed. 'Whichever is abstractly right, the English feeling—by which I do not mean mob and press, but the feeling of Parliament and Government—must govern. . . . At all events I hope you will not stir a soldier beyond the frontier (treating Khelat as within it) without obtaining our view on the matter first.'[5] As it was, Salisbury was having enough trouble with the Lawrencians on his Council over the British troops the Viceroy had sent to Quetta after the Treaty of Khelat. Salisbury now wished that he had advised Lytton 'to locate your Khelat escort at some place not far from Quetta—but which was not Quetta. It is a name to conjure with,—and its precise virtue is to make respectable elderly gentlemen go very mad.'[6]

It must always be hard for the man on the spot who knows, or thinks he knows, so much better than those governing from a distance, to obey instructions which he feels to be totally at variance with the facts. Lytton could sense a stirring among Mahometans in India, and had become very much aware since he had been there that the Mutiny had been a purely Mahometan uprising and that the people of the north might be very willing to join with the Afghans and the Frontier tribes in a holy war instigated by Russia. But he was hamstrung by Salisbury from taking any preventive action.

The Lyttons had again taken The Gables at Mashroba for weekends where they always felt happier and in better health than at Simla. In the middle of June Robert chose the site for a new Government House on Observatory Hill, west of the ridge. (It was not

Famine

finished until 1888 and the Dufferins were the first Viceregal couple to live there.) Some ground was levelled immediately and lawn tennis courts made which were 'a great resource'. The Lyttons had moved back into Peterhof by the time Val Prinsep arrived at the end of the month. Since the Delhi Assemblage he had been touring the native States, painting full-length portraits of their rulers in Durbar dress to go into his picture. The day after he arrived he went to a ball at Peterhof 'to see the beauty and fashion'.[7] Edith, the year before, had noted that the ladies of Simla were either dowdy or fast. Prinsep was able to describe the fast set:

Simla is like an English watering place gone mad. . . . Real sociability does not exist. People pair off immediately they arrive at a party. . . . Rinking is greatly on the increase being the only exercise that many men and all ladies can take. There is a great crowd and constant collisions occur, and it is not an uncommon thing to see a young lady throw her arms wildly round a stranger's neck to support herself. Of course people gamble and do what they ought not. They do that everywhere. The play is very high, the whist execrable. All are bent on enjoying themselves, and champagne flows on every side. Every evening at eight the roads are full of *jampons* conveying the fair sex to the festivities.

Towards the end of July Prinsep was painting Edith who was to be prominent in his picture, and Betty and Conny who were hardly visible. He could not begin on the Viceroy until his robes arrived from Calcutta, but by August 5 he had begun the picture:

As far as his head goes he will be easy enough to do, for that is decidedly good; but his drapery is most voluminous and apt to make the Grand Master of the Star of India look like a bundle of clothes. I regret to say that the first conversation I had with Lord Lytton had been a very disagreeable one for me, for in it he informed me that reasons of state would necessitate him being seated in my picture. Now I have always had my doubts about his standing while the rajas were all seated, but as he did it at the great Assembly I thought I might do it in my picture.*

It seems from this that the Viceroy had been criticised for allowing the princes to sit while he was standing. A few days later Prinsep

---

*Prinsep's huge picture of the Imperial Assemblage was exhibited at the Royal Academy in 1881. It now hangs in the Banqueting Hall in St James's Palace.

was writing again: 'Lord Lytton has certainly not an iron constitution but he stands more work than most people, for he does not require exercise to keep him in good health. I doubt whether he ever took exercise even when young. Now he is sometimes days without going out. He writes day and night.'

Lytton's chief preoccupation that summer had been with the famine which had now developed into one of the worst calamities of its kind experienced in India since the beginning of the century. As well as the monsoon, the April rains had failed completely, affecting crops in vast areas of the Bombay and Madras Presidencies and the native States of Hyderabad and Mysore, some 200,000 square miles altogether, containing a population of over thirty-six million. There were large stocks of grain in Bengal, Burma, the Central Provinces and neighbouring countries but transport was inadequate to carry them to where they were most needed, and, anyway, the people in the south if unemployed could not afford the inflated prices.

Wodehouse's policy in Bombay, now whole-heartedly adopted by the Supreme Government, of starting large public works to give employment and wages, as well as to show some general good for the money spent, was working very well. Lytton believed that the supply of food, whether imported or home grown, should be left to private enterprise, but that it should be distributed, under Government control, to those who would most benefit by it. This, to his mind, meant those who were most able and willing to work for it. To attempt the task of saving life irrespective of cost, or of preventing suffering, was utterly beyond the power of the Government.

The Duke of Buckingham in Madras had adopted a very different policy from Wodehouse's. He had made huge purchases of grain, shipped from Calcutta, in order to keep the price down artificially, and demanded the minimum of work from those who benefited by it. He had opened relief camps all over his Presidency, not only for women and children and those too old or weak to work, but also for the able-bodied who soon became demoralised and diseased from overcrowding.

Conditions in Madras had improved a little while Sir Richard Temple was there (it may be remembered that the Viceroy had sent him to Madras from Delhi) but when he left to take up his appointment as Governor of Bombay on the retirement of Wodehouse, conditions grew worse again and the death-rate rose sharply, whereas in Bombay, where the scarcity was as great, the mortality was far less. Any remonstrance to the Duke of Buckingham, who had been deeply humiliated by Temple's interference, merely aroused his anger. As well as being proud and stubborn, he was greatly influenced by one member of his Council. Intervention in the matter was difficult even for Lord Salisbury.

The battle of the policies was fought out in the Madras and Bombay newspapers. The Bombay press charged the Madras Government with inefficiency and gross extravagance while the Madras papers accused the Bombay Government as well as the Supreme Government of heartlessness, of counting rupees as of more value than human lives. They maintained that the Duke of Buckingham was being very badly treated by the Viceroy and his Councillors who knew nothing of Madrassee conditions. Complaining that he had been denied funds by the Central Government, the Duke had made a personal appeal to world charity.

Conditions in the distressed areas were, of course, appalling. It was the vast agricultural population that was starving and destitute. The *ryots* (peasants with small holdings) had sold or pawned everything they possessed to buy food; they had even torn the straw off the roofs of their houses to get a few *pice* for it. Women, who would rather die than go into relief camps, sold their babies to other women who were then entitled to an extra ration in the camps as nursing mothers. Men were hiring out their wives and daughters as prostitutes. Only the vultures, wolves, jackals and wild dogs grew fat, for people were dying every day in the streets as well as in the country. Cannibalism was so widespread that the police could not control it. There were instances reported of men killing their own children and eating them and drinking their blood. In the relief camps the enemy was disease, due to overcrowding. The camp hospitals overflowed although so many died that they had to be buried in communal graves.[8]

In answer to a suggestion of Salisbury's that a 'famine dictator' should be appointed, Lytton replied:

There never has been yet, and I doubt if there ever will be again, in India an occasion so urgently needing such a dictatorship, but no one in India is able to give the word of command. . . . The adequate management of such a famine urgently requires all the ability and experience which can be found in India, and our line of battle had been completely broken at Madras.[9]

It was at this point that Sir John Strachey conceived the strangely imaginative idea that the Duke himself should be asked to fill the role of dictator, act independently of his Council and secure the help of all the ablest men who had controlled the Bombay famine. It seemed to be the only chance of inducing the Duke to change his policy without losing face. Lytton seized on this plan, obtained Salisbury's sanction for it and decided to go himself to Madras to try to persuade the Duke to adopt it.

Dr Barnett would not allow the Viceroy to undertake the journey south at the height of summer until he had undergone an operation for piles. Prescott Hewett in London had always been against such an operation, so it is no wonder that Edith could hardly sleep the night before it took place on July 20. Doctors Barnett, Bellew and Hervey were all present at the operation which was over in a quarter of an hour, but Robert had bouts of such terrible pain afterwards that Edith was really frightened. There was no pain after the first day, however, and the operation proved entirely successful.

Robert now had a fresh anxiety: Strachey was suffering from severe inflammation of the eyes, as well as a deterioration in his general health, and was told that he must lie in a dark room or face the possibility of going blind. It was obvious that he would not be able to go with the Viceroy to Madras.

Lytton had little hope for the success of his mission. He wrote to Stephen shortly before his departure, 'The weather is hideously hot, and I start on my journey with a profound sense of discouragement, having little assistance here.'[10] The members of his Council were opposed to his scheme (with the exception of Strachey, of course) and this naturally made him more fearful of failure. About Strachey he wrote to Salisbury: 'He is the only man in the Government of India who thoroughly understands the problem we are now dealing with. . . . His courage is indomitable; and if he were stone-blind he would still see further, clearer and quicker than any other man in India. But I feel very unhappy about him, not only because he is my ablest adviser, but also because I love him as a true friend.'[11]

Famine

On August 6 Robert confided his misgivings to Edith who was at Mashroba. He had grave doubts of his legal powers to take the Madras famine into his own hands should the Duke refuse the offer to become 'famine dictator'. Lytton had no faith in Salisbury's promised support. 'He will support me only till the Duke positively resists and then he will throw me over. If therefore I fail to effect a satisfactory agreement with the Duke I see nothing for it but to make the S. of S. [Secretary of State] choose between him and me, and recall one or other of us. The situation is most critical, and the result of the conflict in which I am about to engage, absolutely uncertain.'

By this time some cheering news had reached India. The Russians, having carried all before them, had at the end of July, been unexpectedly halted by Osman Pasha, the Turkish Commander, at Plevna in Bulgaria. This was regarded in England as a sign of Russian weakness. The threat to Constantinople receded and tension between England and Russia relaxed. The war was expected to come to a halt in the winter and to be resumed in the spring. Disraeli had pressed the Cabinet to inform Russia that England would not remain neutral in the event of a spring campaign, but no decision had been reached. The Cabinet was divided. In particular, Lord Derby, the Foreign Secretary, was strongly against making any such threat.

Lytton set off for Madras on August 16 with Colonels Colley and Burne, two aides-de-camp, Dr Barnett and Sir Alexander Arbuthnot, the member of his Council for Home Affairs. Robert and Edith wrote to each other every day while he was away, having decided that in all his telegrams to her he would refer to the Duke as Sardam—Madras backwards. Edith headed her first letter to him 'Black Thursday'; she was utterly wretched the whole time he was away.

At Durhampore on the 17th Lytton sat next to Steuart Bayley at dinner, who, as Secretary of the Government of Bengal, had had experience of famine at Patna in 1874. Lytton found him a most agreeable companion. 'We talked metaphysics, psychology, Darwin, Herbert Spencer and for a while forgot the famine.' It was yet another instance of an immediate mutual attraction, and Lytton took Steuart Bayley with him to Madras as his personal assistant.

At Poona he was joined by Sir Richard Temple from Bombay and General Michael Kennedy, Secretary of the Bombay Public Works Department, who had done more than any other single man to control the famine in that Presidency. All next day at Poona Lytton was busy writing letters for the English mail and to the Duke of Buckingham. The next morning he was to have a Railway Conference. He ended his letter to Edith: 'I am so anxious and miserably unhappy about Strachey.'

The Railway Conference was necessary because at Jubblepore there were 24,000 tons of imported grain piled up, waiting to be transported south, the railway being unable to carry more than 1,000 tons a week. By talking to managers of the railway lines, and with the help of the Department of Public Works, and by buying and borrowing rolling stock, Lytton was able to relieve the block to a certain extent. The pressure of famine traffic was beginning to impede foreign export traffic, and fear of a commercial crisis in Bombay was a fresh anxiety.

In another letter to Edith from Poona, where Robert had decided to stay until August 25 in order to plan his campaign against the Duke, he told her that Temple, who had returned to Bombay, had surrendered General Kennedy with a very good grace to go with him to Madras. The next day he wrote again:

I start for Bellary (where I meet the Duke) to-morrow evening at 10 p.m. My legal powers are much fewer and feebler than I supposed. Nothing left but sheer diplomacy to rely on. I go into battle as L. [the Emperor, Louis Napoleon] went to Sedan—without hope. But we must do our best. You excruciate me, by not telegraphing (as I implored) true and full news of Strachey's health. Anxiety about him weighs on me like a nightmare and is breaking my heart. Could you only assure me he is well, I should have felt twice as strong for the coming conflict with this imbecile Duke.

At Bellary, north west of Madras, Lytton had a long interview with the Duke: 'He is very dull and difficult to keep to the point when it is not one of detail. But I think he means to be loyal. . . . But the real fight will be in Madras whither Sardam returns early tomorrow morning [for a Council meeting] and I rejoin him on Wednesday [the 29th]. All is yet rather vague and we are by no means out of the wood. . . . I continue wonderfully well, but intolerably nervous about the whole business.' That night Lytton, anxious that his views should be clearly stated to the Duke before he met his Council, sat up to write a twelve-page letter to him. He finished it at 3 a.m. and it was delivered to him before he set off. Lytton had been fortified by receiving better news of Strachey.

On August 30 Robert was able to write from Madras: 'Hurrah! I think, my love, I may safely inform you that everything has been satisfactorily settled between the Duke and myself', to which Edith replied, 'I always prophesied that you would carry all before you if you could only have personal interviews.' It had been arranged that the Duke should take the famine into his own hands with the sole help of a secretary and General Kennedy and should adopt the policy of the Supreme Government: all the able-bodied people should be taken out of the relief camps and employed on public works, and the food ration in the camps, which General Kennedy considered unnecessarily generous, should be reduced.

Kennedy wrote to Strachey, 'The difficulties would have been insurmountable had they not been met with rare tact and address from his lordship, whose management of the Duke has been simply admirable, and he has carried him entirely with him from first to last.'[12] Lytton had done more—he had carried the press with him. The Madras *Times* commented that now the Viceroy had seen for himself what conditions were like in Madras and how well the Duke was coping with them, he had gone away perfectly satisfied, leaving his Grace in full charge. The Madras *Mail*, which had pointed out that Lord Lytton was the first Viceroy to visit the Presidency since Lord Dalhousie had spent a holiday there in 1849, believed that he had come to make an *amende honorable* to the subordinate Government. The Duke's face had been magnificently saved and everyone was satisfied except, no doubt, the inmates of the refugee camps.

Robert told Edith in a letter of September 2 from Madras that his mission had succeeded far beyond his expectations. The Duke had 'behaved uncommonly well and very much like a gentleman'. Lytton had now been over most of the relief camps round Madras. 'You never saw such "popular picnics" as they are,' he wrote to Edith in this same letter. 'The people in them do no work of any kind, are bursting with fat, and naturally enjoy themselves thoroughly. The Duke visits these camps like a Buckingham Squire would visit his model farm, taking the deepest interest in the growing fatness of his prize oxen and pigs. . . . But the terrible question is how the Madras Government is ever to get these demoralised masses on to really useful work.'

In his next letter Robert told Edith that he had received two anonymous letters in Madras, obviously written by women, 'one expressing a lively interest in the state of my soul, the other a tender regard for my body'. He went on, 'Dear Owen [Burne] has been more than ever sympathising and helpful. My plan of campaign with the Duke which has been so successful was laid out by Colley.'

Telegrams had now arrived from the Queen, the Prince of Wales and Salisbury all congratulating the Viceroy on the success of his mission. Before returning to Simla he went with the Duke, via Bangalore and Mysore, to Ootacumund, the hill station for Madras. It was not a successful trip; Robert had a headache the first day which prevented his seeing anything, and after that it poured with rain. Only as they were leaving did the clouds clear. 'The morning was fine,' he told Edith, 'and for the first time I have seen Ootacumund. *Having* seen it I affirm it to be paradise. The road was muddy but such beautiful English mud. Imagine a combination of Hertfordshire lanes, Devonshire downs, Westmorland lakes and Scottish trout streams.'

Before Lytton reached Simla on September 26, Strachey had been ordered by his doctors to take a long leave. He was on his way down from the hills when he met Lytton coming up; the two men had half an hour's conversation together on the road.

By October the Viceroy was able to inform the Queen that there was already a marked amelioration in conditions in Madras and Mysore, an improvement in the health of those put on to public works and a reduction in the death rate. He added that these improved conditions were mainly attributable to General Kennedy: 'It is entirely owing to his foresight and energy that whilst the Madras famine has cost the Government of India over ten millions [pounds], the Bombay famine under his management has cost only four millions, although a much larger saving of human life.'[13] (Kennedy, on Lytton's recommendation, was knighted the following year.)

Fortunately the rains came abundantly that autumn and the numbers on famine relief which in September were over two million had fallen by December to 444,000. Sums collected in England and India by the Madras Charitable Relief Committee, initiated by the Duke of Buckingham, were used in helping the *ryots* to buy back the implements they had been forced to sell to buy food. (The Viceroy had contributed £1,000 to this fund out of his own pocket, and over £200,000 had been raised by the Lord Mayor's fund in England.)

But Lytton realised that something much more drastic must be done; each famine could no longer be dealt with empirically when it occurred. In the next Budget, therefore, measures were introduced to provide for the cost of future famines and for the construction of irrigation works, railways and canals. By putting more taxes on land, a licence tax on traders and an income tax on those who did not own land, £1,350,000 was raised annually for a Famine Relief Fund. Lytton also set up a Commission which resulted in the formulation of a Famine Code. This ensured that in all subsequent famines certain measures should be put into operation immediately without wasting time arguing over policy.

11

Tension

On the way back to Simla Lytton had received a report from Sir Richard Pollock that the depredations of the tribes on the North-West Frontier were becoming more outrageous than ever. The frontier officials seemed quite incapable of dealing with the situation, yet something had to be done to protect the lives and property of those British subjects living near the border. Lytton decided to send Colley unofficially from Ambala to Peshawar to confer with Pollock and report on what measures could best be adopted. The Viceroy telegraphed to the Commander-in-Chief at Simla to instruct the Brigadier-General at Peshawar to give Colley every assistance. Haines at once complied, but privately protested to the Viceroy against 'the intervention of an irresponsible officer' between himself and officers under his command.[1] This was the first of many clashes between the Viceroy and the Commander-in-Chief.

The tribe which was being most obstreperous at that time was that of the Jowakis, who occupied a part of the frontier south of Peshawar, sticking out into India from west to east, and controlling the Kohat Pass into Afghanistan. Up till now the frontier policy in trying to control the tribes had been to take punitive measures by attacking the villages across the border with a large force in broad daylight from the front, with the result, in Colley's words, that 'as soon as the fighting men of the village think they have had enough they quietly slip out behind and leave us the proud possessors of a lot of empty stone huts'.[2] After burning the villages there was nothing for the British to do but retire ignominiously. Lytton was very much against this policy which he felt perpetuated barbarous reprisals, rarely punished the guilty party and fell heavily on the innocent.

The new plan, which Major Cavagnari, the Deputy-Commissioner, had worked out and communicated to the Viceroy and Colley, was for a small picked force to set out secretly at night, approach the village in a surprise attack from the rear and capture the men and their arms. As a result of the conference which Colley attended, this plan was adopted with great success in dealing with the small tribes, and it was decided that operations against the more important Jowakis should be carried out on somewhat similar lines. An advance was made into Jowaki country on November 9 with a force of 2,000 men. None of the other tribes came to the rescue of the Jowakis; nevertheless, it was not until the following March that they were finally subdued.

Lytton could now successfully pursue his frontier policy which was, in his own words, 'aimed at the establishment of direct personal relations between our frontier officers and the trans-frontier tribes, and the encouragement of the freest intercourse between them'.[3] It also aimed at obtaining the most accurate geographical information about the country beyond the border. Since the beginning of Lord Lawrence's Viceroyalty until Lytton came to India it had been strictly forbidden for any white man to mix with or communicate with the trans-frontier tribes, and there were no maps of the district. Cavagnari had once entered the Afridi hills where he was hospitably received by the tribes, only to be strongly reprimanded on his return.

This reorganisation of the whole frontier policy was Lytton's great achievement in India although he was bitterly maligned for it in some quarters. White men could thereafter safely enter the passes and there were no more raids across the border.

Colley was back at Simla on October 11. Colonel Burne, who had only been 'lent' to the Viceroy, was due to return to London in March, and since arrangements had to be made in advance, Colley was now offered the Private Secretaryship when Burne left, and George Villiers (just gazetted Colonel) that of Military Secretary in Colley's place. Both men accepted with the proviso that they should be free to return to their regiments in the event of war. But before Colley took up his new position he was to have three months' leave in England; before this he went with the Lyttons on a three weeks' tour, ending in Calcutta. Colonel Burne did not go with them. His wife was expecting another baby in February and was returning to England with her children. He accompanied her to Southampton and then immediately returned to India.

Leaving the children at Simla, the Lyttons and their staff and servants set off on November 5. There were two additions to the party this year—Steuart Bayley, who had gone with Lytton to Madras, and Bonsard, the chef, whose dinners were 'quite admirable' during the tour.

This time their route through the hills took them to Mussorie, a hill station 150 miles south of Simla, where they arrived on November 20. Here official life began again. From Mussorie they went to Agra for the second time and were met there by four Hindu princes—Sindhia of Gwalior, Jaipur, Bhurtpore and Dholpore (a boy of eleven). They stayed three days with Alfred Lyall and his wife. Lytton and Lyall, who had mutual friends in Morley and Stephen, were at once drawn to each other. Lyall was a friend after Lytton's own heart—a poet, a writer, a man of wide culture and broad outlook, in spite of having lived in India for twenty years. He was at this time Resident in Rajputana. (The Residents in native States were political officers who came under the Foreign Department of which the Viceroy was the head; two thirds of them were recruited from the army.) Lord Northbrook had promised Lyall the Foreign Secretaryship when it became vacant. From a personal point of view there was no man in India Lytton would rather have had to travel with him everywhere he went, but in politics Lyall was a radical, and could hardly be expected to favour the forward policy for Afghanistan. However, Lytton took a chance on him; he became Foreign Secretary the following spring and thereafter the two men worked together in almost complete harmony.

Cawnpore was the Lyttons' next stop. Here, memories of the Mutiny were as all-pervading as at Lucknow. They drove to see the *ghat* where the massacre in the boats had taken place and where a commemorative church had been built containing tablets bearing the names of the victims.

And so to Calcutta where they arrived on November 29. It was already 83° in the shade; the *punkhas* were not yet working and the mosquitoes attacked Edith cruelly. The Calcutta house seemed like a great prison to her, though very grand. Robert was in good spirits, she told her mother, but hard at work, sitting up till 6 a.m. sometimes. They had heard *en route* that he was to have the G.C.B. in recognition of his services during the famine. He had also received very flattering dispatches, thanking him, and had been told that Disraeli spoke most cordially of him. They had also heard that Edith was to have the Order of the Crown of India, the first lady 'after the Royals' to receive it. The children joined their parents on December 3. The elder girls had grown considerably and were 'such dear companions'. Emily was very fat and jolly and little Victor had become a real beauty.

A week later came the disturbing news that the Russians had broken through at Plevna, where they had been held by the Turks for over four months, and were advancing towards Constantinople. Disraeli immediately called the Cabinet and asked them to agree to an early summoning of Parliament.

While war excitement was intense in England and people in the streets of London were singing the music hall hit: 'We don't want to fight; but, by Jingo, if we do', the Viceroy, on January 1, 1878, held his first investiture. Maharaja Sindhia of Gwalior was invested with the G.C.B. which had been conferred on him at the time of the Delhi Assemblage; the Maharajas of Bhurtpore and Benares and General Kennedy were made Knights of the Star of India, and Colonel Burne, just returned from England, was made a Companion of the new Order of the Indian Empire. As well as Edith, Lady Strachey and Lady Temple were given the Order of the Crown of India, though no lady was invested that day. (When, the following April, Edith's decoration arrived at Simla with a charming letter from the Queen, she knelt before Robert and was invested at a little ceremony with only a few friends present.)

On January 4 the Lyttons gave a large 'Queen's Ball'. Mademoiselle was invited and allowed to ask all her German friends. Edith wore one of her new dresses from Worth of white tulle trimmed with red berries and wild roses, but her smart satin shoes were 'torture' on the marble floors. One lady came in a high black silk dress, which was against the rules, but she was not turned away. General Roberts, who had just been appointed Commander of the Punjab Frontier Force by the Viceroy, remarked to Edith how happy she looked. In fact she was feeling very much the reverse for she had been crying all day for poor Colonel Burne who had just received news that his wife was dangerously ill. It was decided that he must go home by the next mail steamer from Bombay, two months before his time.* 'R. is so good and patient, though it is a great trial to him, as he has always felt Colonel Burne helped him immensely, and was like a dear tender nurse to him, and he wanted him more than ever with Colonel Colley away.' Steuart Bayley agreed to act as Private Secretary until Colley returned.

The Lyttons were soon to hear by telegram the unwelcome news that Colley was engaged to be married; moreover, he asked for his leave to be extended until the end of April. 'A great surprise,' Edith commented, 'and knowing nothing of her not altogether a pleasant one.' Her dismay was understandable. No one likes to lose by marriage a charming bachelor friend. Lytton wrote him an extremely warm letter, ending, 'Whatever makes you happy makes me happy'.[4] Edith Hamilton, daughter of General Meade Hamilton, was an Irish girl with whom Colley had been corresponding since he left England for India, and a neighbour of the Colley family in Ireland. They were married on March 14 and travelled out to India in a leisurely fashion via Italy and Egypt.

Two days after the news of Colley's engagement arrived Mademoiselle announced that she wanted to marry a German, Herr Seeback. Satisfied that they really cared for each other, Edith gave her consent although it would be 'a sad loss' for her and the girls. (After she left, a German governess, Mlle Oppermann, arrived from Europe. Edith described her as like 'a bright ray of sunshine'.)

The opening of Parliament on January 17 produced no decision with regard to the war. It was not until January 21, when an armstice was signed between Russia and Turkey at Adrianople, the terms of which were unacceptable to England, that the Cabinet at last took action: the fleet was ordered to the Dardanelles. War between Russia and England was again imminent and if the Russians had taken Constantinople it would almost certainly have broken out. On March 3 Russia forced a treaty on the Turks at San Stefano, a small port just west of Constantinople. The British Government then

---

*Burne arrived in England to find his wife dying of 'rapid consumption' as the result of a cold caught on the voyage home. She gave birth to a daughter on February 20 and died on April 22, aged thirty-seven. Poor Mrs Burne—could she have been consumptive all along? Was that the reason for her constant dullness? Burne, who was knighted in 1879, married again in 1883 Lady Agnes Douglas, daughter of the Earl of Morton. In 1887 he was appointed a member of the Indian Council in London.

demanded that the terms of the treaty, which had been kept secret, should be submitted to the arbitration of the Great Powers. The situation was tense in England while Russia's reply was awaited.

It was in this atmosphere of uncertainty that the Viceroy brought before his Legislative Council a new Bill which he had been busy drafting that winter. This was the Vernacular Press Bill which was bitterly opposed, not only by Indians but by the whole of Liberal opinion in England. In 1835, Macaulay, then the legal member of the Viceroy's Council, had released the Indian press from all censorship, since when the Indians had come to regard a free press as a sacred right. With the spread of education many newspapers in different native languages had been started; by 1878 there were about 200 in almost as many languages. The press had been muzzled during the Mutiny but at that time restrictions had been imposed equally on English and vernacular papers and had been withdrawn immediately after the restoration of law and order. Through the press the people were able to vent their grievances against the Government, and it was an excellent way for the Government to discover what those grievances were.

For the past ten years there had been a growing dissatisfaction on the part of the Government, who accused the native papers of daily publishing mischievous falsehoods, and before Lytton arrived in India there had been much talk of what measures should be taken to censor them. Most of the attacks on the Government were on subjects such as the larger jurisdiction given to Europeans, the inequality of punishment meted out to Europeans and natives for the same offence; the general unfriendliness and haughtiness of the Europeans; the overbearing conduct of the British Residents in the natives States. But now the native newspapers were publishing undeniably seditious material, even going so far in a few instances as to encourage the *sepoys* (infantry) to turn on their officers as they had done in the Mutiny. Such sedition, the Government felt, could no longer be tolerated, especially at this time of tension between Russia and England.

There was already an existing law of 1867 prescribing that the proprietor of a paper, whose name had to be registered in the Government record, was responsible for all seditious articles published and was liable to be fined, but no distinction was made between English and native papers. This law could be evaded by the real proprietor registering his paper in the name of some poor student who had no means with which to pay the fine. To circumvent this, the new Bill called for the laying down of a bond of Rs. 10,000 by all *native* proprietors who would be compelled to re-register their papers. If any seditious matter was published the local Government was to warn the proprietor concerned; any repetition of the offence would result in the seizure of the plant and forfeiture of the bond. All the small papers which could not afford such a deposit would be forced out of business. The reason given for making the distinction between English-language papers and those in native languages was that the latter were circulated among people who were likely to believe anything they read, whereas those who could read English were capable of judging the contents for themselves.

The Bill, which was approved by Lord Salisbury on March 8, was introduced by Sir Alexander Arbuthnot on March 14. All those who spoke were in favour of it, though expressing their regret for the necessity of such a law in a British dependency, and it was passed at a single sitting. The Act was applied only once before it was repealed in 1881 by Lytton's successor, Lord Ripon. Nevertheless, the protests against it during the three years it was in force brought Indians together in a way they had never been united before. The fight for Indian freedom by the educated masses can really be said to date from the Vernacular Press Act.

12

Secret Instructions

The children, who had been ill on and off all the winter, had been sent to Simla on February 16, and on March 18 the Lyttons and their party left Calcutta, without a single regret this year as far as Edith was concerned. After two nights in the special train they arrived at Saharampore in the north, not far from Ambala, and from there began the usual tour of day marches and nights in camp. Alfred Lyall, the new Foreign Secretary, was with them this time.

From Rampur they crossed the Jumna into the territory of the Raja of Nahun and drove on March 26 to a camp he had prepared for them at Marjura. Edith described a tiger shoot arranged next day by the Raja for the Viceroy's staff (Robert himself hated shooting):

The gentlemen came in at two very excited having been out since seven. On arriving at the spot they were told they were to go on foot which is most dangerous and all acknowledge to having been much frightened but none liked to say they would not go. Lord William said he prayed all the time that a tiger might not come near him for he is a bad shot and says he must have been killed either by an animal or the native guns who stood behind him. The party got three tigers and a bear—the latter Dr Barnett shot. Captain Rose was looking at a tiger cub he had shot lying dead in a little dell, when he heard a tremendous roar, and a large tigress rushed past, taking his Khitmagar by the arm and dragging him down a small khud, literally rolling together, and Captain R. thought the man must be dead but the tigress left him, then Captain Rose shot her dead but they were really all in great danger. The Raja shot the second cub, and the natives with him, giving some extra shots, fired on a poor sepoy and shot him in the arm and leg. Dr Barnett got much chaffed for having some luck with surgical cases as well as other sport. George [Villiers] looked rather low at having no chance, but considering the danger I thought he was very lucky to have had an uneventful day.

The Viceroy's day had been far from uneventful. He had received exciting news from home. Russia had declined to submit the Treaty of San Stefano to the Powers, whereupon Disraeli had called out the reserves and telegraphed to Lytton instructing him to send 7,000 native troops to the Mediterranean, but to observe complete secrecy in making the necessary preparations until Parliament adjourned in three weeks' time. If the news came out while Parliament was sitting, the pressure of questions would be so great that it would be difficult to maintain secrecy. This was the first time that native troops had ever been sent abroad.

On the evening of that same day, March 27, Lord Derby resigned, Lord Salisbury became Foreign Secretary and Gathorne Hardy (who was soon created Viscount Cranbrook) was appointed Secretary of State for India. (Salisbury and Lytton wrote warm letters to each other on the occasion of these changes of office; their relations were never outwardly anything but cordial.)

Lytton could not, of course, make any open preparations, but was able secretly to plan his course of action with Sir Edwin Johnson, military member of Council, whom he asked to join him on tour, and who, together with the Commander-in-Chief and Sir Richard Temple, Governor of Bombay, were the only people he was permitted by Disraeli to take into his confidence. The troops would have to be transported from Bombay. They were concentrated near that city and it was given out that they were being moved for a land expedition. Temple had secretly to arrange transport for 1,300 horses as well as 7,000 men. It was planned to send one brigade of white troops to two of native. No Mahometans were to be sent, only Sikhs and Gurkhas.

The Lyttons arrived at Simla on April 4 in 'excruciating uncertainty between war and peace' as Robert put it. Edith and the children were overjoyed to see each other again and 'jumped and ran about together'. She had never thought to see them so well in India again. Life went on normally under the threat of war. 'This month has been such a happy one as we have not received,' Edith wrote in her diary on Good Friday, April 19, 'and I have been able to enjoy my pets. I have also had charming scrambling walks with dear R. Oh, I hope this may be a happy season and that our nice staff won't all be taken away to a war. We are quite uncertain whether there will be any or not.'

Secret Instructions

Lytton had redecorated the Simla theatre and had had three boxes built—for the Viceroy, the Commander-in-Chief and the Lieutenant-Governor of the Punjab. The amateur theatrical season that year began with a production of Bulwer-Lytton's *Walpole*, a play in rhymed verse on the subject of Robert Walpole's dictum that 'Every man has his price'. The Viceroy himself superintended all the rehearsals. He also had the roads improved at Simla that summer, making an easier way down to Allandale, a new carriage road up to Peterhof and a carriage road round Jacko.

On April 15 Parliament adjourned and the next day it was announced that Indian troops were to be sent to Malta. (This move was denounced by the Opposition as unconstitutional.) Lytton's secret preparations were so far advanced that the embarkation of the whole force was completed by May 1. On that day he wrote to tell Lord Cranbrook, his new Chief, that the fighting elements in every part of India had been telegraphing for permission to be employed in any service against Russia. The Begum of Bhopal had offered to put all the resources of her kingdom at the disposal of the British in the event of war; the Maharaja of Kashmir had offered his best troops for the defence of the North-West Frontier; Nepal had offered its whole army for garrison work, and Maharaja Sindhia, who was an honorary Colonel in the British army, was 'fretting' for permission to furnish and lead a regiment.[1] Lytton saw this enthusiasm to serve the British as a direct result of his wooing of the princes at the Delhi Assemblage, and he felt justly proud of the loyalty he had inspired in them, particularly with this evidence of loyalty in Kashmir.

When towards the end of April Colonel Colley arrived at Bombay with his new bride he saw ships being hurriedly engaged and found war excitement running high. The move of Indian troops seemed more than anything else to have convinced Russia that England was not bluffing, and she agreed to a Congress of Powers to consider the Treaty of San Stefano. It was eventually decided that the Congress should be held in Berlin.

The Colleys went straight to Simla where they arrived on May 2. Both Edith and Robert were delighted with Mrs Colley who was graceful and pretty as well as having 'an easy way of chatting'. Thereafter Edith had a woman friend, the only one she had made in India, and she needed a friend when she realised at the end of the month, to her intense dismay, that she was going to have another baby. She felt very ill for some weeks after that and was obliged to give up many of her official duties.

Colley could no longer, of course, be quite the same ever-present friend to the whole Lytton family as he had been as a bachelor. Robert was particularly glad to have him back, though, because John Strachey had fallen ill again and had to go home on six months' leave. While he was away, his elder brother, General Richard Strachey, took his place as financial member of Council. General Strachey had had a long distinguished career in India before retiring from the army in 1875. He had returned to England and had been on the Indian Council in London until 1877 when he came back to India to arrange the purchase of the East India Railway for the Government. Lytton then made him chairman of the Famine Commission. When he agreed to stay on as Finance Minister, his wife decided to join him. Before she arrived she had been very critical of Lytton's Afghan policy in letters to her husband[2] (*all* the Stracheys were Liberals), but as soon as she met him she was captivated and they became firm and lasting friends, sharing a particular love for amateur theatricals. When her fifth son was born in England in 1880 Lytton was asked to be his godfather, and the child was called after him.

General Strachey had supported Lytton on the London Council. After he left for India the Council began to harass the Viceroy.

Each of us has a thorn in the flesh in the shape of a Council [Lytton wrote to Cranbrook in May]. In this respect I fear your thorn is bigger than mine, your Council being more numerous [fifteen], and then there is Parliament behind it. When I first joined my own Council, I found it in a very cantankerous, and hostile disposition towards any advice or instruction from home.... I think I have now got the Council here sufficiently in hand to be able to assure you that, on any question of importance, you need fear no frivolous, or factious, opposition from the Government of India.... I have only to consider what is best for India; you have also to consider what is possible in England.... But I must confess to you, my dear Lord, that the recent attitude and conduct of the India Office Council causes me some anxiety. The disposition of that Council is to reject summarily every proposal, however important, or however trivial, which emanates from the Government of India.... I cannot, of course, and do not, expect unanimity of opinion, or support, from fifteen gentlemen, whose chief function is negative criticism. But I do feel very strongly that, in the ordinary current details of its administration, a great Government such as the Government of India, ought not to be and cannot safely, be, subjected to the uncontrolled interference, and invariable veto, of a distant, and practically irresponsible, body sitting in England.... I should not dream of exercising in the affairs of the smallest local Government of India, the same amount of detailed interference, which has lately been exercised by the India Office in the affairs of the Supreme Government. Every administrative question, however trivial, has a financial side to it, and must therefore be submitted by the local to the central authorities in whom the financial control is vested. But were I to stretch the technical right of using financial supervision for the purpose of administrative interference, in my relations with the local Governments, as far as it has been lately stretched by the India Office in its relations with the Government of India, the whole machinery of Indian administration would soon break down.[3]

In this letter Lytton gave some instances of the interference he complained of. They were small administrative matters which the Council in London persuaded themselves had a financial implication and therefore came within their jurisdiction. Lytton also went on to tell Cranbrook that he had 'a vague impression' that the hostility of the Council was 'personal to' himself, and if Cranbrook could find out his sins of omission or commission he would be anxious to repair them. He wrote to Burne that the only hope for the Council in London was to fill up all the vacancies with younger men who still had a career to make instead of retired civilians with nothing left to do but 'air their crotchets and prejudices'.[4]

Shortly afterwards Lytton was writing again to Cranbrook to tell him that Sir Henry Norman, who had been military member of his own Council and was now on the Indian Council in London, had been behaving in the most outrageous way. He had written to General Roberts, in command of the Punjab Frontier Force, and to Sir Edwin Johnson 'vehemently denouncing' the whole of Lytton's frontier policy and 'urging them to resist it', and also charging the Viceroy with having caused the alienation of Afghanistan, 'although', as Lytton said, 'he must be well aware that this was an irretrievable *fait accompli* long before I came to India'.[5]

It seems probable that it was Sir Henry Norman and Sir William

Muir, both of whom had been overruled by the Viceroy when he first came to India, who had managed to communicate to the other members of the Secretary of State's Council their own personal dislike of Lytton.

The Congress of Berlin, which was to last a month, was convened on June 13, but before it opened England had entered into a secret agreement with Turkey whereby, in exchange for a defensive alliance, Turkey agreed to the occupation of Cyprus by the British. It was an answer to Russia's acquisition of the Black Sea port of Batum under the terms of the Treaty of San Stefano.

Just as a major war receded with the opening of the Congress a little war was started in South Africa with the Kaffir tribes (it was the ninth Kaffir War). Edith reported that on June 23 Lord William 'suddenly settled to start for six months leave for the Kaffir war as he is restless'. He left that evening after a sad parting, with 'everyone shedding tears over him', but two days later he was back again having heard by telegraph at Ambala that the war was over. 'Only waiting to dine he rushed back to be in time for a ball we had and Oh how ill and faint I felt at it.' The ball was a success all the same and 'the people danced like mad creatures, as if they had never danced before'.

Miss Marianne North came to Simla in June and lunched at Peterhof to show the Lyttons her drawings. 'She is a most curious character,' Edith wrote, 'and has travelled a great deal. She has an exhibition of 500 drawings at South Kensington; and one of the lovely Amhersitia among them.' Edith liked some of her sketches very much, 'especially of the dear Taj', but found the colouring rather hard.* She considered that Colonel Colley could sketch just as well and only wished he had more time for it. Marianne North gives a vivid picture of the Lyttons at Simla. She complained that 'Lord Lytton set a bad example, keeping up very late at night'. She

---

* Marianne North (1830–90) travelled all over the world painting flowers in their natural habitat. Encouraged by Charles Darwin and Sir Joseph Hooker, director of Kew, she had a gallery built in Kew Gardens at her own expense to house 848 flower paintings and landscapes. Designed by James Fergusson it was opened to the public in 1882. Though not impressive from the outside, the gallery is delightful inside with small, brilliantly coloured oil paintings so closely covering the walls as to give the appearance of an enchanting wallpaper. The Amhersitia, which Edith had greatly admired in the Botanical Gardens in Calcutta (a Burmese plant) and the picture of 'the dear Taj' are in the collection at Kew.

was staying with the Lieutenant-Governor of the Punjab, Robert Egerton:

One afternoon he proposed going to the Simla Monday Popular Concert, and before I knew where I was, I found myself sitting in a great arm-chair next the gorgeous and lovely Lady Lytton in front of everybody, in my old looped-up serge gown and shabby old hat. I consoled myself by thinking it was quite distinguished to be shabby in Simla; and the Queen of Simla made everybody believe she was entirely devoted to them and interested in their particular hobbies while she talked to them.... The concert was chiefly an amateur one, and because one of the ladies was nervous, Lady Lytton made the Governor encore her song to encourage her. It was impossible not to love that beautiful lady. I took my paintings one day and had luncheon with them, in the middle of which entertainment the Viceroy lit his cigarette. He was interested in my work, and spent an hour or more looking at it. One night I went to a tremendous dinner there. About fifty sat down in the great dining-room, and a band played all the while. The table was quite covered with green ferns and ivy laid flat upon it, with masses of different coloured flowers also laid on, in set patterns. The yellow bracts of the bethamia, with bougainvillia, hibiscus, etc., formed separate masses of colour. The ladies' dresses were magnificent, Lady L, herself so hung with artificial flowers that she made quite a crushing noise whenever she sat down. Lord and Lady L. came in arm and arm, just as dinner was announced. After dinner an A.D.C. carried a small chair for Lady L., who went about talking to everyone in turn. The Viceroy also did his best to be civil to people.[6]

Edith's graciousness, which had so charmed Miss North, had been noted by Val Prinsep at Delhi and was to be confirmed by Wilfred Blunt the following year when he stayed at Simla. It is a pity that her letters and diary entries give so little idea of how she must have appeared and the charm she must have exercised. Her photographs, however, show her dignity and strength of character. She was greatly loved by her children and her many grandchildren.

13

The Russians at Kabul

The Treaty of Berlin, signed on July 13, was a diplomatic triumph for Disraeli, and although he had to compromise over certain issues he got his way in most things. (Russia kept Batum but England kept Cyprus.) Above all it prevented the occupation of Constantinople by the Russians, and, as Disraeli believed, halted the Russian advance in Central Asia. But all this time Russia had been drawing nearer the Afghan border, and while the Congress was still sitting, rumour had reached Simla, through native spies, that the Tsar was sending a Russian mission to Kabul. The Amir, it was said, had tried to stop it, only to be informed by General Kaufmann from Tashkent that it was too late to recall it and that the Amir would be held responsible for its safe-conduct through Afghanistan and honourable reception at Kabul. Sher Ali had then given orders that no obstacle should be placed in its way.

On receipt of a telegram to this effect from the Viceroy to Cranbrook, the British Government sent an enquiry to St Petersburg and was assured that no Russian representative had been, or was intended to be, sent to Kabul, either by the Russian Government or by General Kaufmann.[1] When this assurance was relayed to Lytton at Simla he telegraphed back on July 30 that the representative was coming, by whomsoever sent: in these circumstances he proposed, with Cranbrook's consent, to insist on the immediate reception by the Amir of a British mission.[2]

On August 2 the Viceroy sent another telegram to Cranbrook confirming that the Russian Mission under General Stoletov had arrived at Kabul in spite of Russian assurances to the contrary and had been received with honour by the Amir. The telegram continued:

To remain inactive now will, we respectfully submit, be to allow Afghanistan to fall certainly and completely under Russian power and influence. We believe we could correct situation if allowed to treat it as a question between us and the Ameer, and probably could do so without recourse to force. But we must speak plainly and decidedly and be sure of your support. Ameer knows that we are more powerful for good or harm in Afghanistan than Russia but he believes Russian policy bolder and more resolute and therefore had granted to Russia what he has refused us.[3]

After a meeting of the Cabinet on August 3, Cranbrook telegraphed to Lytton: 'Assuming the certainty of Russian officers in Kabul your proposal to insist on reception of British envoy approved. In case of refusal you will telegraph again as to step you desire to take for compelling Ameer to receive your Mission. I presume you would not employ force by Khyber Pass.' To this Lytton replied, 'No hostile action will be taken without previous communication to you, and no employment of force in Khyber is contemplated.'

General Sir Neville Chamberlain (no relation of the British Prime Minister of that name), Commander-in-Chief at Madras, was asked by the Viceroy to head the Mission—'an able resolute man of exceptional experience of all frontier matters', as Lytton described him, and, moreover, one who had lived in Afghanistan for four years altogether and was personally acquainted with the Amir. (Lytton had chosen him particularly because he was 'a hero of the Lawrence school', thereby hoping to placate the Opposition.)[4] Chamberlain was to be accompanied by Major Cavagnari as his second in command, a Major St John, Dr Bellew, two Indian nobles (a Mahometan and a Hindu) and an escort of 250 Guides (the number of the Russian escort) under the command of a Colonel Jenkins. (The Guides were the cream of the Indian army, and, incidentally, the first soldiers ever to wear khaki.) The Mission was to carry expensive presents for the Amir to show its friendly nature. 'Its safe-conduct through the Khyber Pass,' Lytton wrote to Cranbrook on August 3, '(for which negotiations are already being opened with the Khyberis), is only a question of money.'[5]

On August 14 a native Mahometan nobleman, the Nawab Ghulam Hassan, was entrusted with a letter from the Viceroy to the Amir announcing the coming of this friendly Mission. Four days later Lytton telegraphed to Cranbrook to say that Chamberlain had accepted charge of the Mission and would probably leave Peshawar for Kabul on September 8. On August 21 news was received at Simla that the Amir's favourite son and heir, Abdulla Jan, had died on the 17th; in consequence the Nawab was held back until August 30. On that day he left Peshawar with an additional letter to the Amir of condolence from the Viceroy. (This letter of condolence was never answered, an unpardonable affront to the Viceroy according to native etiquette.) The Mission was also held back so that it would not arrive at Kabul until the end of the forty days' period of mourning.

During this interval of waiting, Sir Neville Chamberlain and Cavagnari went up to Simla on August 25. The day before they arrived Lytton telegraphed to Cranbrook for approval of Chamberlain's orders. Cranbrook replied, 'Must leave wide discretion to you,' whereupon Lytton telegraphed back by return, 'Grateful thanks for confidence placed in my discretion.'[6] He now felt he could go ahead with his plans without any interference from London. He heard on August 31 that General Stoletov had returned to Tashkent leaving two officers behind at Kabul and promising to return there himself in forty days' time. On that day Lytton wrote to Cranbrook that Haines, the Commander-in-Chief, was advocating 'gigantic preparations for gigantic campaigns' in the event of the Amir's refusing to receive the Mission.[7] Lytton himself did not believe that he would dare refuse it.

Lytton also wrote to the Queen on August 31 giving her a detailed report on the situation, and concluding:

Such are the difficulties and anxieties of the position in which we are landed at last by seven years of the policy, pertinaciously imposed by Mr Gladstone on successive Governments of India in the conduct of their relations with Afghanistan. A small stitch taken in time, even a few years ago, would have certainly saved the nine big ones which may have to be taken now. As that eminent man, and his personal supporters in office, are the direct authors of all our present difficulties in Afghanistan, I trust that, at least, they will now have sufficient patriotism to abstain from factiously opposing, and weakening, the efforts of those, to whom they have bequeathed the dread responsibilities of their own neglect.[8]

This criticism of the Queen's former Prime Minister was not, to Lytton's mind, involving her in politics but simply acquainting her with what he believed to be the true facts. All the same, it seems

remarkable that he should have felt free to blame Gladstone so un-
equivocally to the Queen. No doubt he felt more free to do so on
account of her well known detestation of Gladstone.

Edith, who had given up her room at Peterhof to Sir Neville
Chamberlain, was feeling better and able to take part in all the entertainments arranged in his honour. 'I have quite lost my heart to
Sir Neville,' she wrote, 'he is such a great gentleman, and immediately on arriving he made R. such a nice speech, saying that whatever policy he had formerly held, and however much his sympathies
had been with Lord Lawrence, they were views of thirty-five years
ago, and he would most loyally carry out all R. said to him.' But
in spite of Sir Neville's charm she was glad to get her room back
when he and Cavagnari left for Peshawar on September 8.

On that day Lytton telegraphed to Cranbrook, 'Chamberlain's
instructions considered and approved in Council yesterday, is to
leave Peshawar about 16th to march to Kabul disregarding objec-
tions or remonstrances en route, and not stopping unless resisted
by force. On reaching Kabul is to deliver Viceroy's letter in Durbar,
ask explanation of reception of Russian Mission after refusal of
British one and insist on dismissal of Russian Mission. British
Government engages protect Ameer against consequences from
Russia.'

On the same day Lytton wrote Cranbrook a most revealing letter:

Sir Neville Chamberlain left Simla early this morning, in good heart and
hope. I am greatly pleased by all I have seen of him during his stay with
me: and I do not think the Kabul Mission could have been confided
to safer, or firmer, hands than his. His second in command (Cavagnari)
is one of the very few Indian officials who have a really political head:
a possession he probably owes to his Genoese parentage. . . . The impression at Peshawar is that the Ameer is anxiously awaiting Kauffman's reply
to an urgent enquiry, from himself, as to what practical assistance the
Russians are prepared to give him, if he breaks with us: and that, pending
the receipt of this reply, he will be fertile in pretexts, either for not receiving the Mission, or for evading its representations. This is probable. . . .
By his reception of a Russian, after his refusal to accept a British, Mission,
the Ameer of Kabul has inflicted upon us a public, and very significant
affront, in the face of all Asia, and all India. . . . Utterly disbelieving,
as I do, both in the efficacy of British diplomacy at St Petersburg, and

also in the necessity of making a European *casus belli* about Russian misdemeanours in Central Asia, I thank you sincerely and cordially, for the large discretion you are disposed to leave to the Government of India in dealing with the present crisis which I certainly believe to be more seriously dangerous to our position in India than anything else that has yet happened since the mutiny. I am confident ... that the Government of India is the only executive authority to deal with those difficulties efficiently, yet inexpensively, that I do not shrink from any amount of responsibility.... But scalded cats mistrust cold water; and I cannot help remembering that, although, for more than twelve months, Lord Salisbury, in his private letters and telegrams, unreservedly approved, and encouraged, every detail of my policy and action in regard to frontier affairs, yet when these were publicly challenged, he threw me over the parapet without a moment's hesitation; and the language he then publicly held to others was absolutely irreconcilable with that which he had been privately holding to myself.... I sincerely believe, that on this particular question of Afghan Policy, I am at the present moment, the *least* bellicose man in all India. I trust that my accompanying minute will satisfy you that I am really not the reckless military fire-brand which your Council, I know, supposes me to be. Here, at least, I am daily made to feel the resentment with which my military advisers regard my constant repression of their martial ambitions.[9]

On this same day, September 8, the Viceroy issued a long public communiqué announcing that a Mission to the Amir, headed by Sir Neville Chamberlain, was to leave Peshawar on September 17 and proceed to Kabul through the Khyber Pass; the communiqué, which also gave in detail the reasons for this step, was published in the London *Times* on September 10. What Lytton did not know was that on August 19 the British Government had sent a letter of remonstrance to St Petersburg requesting an explanation for the sending of Stoletov's Mission. It came as a shocking surprise to him, therefore, when on September 14, only three days before Chamberlain's Mission was due to set out, he received a telegram from the India Office informing him: 'Official reply to remonstrance at St Petersburg on way to London. Important to secure this before Chamberlain starts. Await further telegram.'

The extraordinary truth of the matter is contained in a letter from Cranbrook to Disraeli dated September 13: 'I was not aware, nor could Lord Lytton be, that any remonstrance had been addressed to M. Giers [Russian Foreign Secretary].'[10] The only explanation for having neglected to inform Cranbrook (and therefore the Viceroy) of the remonstrance was that the Cabinet was scattered for the summer holidays; Disraeli, a sick man, was resting at Hughenden after his exertions in Berlin; Cranbrook was deer-stalking in Scotland, but could easily have been reached. It was Lord Salisbury in London who was the first member of the Government to see Lytton's telegram of September 8 announcing the date of Chamberlain's departure, and it was he who sent it to Disraeli. On the day the Viceroy's communiqué was published in *The Times*, Salisbury, believing that there was need for immediate action, went to Hughenden to confer with Disraeli, and then wrote to him next day, '. . . the information which reaches me is that Cranbrook's views are inclined to be bellicose with respect to Afghanistan. In order, therefore, to ensure full consideration I have officially requested the India Office to prevent any action being taken in India until we have received and communicated a letter from de Giers on this subject.'[11] In fact Salisbury had written to Cranbrook in Scotland requesting him to stop the Mission, and it was Cranbrook, on Salisbury's instructions, who had ordered the India Office to telegraph to Lytton.[12]

Disraeli, much perturbed, hastened to write to Cranbrook on September 12:

What injurious effects Lytton's policy, ostentatiously indiscreetly, but, evidently officially announced in the Calcutta correspondence of *The Times* of yesterday [actually the 10th], may produce, I cannot presume to say. But I am alarmed, and affairs require in my opinion, your gravest attention. If Ld. Lytton has ventured on these steps with full acquaintance with our relations with Russia on the subject of Afghanistan, he has committed a grave error; if he has been left in ignorance of them, our responsibility is extreme.[13]

The responsibility for not acquainting either Cranbrook or Lytton with the facts was surely Salisbury's, and it does seem a quite unaccountable lapse on his part for which he never, apparently, offered the Viceroy the slightest apology. The next day Disraeli wrote to Cranbrook again: 'Our despatches crossed. . . . I have read all your documents, printed and M.S. Lytton grapples with his subject like a man. I always thought highly of his abilities, but this specimen of them elevates my estimate.'[14]

1878

Cranbrook, who could not come south to confer with his colleagues in this crisis because he had to go to Balmoral, replied by return to Disraeli's letter of the 12th: 'I am sorry that Lytton has so ostentatiously proclaimed his intentions ... but I think to stop the mission would be most prejudicial after what has occurred.... It is time to come to some understanding about the position of Afghanistan in relation to ourselves, and inactivity will not meet the case.'[15]

In truth neither Disraeli nor Salisbury had been perturbed by the Russian Mission to Kabul. They had looked on it as retaliation for bringing Indian troops into the Mediterranean and believed that now peace had been established by the Treaty of Berlin the Mission would be recalled. Stoletov had indeed left Kabul on August 23 but had left behind two officers belonging to the Mission who remained there until December.

By the time Lytton was told about the remonstrance to St Petersburg his preparations were complete and had been publicly announced. He was in a very awkward position. Nevertheless, he held up the Chamberlain Mission for four days. Any further delay, as he told Cranbrook, would lose it the help of the Khyberi tribes whose promise of safe-conduct through the Pass had been secured by Cavagnari. There had never been any doubt in Lytton's mind but that the Mission should go by the most direct route to Kabul, through the Khyber Pass. Later he was accused by Disraeli of disobeying orders; he had been told, Disraeli averred, to send it by Kandahar and on no account by the Khyber. No such instructions had in fact reached Lytton. He had merely been told not to employ force in the Khyber, and this he never intended to do. Cranbrook had known since the beginning of August that it was to go by the Khyber. To have sent the Mission by the circuitous route by Kandahar was the difference between 460 miles and 166 miles. As Lytton afterwards told Cranbrook it would have taken the Mission '150 days to complete its business' had it gone by Kandahar.[16]

Disraeli's objection to the Khyber route was never explained. The passes did not belong to the Amir and he had only been allowed to keep them as a friend of the British, and on the understanding that he kept them open.[17] He had shut them against the British long before Lytton came to India.

134

14

War and Peace

On September 17 Lytton heard unofficially (probably from Colonel Burne at the India Office) that an answer had come from St Petersburg, and that it was unsatisfactory.[1] He also heard on the 17th that the Nawab had delivered his letters to the Amir at a private audience, and that the Amir was much displeased and objected to the coming of the Mission. Chamberlain, who had relayed this message to the Viceroy from Peshawar, gave it as his opinion that the Amir was trifling with them.

Lytton decided to wait no longer. Although he had not heard directly from the Amir nor received authority from London he gave orders to Chamberlain to set off from Peshawar on September 21. To Edith, who was now in camp at Narkanda with Mrs Colley, Robert excitedly recounted the progress of the Mission in a letter begun at 1.45 a.m. on the 22nd:

Last night Chamberlain reported that he had at last completed negotiations with the Khyberis to escort the mission as far as Ali Musjid (a fort half way through the Khyber Pass [ten miles inside the Pass] which is held by the Ameer's troops under the command of Faiz Mohamed). He proposed to send Cavagnari on with the Khyberi escort to Ali Musjid to demand from Faiz Mohamed whether he would let the mission pass beyond or not—with orders to insist on a plain yes or no: he himself remaining at Peshawur with the rest of the mission. I telegraphed back to this effect: 'No, you must leave Peshawur with the whole mission and enter the pass,—be it only a few inches,—in order that if the Ameer's authorities oppose your further progress—or refuse safe conduct beyond Ali Musjid, the *return* of your mission to Peshawur may furnish me with a definite *fact* which the public can understand. But you need not proceed further than Jamrood (the first station-fort in the pass within a few miles of our frontier). Halt there and send Cavagnari, with small escort to Ali Musjid with the instructions you have proposed. If the reply of Faiz

Mohamed is satisfactory move on the whole mission at once. If unsatisfactory I shall be prepared to withdraw the mission and break off negotiations.' This morning Chamberlain telegraphed that the mission had moved out of Peshawur to Jamrood: was camping there: and that Cavagnari had gone on as proposed, with an ultimatum, to Ali Musjid.

So matters stood when I went to dine with the Stracheys [the Richard Stracheys] this evening. At dinner I received the following from Sir Neville: '8.4 p.m. Cavagnari reports that he has received a decisive answer from Faiz Mohamed after a personal interview, that he will *not* allow the mission to proceed. He (F. M.) crowned the heights with his levees, commanding the way: and, though many times warned by Cavagnari that his reply would be regarded as that of the Ameer, he said he would not let the mission pass. I now go to Jamrood for the night. Shall I make another attempt tomorrow morning, to bring Faiz Mohamed to reason, or make him fire on us?—A reply can reach me before morning. P.S. I have just met Cavagnari, who has given me full details. I am positively of opinion that any further attempt will only bring more disgrace on us.'

To this immediately after dinner I replied (without the smallest hesitation in my own mind) as follows:— 'Your tele. received. Accepting Faiz Mohamed's reply to ultimatum by Cavagnari as positive refusal by Ameer to let the mission pass, I consider you should now withdraw, and spare no effort to detach Khyberis from Ameer. Simultaneously communicate briefly to Ghulam Hassan [the Nawab who had taken the letters to the Amir] what has occurred and instruct him to return immediately.'

By the time I had ciphered this and sent a copy of it (and Chamberlain's telegram) to Colley [Colley had left Simla that afternoon to spend a few days at Narkanda with his wife so Lytton was acting entirely on his own initiative] it was past 1 p.m. I then came home, and found here George Villiers [Military Secretary] with a long face, and a message from Lyall [Foreign Secretary] to the effect that he (Lyall) was frightened by the decisive character of this instruction and begged reconsideration, but as Lyall could suggest no practical alternative, and as it was necessary to answer Chamberlain before daybreak, I have maintained my own instruction; and I think it is justified by the following telegram from the Commissioner [Pollock] which reached me while I was writing this:— 'Cavagnari attended by whole native staff had 3 hour interview with Faiz Mohamed who positively refused to allow passage of mission. Was blamed for allowing Nawab to pass. Consequences were explained, but refusal was absolute.'

The alternative to the 'decisive' instruction to withdraw the

Mission could only have been to temporize by leaving it at Jam-rood or Peshawar in the hope that the Amir would relent.

Immediately after these events Chamberlain wrote to the Viceroy, 'Nothing could have been more distinct. Nothing more humiliating to the dignity of the British Crown and nation ... and I believe that but for the decision and tact shown by Major Cavag-nari at one period of the interview even the lives of the British officers, as also the lives of the small native escort, were in consider-able danger.'[2] The Afghan soldiers had begun to pull back their sleeves in a manner recognised by Cavagnari as being a prelude to drawing their swords. Chamberlain, on withdrawing the Mission, guaranteed the full aid and protection of the British Government to the Khyberi tribes who had escorted Cavagnari to Ali Musjid should the Amir take revenge on them.

As Lytton wrote to the Queen, 'This public and deliberate affront, which has produced a profound sensation throughout In-dia, precludes all further hope of amicable relations with Sher Ali. To leave it unavenged would dangerously shake the confidence in the power of your Majesty in your Majesty's subjects.'[3] He also wrote to Cranbrook, 'The Amir's policy was to make fools of us in the sight of all Central Asia, and India, without affording us any pretext for active resentment.... The affront offered to the British Government ... is no greater than any of the numerous affronts from the Ameer accepted during the past seven years. The dif-ference is that it was impossible to conceal this particular one from the British public.'[4] The Amir had now been forced to show his hand.

Although Disraeli had known since September 16 of the unsatis-factory reply from de Giers, the Russian Foreign Secretary, it was not until the 24th that the Viceroy was at last officially informed of it from London.[5] It was as might have been expected: the British Government was assured that the Russian Mission was not of a nature to excite English suspicions; it was purely courteous, and did not clash with Russia's former promise that Afghanistan should remain outside her sphere of influence.[6] This reply did nothing to allay Lytton's suspicions. Despairing of ever establishing friendly relations with the Amir and genuinely fearing Russian en-croachment, he believed that the subjugation of Afghanistan was now the only means of preventing Russia from ultimately occupying that country herself. He wanted to declare war on Afghanistan immediately but was restrained by Cranbrook until the matter had been discussed by the Cabinet who were still scattered.

Lytton's distrust of Russia could hardly have been greater had he known the truth, which was that General Stoletov had advised Sher Ali not to receive the British Mission, that he had signed a treaty with him on August 21 and that on leaving Kabul two days later he had promised to return soon with 30,000 troops.[7] Stoletov was probably exceeding his authority, for since the signing of the Treaty of Berlin in July the Russian policy of fomenting an uprising in Afghanistan against the British, in view of the expected war with England, had been postponed if not abandoned altogether, but Sher Ali was not to know this and was relying on Stoletov's promises when he refused Chamberlain's Mission. Nor, it seems, were the Russians being anything but devious in their protestations that their Mission to Kabul had been purely courteous, for on September 22, the day after the British Mission had been turned back, and more than two months after the signing of the Treaty of Berlin, General Miliutin, who had far more influence with the Tsar than Prince Gorchakov, the Chancellor, was making this entry in his diary:

In London they cannot digest it that Shir Ali received very cordially the Russian embassy of Stoletov, while refusing to admit the British embassy. But what an outcry will be raised when it is learned that the ruler of Afghanistan himself has sent his embassy to Tashkent with the request to take Afghanistan under Russian protection and the declaration that he will not receive the English at Kabul without General Kaufmann's 'permission'.[8]

Not, of course, knowing any of this, Disraeli was furious with the Viceroy, writing to Cranbrook on September 26:

He [Lytton] was told to wait until we had received the answer from Russia to our remonstrance. I was very strong on this, having good reason for my opinion. He disobeyed us. I was assured by Lord Salisbury that, under no circumstances, was the Khyber Pass to be attempted. Nothing would have induced me to consent to such a step. He was told to send the Mission by Candahar. He has sent it by the Khyber, and received a snub, wh. it may cost us much to wipe away. When V-Roys and Comms.-in-Chief disobey orders, they ought to be sure of success in their mutiny. Lytton, by disobeying orders, had only secured insult and failure. What course we ought now to take is a grave affair. To force the Khyber, and take Cabul, is a perilous business. Candahar we might, probably, occupy with ease, and retain. These are only jottings. I have the utmost confidence in your judgment and firmness, but I shall never feel certain now, whether your instructions are fulfilled.[9]

Chamberlain came to Simla on September 28 'breathing fire and revenge against the Amir' as Robert told Edith. Edith returned from Narkanda on October 1 to find Chamberlain again occupying her room at Peterhof, so she was amused to read in the London *Spectator* that the Viceroy dispersed the Mission and sent Chamberlain back to Madras without exchanging a word with him. (Chamberlain declined the Viceroy's offer to put his name forward for a peerage.) The *Spectator* also pronounced that Lytton had deliberately created the situation resulting in Chamberlain's rebuff for reasons of ambition and self-aggrandisement.

On the evening of Edith's arrival Robert told her of 'the terrible scrape poor George Villiers had got into'. She gives no hint as to the nature of this scrape but it was probably to do with a woman (see p. 155). 'One of the gravest charges brought against Lord Lytton,' wrote a Civil Servant in India at this time, 'relates to the laxity of his entourage. At least one very scandalous case occurred which was not only the talk of Simla but of every regimental mess throughout India.'[10] The fact that Villiers was the Viceroy's Military Secretary as well as a first cousin of his wife must have made the scandal all the more salacious. Edith had written 'poor George Villiers' so he evidently received sympathy from the Lyttons. One would expect no less from Robert's understanding heart.

Villiers does not seem to have been dismissed from the staff, but he was soon to go up to fight in Afghanistan, as were also Lord William and Fred Liddell. William Loch did leave the staff, however. He was engaged to be married and had accepted an offer to become Principal of the Mayo College in Ajmer, an appointment derived from his prospective marriage.

While Lytton waited impatiently for the Cabinet to meet he was making his military preparations. His impatience was fed by Alfred Lyall who told him that 'To sit idle on the threshold of Afghanistan until next spring would' in his opinion 'be almost too ruinous a policy to be even mentioned; we should lose the tribes, lose our reputation, and give the Amir the immense prestige of having defied us for a whole season of campaigning'.[11] If the troops did not cross the border before the end of November the passes would be snowed up for six months, therefore all must be ready the moment Disraeli gave the word.

Although the Commander-in-Chief agreed with the Viceroy's general policy, there were many differences of opinion between them as to the number of troops required and the scale of preparations. It was the age-old dispute between the civilian and the professional (Haines in this case regarding Colley as a civilian since he had never commanded a regiment). Lytton and Colley wanted to confine the operations to a small offensive, relying on speed, superior guns and the element of surprise in attacking in winter. Lytton complained that Haines was saturated in traditions and prejudices; he refused to move until he had covered every contingency, brought up reserves and made provisions for supplies, transport and warm clothing for the troops. He believed, rightly, that the Viceroy was far more influenced in military matters by Colley than by either himself or Sir Edwin Johnson. Chamberlain, who remained at Simla for these strategical discussions, noticed the same thing. Colley, he found, was always present at military consultations, 'but sits away and says nothing. I feel all the time that he has given the Viceroy the key to the discourse, and is his real military mentor,—and one cannot help admiring his reticence and apparent indifference to all that is said, and his being content to be a nobody.'[12]

Lytton assured John Strachey in England that the cost of the military measures he had sanctioned would be small. He was more frightened of Haines than of Sher Ali: 'The Commander-in-Chief is daily urging on me gigantic operations on a scale of unlimited splendour,' he wrote, 'regardless of expense, and my refusal to sanction these operations has caused on his part an intense soreness and irritation. He considers, apparently, that the responsibility rests with him and not with me, and that he is very ill-used.'[13] Haines was influenced by the report that the Amir had 60,000 troops, but he knew nothing about Afghanistan or mountain warfare; Chamberlain, who did, understood the difficulties of transport and

War and Peace

supply in mountainous country. Too large a force would endanger the whole operation. If it had not been for Chamberlain's support Lytton would have found it far more difficult to get his own way with Haines.

*　*　*　*　*

The advance into Afghanistan was planned to be in three columns. One force, commanded by Sir Sam Browne (who had lost his left arm and won the V.C. in the Mutiny, and who was, incidentally, the originator of the sword-belt) was to enter the Khyber Pass; the second, under General Roberts, was to go by way of the Kuram Valley, south of the Khyber, with the Peiwar Pass in view, and the third column, under General Biddulph, was to go via Quetta and the Pishin Pass to Kandahar. General Donald Stewart (who was to become Commander-in-Chief in India after Haines) was to bring up a division from Multan, join General Biddulph and take command of the force moving on Kandahar. Including reserves, the Quetta force was to number nearly 13,000 men, the Khyber force 16,000 and the Kuram force only 6,000. For once Haines was moderate and believed that this small force would be amply sufficient for the Kuram. (He was unlucky in the event: the Peiwar Pass was the only place where any serious fighting took place). It was never intended that the three columns should advance far into Afghanistan. Lytton firmly believed that as soon as the Amir realised he was at their mercy he would capitulate, whereupon the forces would be immediately withdrawn.

In spite of Disraeli's anger he was praising Lytton in a letter to Salisbury of October 3:

I have been obliged to summon the Cabinet. . . . I have given the deepest attention and study to the situation and read with becoming consideration all Lytton's wonderful M.S. pamphlets; wh. are admirable both in their grasp and their detail; and this is my opinion. His policy is perfectly fitted to a state of affairs in which Russia was our assailant. But she has sneaked out of her hostile position, with sincerity to my mind, but scarcely with dignity, and if Lytton had only been quiet and obeyed my orders, I have no doubt that, under the advice of Russia, Shere Ali would have been equally prudent.[14]

Would he?—fortified as he was by promises from Stoletov, backed by General Kaufmann?

The Cabinet meeting which Lytton had been so eagerly awaiting was held on October 5, but nothing was decided. A short telegram merely was sent to the Viceroy by Cranbrook: 'Cabinet assembled to-day. Noted with regret your action in sending forward Mission without awaiting further telegram as directed September 13.'[15] Lytton was not reprimanded for sending the Mission by the Khyber so presumably Disraeli had realised by this time that he had never received orders to send it by Kandahar.

On receiving this curt telegram Lytton wrote to Cranbrook with understandable bitterness:

It contains nothing which can guide, assist or support me—very much which seems deliberately calculated to discourage, confuse and embarrass me, in the execution of a task from which it still leaves me unrelieved. For it neither recognises, nor mitigates, my responsibilities. Every word of it breathes mistrust, suspicion, timidity and a fretful desire to find fault on the most frivolous pretext. Yet not a single word of it affords me the faintest clue to a leading idea, a governing principle, or an intelligible object and purpose on the part of Her Majesty's Government, to which I may direct the efforts of the Government of India.... If Her Majesty's Government do not approve, and are not prepared to support, my frontier policy and measures, I will, after learning what is the policy, and what are the measures, they desire to substitute for mine, endeavour to carry them out with complete loyalty, or will frankly inform them, without loss of time, of my inability to do so.[16]

To John Strachey Lytton was writing shortly afterwards: 'I believe that thus far, I have probably had the good will of Lord Cranbrook and the P.M., but Cranbrook is not master of the question, and he seems to be weak and lazy, and Lord Beaconsfield is reported to be ill and worn-out. Lord Salisbury is obviously opposing me, and doing all he can to trip me up, and the Cabinet is treating me with a singular combination of cowardice and meanness.'[17]

Salisbury put his own point of view in a letter to Disraeli dated October 22: 'That a breach with the Amir was inevitable sooner or later I quite believe, but the time has been chosen with singular infelicity. It would have strengthened us much in our struggle to get Russia out of the Balkan Peninsula if we could have deferred this affair for a year. But we are in a mess and must get out of it.'[18]

War and Peace

In that year might not Russia's hold on Afghanistan have become impossible to dislodge?

On October 19, a month after Chamberlain's Mission had been turned back, the Nawab Ghulam Hassan at last returned from Kabul with a reply from the Amir to the Viceroy's letter sent on August 30. It was so evasive that had Chamberlain waited for it at Peshawar the situation would not have been changed in the least.

During the weeks between the failure of the Mission and the decision of the Cabinet, long letters appeared in *The Times* from Lord Lawrence and Lord Grey condemning Lytton's actions. These were answered by equally long ones from Fitzjames Stephen and Sir Bartle Frere defending him. Lytton did not have as much support in England for his policy as Colonel Burne at the India Office had led him to suppose. Lytton's brother-in-law, Henry Loch, gave him the best idea of how the country was divided over the issue:

I have never known such strong feelings to exist on any question as on this [Afghanistan] and the Turkish question—friends of years standing become bitter foes—members of the same family don't speak one to the other ... and it is all *purely personal*, the divergence of opinion not being so much on the merits of the questions which seem seldom understood, but on the feelings that are entertained either towards Lord Beaconsfield or Mr Gladstone.[19]

Lytton, as the instrument of Disraeli's policy, was as much abused by Gladstone's adherents as was Disraeli himself. But quite apart from the bitter difference over Afghan policy, Lytton was personally a splendid target for Gladstone's vituperation. In Gladstone's eyes the Viceroy appeared irreligious, worldly and immoral as well as being a dilettante and an amateur in politics. If Gladstone believed that his own was the voice of God, Lytton must have seemed to him the mouthpiece of Mammon. Lytton was later to tell the Queen some of the abominable accusations Gladstone had publicly made against him. Even so, Lytton was fair enough to concede that Gladstone was a superb orator.

The Cabinet met again to discuss Afghanistan on October 25. Disraeli wrote a long account of the meeting to the Queen, characterising it as 'one of the most remarkable meetings' he remembered.

Salisbury had been Lytton's severest critic at the discussion. He had maintained that the Viceroy 'was forcing the hand of the Government and had been doing so from the very first; he thought only of India, and was dictating by its means the foreign policy of the Government in Europe and Turkey.... He spoke with great bitterness of the conduct of the Viceroy and said that, unless curbed, he would bring about some terrible disaster. . . . Suddenly Lord Cranbrook startled us all by saying ... his own opinion was for war, immediate and complete ...'. Cranbrook defended Lytton and managed to convince the Cabinet that there was a *casus belli* 'formed by an aggregate of hostile incidents on the part of the Amir'.[20]

Shortly before the meeting Salisbury had written devastatingly and most unjustly to Disraeli about Lytton: 'He [Cranbrook] does not realise sufficiently the gaudy and theatrical ambition which is the Viceroy's leading passion.'[21] Ambition to be recognised as a poet Lytton certainly had, but not to shine in public life. He had never wanted to be Viceroy, and had only accepted the offer out of a strong sense of duty.

At last, on October 26, the decision of the Cabinet reached the Viceroy by telegram: an ultimatum should be sent to Sher Ali announcing that military operations against him would begin unless a letter of full apology and a declared willingness to receive a British mission was received by sundown on November 20. After some revision the ultimatum was dispatched on November 2.

On November 18 the Lyttons moved to Lahore, the capital of the Punjab, leaving the children at Simla. The Council was dispersed; the Viceroy was to act alone in consultation with the Commander-in-Chief, the Lieutenant-Governor of the Punjab (Robert Egerton), General Strachey (acting Finance Minister), Alfred Lyall and his military member of Council. In the absence of Sir Edwin Johnson on sick leave, Neville Chamberlain agreed to act as military member. George Villiers had already left for Peshawar to join General Roberts, and Lord William and Fred Liddell to join Sir Sam Browne. Colonel Baker had been sent out from England to take Villiers' place as Military Secretary. (Baker was to have a very distinguished future career.)

No reply having been received from the Amir by the evening of November 20 (Lytton had not for a moment expected one), the three columns were ordered to advance at daybreak on the 21st. The delay had not been wasted, for on the 20th a written agreement was signed between Cavagnari and the representatives of the Khyber tribes by which the tribes would detach themselves from the Amir and give up the control of the Pass to the Indian Government in return for monetary compensation. At the same time as the troops crossed the frontier a proclamation was issued by the Viceroy to the Sirdars and people of Afghanistan declaring that the British had no quarrel with them and that on the Amir alone rested the responsibility for having exchanged the friendship of the Empress of India for her hostility.

Sir Sam Browne overcame some strong resistance at Ali Musjid but the garrison escaped by fleeing in the night. He occupied the fort and then advanced into Afghanistan unmolested. On December 20 he encamped on the plain of Jellalabad, south-east of Kabul, where he remained for the rest of the winter. General Roberts, who had moved swiftly up the Kuram Valley, met with unexpectedly fierce resistance at the Peiwar Khotal (Pass). He fought and brilliantly won a ferocious battle lasting for two days, December 1 and 2. He then advanced into Afghanistan only as far as the Shutargardan Pass where he encamped for the winter. General Biddulph had a long arduous march from Quetta through the Pishin Valley. General Stewart met him at Pishin and the two forces, meeting no resistance, reached Kandahar on January 8. The campaign had been entirely successful and there had been few fatal casualties. General Roberts in particular had greatly distinguished himself.

Those members of the Viceroy's staff who were in Afghanistan had taken the war in the light-hearted spirit that was no doubt typical of young British officers. George Villiers wrote very cheerfully; he said the cold was intense, washing was out of the question and he had not taken his clothes off for seven days; he had had many narrow escapes at the Peiwar Pass engagement, where the firing had been very hot, but he had never felt better in his life. Lord William had joined the Lyttons at Lahore at the end of November. He had believed that he could not reach General Roberts by the time of his advance, and so, to his great disappointment, he had missed the fighting at the Peiwar. At Ali Musjid in the Khyber the bullets had whizzed over him but he had soon stopped even ducking his head.

The Viceroy received many congratulatory telegrams and letters from home on the conduct of the war. On December 6 the Queen wrote to him sending her congratulations on the 'brilliant sacrifices of her brave noble soldiers, but it in *no* way surprised her for British soldiers always do their duty'.[22] She was in deep sorrow when she wrote this: two of her grandchildren had just died of diphtheria, and on December 14 came the news that their mother, Princess Alice, Grand Duchess of Hesse, the Queen's second daughter, had died of the same disease on the anniversary of her father's death in 1861.

As soon as it was known that war was a certainty Parliament had been called. (By an Act of 1858 the Government could make war in India without any previous notification to Parliament.) It met on December 5, and on the 9th votes of censure on the conduct of the Government which had resulted in war with Afghanistan were moved in both Houses. The Opposition contended that it was the Viceroy's handling of Sher Ali which had alienated him and that the latter would have been perfectly willing to accept Chamberlain's Mission had he been given time to do so, but that to have sent it without waiting for his consent was a slur on him which he had every right to resent. The Government on the other hand claimed that Sher Ali had gone over to Russia long before Lytton arrived in India as a result of the Liberal policy (the Viceroy's first letter to him which he had repulsed could not have been more friendly or courteous) and that he had been given plenty of time to express his willingness to receive the Mission. Disraeli, Salisbury and Cranbrook spoke as convincingly in the Lords as any member of the Opposition but there was no one in the Commons to match Gladstone's masterly denunciation of 'this evil war'. *The Times* reported that 'The warmth which Mr Gladstone displays has now become so superheated as to imperil the very decencies of Parliamentary intercourse'.

The Government majorities were 136 in the Lords (what Disraeli called unprecedentedly large) after a two-day sitting, and 102 in the Commons after four evening sessions.

Disraeli in the course of the debate expressed himself as perfectly satisfied with the conduct of Russia, although part of the Russian Mission was still at Kabul. (The last Russian officer did not leave until the end of the month.) Either Disraeli was being diplomatic, not wanting to provoke Russia, or else he genuinely believed de

Giers's assurance that the Russian Mission was of a purely courteous nature; he blamed the Amir entirely for provoking the war.
This public declaration of faith in Russia was afterwards used by
the Liberals against Lytton whose policy was based almost entirely
on distrust of Russia.

The Lyttons left Lahore for Calcutta on December 19, meeting
the children at Ambala. On the way, Lytton heard that on the receipt
of the news of General Roberts's victory at the Peiwar Pass, the
Amir's army had begun to desert. Sher Ali, it was to transpire, then
wrote to General Kaufmann beseeching him to send immediately
the 30,000 troops which Stoletov had promised were in readiness
for when he needed them. Kaufmann replied, advising him to make
peace with the British since he could not give him any assistance
in winter.[23] Sher Ali then decided to go himself to St Petersburg
to put his case before the Tsar. Having released from prison his
rebellious eldest son, Yakub Khan, and appointed him regent at
Kabul, he departed with a small retinue towards the Oxus and Russian protection. At Mizar-i-Sherif, near the Afghan border, he fell
ill, and died on February 21, 1879. (According to a young medical
officer in Afghanistan at this time he died of 'mortification of the
leg'. His life might have been saved if he had agreed to an amputa-
tion.) Yakub Khan was then proclaimed Amir.

15

The Treaty and the Massacre

The Liberal press in England went on attacking Lytton. John Morley was now among his most hostile critics, and in January, 1879, Robert sent him a letter from Calcutta which shows how deeply hurt he was:

I cannot say, dear friend of former days, how acute is the pain with which I reluctantly recognise, as irremediable, all that is involved, to my lasting loss, in the fundamental difference between our respective views and feelings.... I confess I have sometimes fancied that had our positions been reversed my confidence in your character and intelligence would have sufficed to satisfy my judgment that there was more honesty and wisdom in your action than in the denunciation of it by persons who could not be fully acquainted with the causes and conditions of it.... How can I find comfort in intimate intercourse with one who conscientiously regards me as a willing, or witless, instrument of a wicked betrayal, or abominable mismanagement, of the highest public interests? And how can you value the esteem, or care to retain the professional friendship, of a man whose conduct irresistibly presents itself to your deliberate judgment in so odious a light?[1]

One cannot imagine Robert making personal attacks on a friend, however opposed he might be to him politically. Whatever his shortcomings, Robert never failed in the warmth and loyalty of his affections. Morley had told Mrs Richard Strachey that Lytton's great misfortune was that he had never been in contact with English public life and consequently did not understand the real forces in the country to which the Executive must yield.[2] There was much truth in this.

The return to India of the John Stracheys in the middle of January was a great comfort to Lytton although it meant the departure of Richard Strachey and his wife to whom Robert had become very attached. The Queen's Ball, which had been postponed because of the Court mourning for Princess Alice, had now been fixed for February 5. Edith, who was nearing her confinement, hoped the ball would be over before she was laid up. It almost was. The baby was born between the first and second suppers.

All came to see me in their finery, dear R. in full uniform, Mrs Barnett dining with me, then Edith Colley rushing in and looking very nice, and the contrast all seemed so horrid to my suffering and lowness, and Oh the dance music was so trying. When R. came back to me after the first supper about 1.30 I was quite exhausted and he ran for Dr Barnett who then gave me chloroform and I was quite happy and in half an hour a fine boy appeared and all was well. All were so pleased to have a second boy, and I was so proud, not having had two boys alive together before. Green, R's faithful servant and friend, rushed downstairs to announce the event, and our healths were drunk with many cheers by the gentlemen and guests, Green and the bandsmen.

The child was christened Neville Stephen—Neville after Sir Neville Chamberlain and Stephen after Fitzjames Stephen. Stephen and John Strachey were the godfathers. Edith had a charming nurse this time, 'English in all her ways', and never experienced a happier time of recovery after a confinement in spite of seeing so little of Robert—'but that was no different from other times, for in India I hardly see anything of him'. The new baby, like Victor, was given over to a native wet-nurse.

At the end of February the ever-restless Lord William went off to the Zulu war which had broken out in South Africa in January, and in which the Prince Imperial, the only child of Napoleon III, was to be killed in June while fighting for the British. As usual everyone shed tears at Lord William's departure.

On March 10 the Lyttons entertained at a big dinner party General Ulysses Grant, the ex-President of America, and his wife who were on a three-year journey round the world. It was the first party Edith had attended since her confinement. She 'dressed in full dress', a dress which was afterwards used to cover a sofa at Knebworth. She found General Grant 'rather dry and simple' but got on well with him. Robert had a very different impression of him:

My last official duty at Calcutta was to entertain General Grant, family and staff [he told John Morley with whom he was still corresponding in spite of their differences], all of whom, on quitting Calcutta I handed over to the hospitality of Sir Ashley Eden. These filthy creatures have now left India for pastures new of sotting and spitting. On their last night at Calcutta General Grant and 'Suite'—with the exception of Mrs G (who was 'incommoded in her inside') dined with the Chief Justice Sir R. Garth and Lady Garth, from whose house they embarked. On this occasion 'our distinguished guest' the double Ex-President of the 'Great Western Republic', who got as drunk as a fiddle, showed that he could also be as profligate as a lord. He fumbled Mrs A., kissed the shrieking Miss B.—pinched the plump Mrs C. black and blue—and ran at Miss D. with intent to ravish her. Finally, after throwing all the Garths' female guests into hysterics by generally behaving like a mûst elephant, the noble beast was captured by main force and carried (quatre pattes dans l'air) by six sailors on board the ship which relieved India of his distinguished presence. The marine officer who superintended the carriage of the General from the house to the ship, reports that, when deposited in the public saloon cabin, where Mrs G. was awaiting him with her cock in her eye [a squint], this remarkable man satiated there and then his baffled lust on the unresisting body of his legitimate spouse, and copiously vomitted during the operation. If you have seen Mrs Grant you will not think this incredible.[3]

The Lyttons left Calcutta on March 14 to return to Lahore while the children went straight to Simla. The new Amir of Afghanistan, Yakub Khan, was now putting out tentative feelers to the British, and Cavagnari had been entrusted with the task of making some kind of peace settlement with him. The Viceroy, wishing to be close to the frontier, had for this reason left Calcutta rather earlier than usual, but not before he had rushed through the Legislative Council a Bill abolishing the 5% customs duty levied on the import of cotton goods from Manchester. This measure was almost as deeply resented in India as the Vernacular Press Act. India had only recently started a cotton industry of her own; cotton mills had been opened in Bombay and were able to compete with Lancashire so long as the import duty remained. It was this very competition, though, that the Lancashire cotton industry feared. Lytton cannot be blamed for abolishing the duty since in 1877 the House of Commons had adopted without a division the resolution to repeal it as soon as financial conditions in India warranted, but he can be blamed for pushing through the measure, on Strachey's advice, against the majority of his Council. This he was able to do under the terms of an Act of 1870—the only instance of the exercise of this power since the Act was passed.

In Indian eyes it was yet another instance of racial discrimination, of putting British interests above those of the Indian people, of strangling their new young industry; another let-down by the Viceroy who had so delighted them on his first arrival by paying an unofficial visit to Moraji's cotton mill in Bombay.

Yakub Khan was not willing to give up any territory, although he agreed to accept a permanent British Mission at Kabul; the British were determined to keep either the Khyber Pass or the Kuram Valley; Cavagnari's negotiations with the new Amir were, therefore, protracted. On March 20 Cavagnari came to Lahore to confer with the Viceroy. He told Edith at dinner one night, 'For years I have held the same policy which I have lately had the pleasure of carrying out under Lord Lytton, but I was only snubbed and laughed at.'

The Viceregal party left Lahore for Simla on April 14 and arrived four days later, having made stops on the way. Towards the end of April, while negotiations with Yakub Khan were still going on, Colonel Colley was sent up to the frontier to inspect the two routes into Afghanistan and help decide which the British should insist on keeping. He rode up the Khyber Pass to Gandamak, west of Jellalabad, where Sir Sam Browne was now encamped, and had interviews with the General and with Cavagnari who had returned there; then back to Peshawar and up the Kuram Valley, riding up the new road which General Roberts had had made, to the Shutargardan Pass where Roberts was still encamped. He rejoined the Lyttons at Simla on May 1 after this very arduous tour of inspection. He was in favour of keeping the Kuram route, the easiest route to Kabul now the new road had been built. This was the cause of another clash between the Viceroy and the Commander-in-Chief who could see no value in the Kuram route.

On May 8 the Amir, Yakub Khan, went himself to Gandamak with a retinue of 400. He was received with every honour, and after much bargaining with Cavagnari signed a treaty on the 26th which gave the British practically everything they had asked for. The Amir agreed to a permanent Embassy at Kabul; the towns of Kandahar and Jellalabad were restored to him and he and his successors were to receive an annual subsidy of six lachs of rupees (about £52,000), but all the passes were to remain under British control.

The Viceroy ratified the treaty on May 31. As he wrote to Stephen next day it had secured the frontier, the friendship and alliance of the Amir and the complete exclusion of Russian influence from Afghanistan—'the propriety of those objects has never been denied even by the Lawrencians who have failed to secure any one of them'.[4] All this had been achieved with the smallest possible loss of life, without any military check, and without any annexation of territory, nor would the original estimate of two million pounds be exceeded. Lytton's object all along had been 'to convert the Amir into an honest friend not merely to reduce him to submission'.[5]

Praise came from England. Even Lord Salisbury wrote, 'I cannot allow the conclusion of this affair ... to pass without warmly congratulating you on the great success you have achieved and the brilliant qualities you have displayed. To my eyes, the wise restraint in which you have held the eager spirits about you [a dig at Haines] is not the least striking of your victories.... The great military success has done us yeoman's service in negotiating with Russia.'[6] (Lytton replied rather coolly to this letter—he had received no help from Salisbury.) And a few weeks later Disraeli, who had just entered into his sixth year as Prime Minister, was writing, '... whatever happens [to his Government], it will always be to me a source of real satisfaction that I had the opportunity of placing you on the throne of the Gt. Mogul.'[7]

It seemed at that moment that Disraeli's forward policy had been fully vindicated and that Lytton, having carried it out so successfully, would return to England when his term of office was up with honour and a sense of great achievement.

*   *   *   *   *

Wilfred Blunt and his wife were at Simla to witness the triumph of the Treaty of Gandamak. They had arrived on May 16 and were to stay with the Lyttons for nearly seven weeks. Blunt had left the Diplomatic Service soon after his time with Robert at Sintra, and in 1869 had married Lady Anne King-Noel, the only daughter of the Earl of Lovelace and his wife, Ada, Byron's daughter. The Blunts had become great travellers, and had arrived at Simla from Persia, bringing with them two Arab mares.

The Treaty and the Massacre

'With his affectionate disposition,' Blunt recorded, 'he [Lytton] was in truth delighted to see me and our intercourse was renewed on all our old footing of intimacy, just as it had been in the days of our first friendship.'[8] Blunt remembered Peterhof 'as being very delightful, between a palace and a villa, with all possible comforts and luxuries, standing in its own shady grounds and gardens, and with chalets for the guests'. He thoroughly enjoyed the 'banquets' prepared by Bonsard, and the 'gorgeous entertainments which twice a week varied the quiet family meals each beautiful summer night'. Lady Anne described Edith as 'more lovely than ever'.[9] Wilfred too was enthusiastic about her:

It was then that I discovered what a very charming and beautiful woman Lady Lytton was. Intimate as I had been with her husband for years she had remained for me a rather unknown region of his life and an influence with him I had imagined not altogether friendly to my own. Now however we made friends—Though always a pretty woman she had not, before she went to India, made her beauty fully felt. Now *elle se faisait valoir* and with admirable effect. She had made an arrangement in passing through Paris, with Worth, the celebrated man milliner, that he should keep her supplied with garments suited to her new high station and he had nobly acquitted himself of what he held to be a sacred trust. Lady Lytton was splendidly attired, and the fineness of her new feathers had made of her a truly lovable and glorious bird. Not that I ventured anything of love with her—her whole heart was devoted to Robert, but she was not displeased that I should find her beautiful and on this understanding we made friends.

Blunt also found that Edith played her part admirably as 'Vicequeen', repairing Robert's mistakes and giving dignity to Government entertainments. Blunt was interested in all the Viceroy's staff. He considered that Alfred Lyall—'a poet, a man of imagination and enlarged ideas'—was the only high ranking official whom Lytton could talk to about 'other than official matters'. He saw Colonel Colley 'as a man of extreme self-confidence, and one who had acquired so great an influence over Lytton that he had persuaded the Viceroy that between them they could direct the whole detail of the plan of campaign from Simla, in the war they were just bringing to a close when we arrived there, in Afghanistan'.

On May 28 Colley received a telegram from his old chief, Sir

Garnet Wolseley, requesting him to join him immediately at Natal as his Chief of Staff. Colley did not hesitate to comply, nor, of course, now that the Afghan War was over, could Lytton stand in his friend's way. George Villiers, who had returned from Afghanistan, was also appointed to Sir Garnet's staff, and he and Colley went off together four days later. 'It was a great trial for all of us losing the latter,' Edith wrote, 'but particularly for poor E. [Edith Colley] who would not be petted, but was quite miserable at first.' And Robert wrote to Colley, 'Your poor little wife looks so sad and forlorn, with her wistful eyes and eager face that my heart aches to the core when I see her. Never since the days of the Odyssey was absent hero more missed.'[10]

On the day of Colley's departure, June 2, Lytton was writing to Lord Cranbrook, 'For the K.C.S.I. I can put no name before that of Colonel Colley, which I have already submitted to you by telegraph.... Next in order, and *facile princeps* beyond all that of other political agents, stands the name of Major Cavagnari.' In his telegram Lytton had 'earnestly solicited' Cranbrook for this honour for Colley as a personal favour to himself, and had asked for permission to tell Colley before he left for South Africa.[11] Colley, Colonel Burne, Cavagnari and General Roberts were all knighted in August.

Colley and Villiers left the day before a big ball at Peterhof. Lady Anne Blunt, who had brought few clothes with her, wore one of Edith's Worth dresses for the occasion which she considered too young for her age (she was forty-two, four years older than Edith and three years older than Blunt). She described the supper at the ball as being 'a triumph of Bonsard's art'. Fred Liddell had come back from Afghanistan in time to help with the ball, looking very handsome with a beard.

Lytton now had the task of choosing a new Private Secretary to replace Colley. He had no hope of getting the man he would have wanted—Steuart Bayley, who had been appointed Commissioner of Assam. 'Batten is the only civilian of adequate standing whose services in this capacity can be secured without involving a considerable additional expense to the Government of India,' he wrote to Edith at Mashroba. George Batten, a brother of Lady Strachey, was the Commissioner of Inland Customs for the Central Provinces. He was already at Simla with his wife for the summer as were most of the senior members of the Civil Service. Mrs Batten and Mrs Plowden were the two most attractive women in Simla, both young, pretty and lively.* According to Blunt, Robert avowed to him 'that both ladies were a temptation he would have willingly indulged, had it been possible without a certainty of scandal', but to his 'chagrin' both ladies 'consoled themselves' with his aides-de-camp. (It seems from this that the scrape George Villiers had been involved in was to do with one of these pretty women.) 'It was a régime which was compromising him without adequate return of amusement,' Blunt continued. 'He had taken Batten as his private secretary, and I warned him of the imprudence and of the opportunity it would give for evil tongues.' Edith was against Batten's appointment because she disliked him personally—'He had such abominable manners and often would get so cocky'—but she never wrote a word against either Mrs Batten or Mrs Plowden. She knew what a flirt Robert was and probably knew also that his amorous activities did not go beyond flirting even when there was no fear of scandal. Blunt on the other hand was a well known seducer (he had an affair with Mrs Batten which did not end at Simla) and it is more than likely that Robert was teasing him when he said that both ladies were a temptation he would have indulged had it not been for the fear of scandal.

Blunt accepted Lytton's assurance that he was innocent, although, as he wrote, all Simla believed Lytton to be the lover of these two ladies: 'Tales were current all over India of his goings on with the wives of his subordinates, and these had been got hold of in England and were being made use of there against him by his political opponents.... The Viceroy was high game for any pretty woman to fly at, and declarations of affection mostly anonymous were no uncommon element in his private post bag.'

As a reaction from all the excitement of the war Robert had been attacked by the 'blue devils' as he called his depressions. He was tired out. He was to tell Mrs Strachey that at this time he had written to the Prime Minister tendering his resignation but that on reflection he had torn up the letter.[12] He seems, though, to have recovered

* Mrs Plowden's friendship with the Lyttons, which was kept up after they left India, had a happy aftermath: her younger daughter, Pamela, the same age as Emily, married Victor Lytton in 1902.

his spirits somewhat when he went into camp at Naldera on June 16 with the Blunts, Edith Colley, the elder girls and Alfred Lyall and his much younger sister, Barbara, who had recently come out to stay with him and who was to become a great friend of both the Lyttons. Robert was able to indulge there in his favourite outdoor pastime of sending up fire balloons. 'He sent up a beautiful new brown holland large captive balloon,' Edith recorded, 'which came from England, with furnace below, and a string to hold it. It rose very fairly three times—and had large dolls in it, to the excitement of the girls.'

Blunt noted that Robert 'augured his military success or failure by the direction of the ascent of fire balloons'. His superstitiousness, Blunt believed, had been inherited from his father, 'and like many men who are materialists in religion believed in omens, and he had the idea that I had been born under a lucky star and valued my presence with him for that reason'. Robert no doubt felt that the success of the new balloon augured well for Cavagnari who had been chosen as the first Envoy and Minister Plenipotentiary to the Court of Kabul. He was to set out for Kabul in July.

Cavagnari came to Simla on the day the Lyttons returned from Naldera, June 20, and was, Edith tells us, treated at dinner that night at Peterhof 'as first guest of the evening before members of Council. He seems full of decision and courage, and is going to Kabul next week in perfect confidence that all will be right'. His wife was to join him at Kabul as soon as he had established himself at the Residency, and he invited the Blunts to stay with him in the spring when Afghanistan was as beautiful as any place on earth with the fruit trees in blossom.

The Blunts left on July 3 in torrents of rain, the monsoon having broken early that year. Blunt dated this visit to Simla as the beginning of his political life. 'He [Lytton],' he was to write, 'made me the confidant of all his affairs private and public and hid I think absolutely nothing from me of what was going on. Thus for those weeks I may truly say that the whole machinery of the Indian Government was laid bare to me with its hidden weaknesses as well as its strengths.' Neville Lytton, who was to marry the Blunts' only child, Judith, maintained that these confidences were betrayed by Blunt in his future campaigns against imperialism.[13] Whether this was so or not Robert certainly bore him no grudge. Although the two men grew far apart politically their poetic sympathies became ever warmer and they remained close friends until Robert's death.

Cavagnari came to Peterhof for the last time on July 6 'feeling rather low at his banishment' according to Edith. He left Simla for Peshawar a few days later. On the 18th Lytton received a telegram from him: 'Cabul Embassy crosses frontier tomorrow. I have the honour to wish Your Excellency good-bye.' It had been decided, at Cavagnari's own suggestion, that his escort should be as small as possible. It consisted of a secretary, William Jenkyns, a military medical officer, Dr Kelly, and a very young Second Lieutenant, Walter Hamilton, in charge of twenty-five cavalry and fifty infantry of the Guides Corps. Hamilton had won the V.C. the year before with Sir Sam Browne's column in the Khyber engagement. Since Yakub Khan had pledged himself to receive the Embassy a larger escort was considered unnecessary.

The Embassy went by way of the Kuram Valley, Colley's advice as to holding on to this route having been taken in spite of Haines's opposition. General Roberts, whose force alone now remained in Afghanistan, accompanied it from his advance post at Alikhel, at the upper end of the valley, as far as the Shutargarden Pass. Roberts was not happy about the Embassy. He believed that the Treaty of Gandamak had been signed too quickly, before the British had instilled 'sufficient awe into the Afghan nation which would have been the only reliable guarantee for the safety of the Mission'.[14] As Cavagnari and Roberts ascended towards the Shutargarden they came across a solitary magpie. Cavagnari begged Roberts not to mention this to his (Cavagnari's) wife if he wrote to her, for she was bound to consider it an unlucky omen.[15]

From the moment the Embassy left the British border it was treated with the utmost cordiality by the Afghan officials. On July 24 it entered Kabul to a salute of seventeen guns and an attempt by massed bands to play 'God Save the Queen'. Mounted on elephants with gold and silver howdahs they rode through the streets thronged with a welcoming crowd to the quarters prepared for them by the Amir. The Residency was inside a walled courtyard adjoining the Bala Hissar, the great fort to the south-east of the city where the Amir had his palace, his treasury, and barracks for some of his troops. Cavagnari had an interview with Yakub Khan that evening and found him very friendly, though he was weak and rather sickly as the result of his long imprisonment. All went well with the Embassy throughout August; Cavagnari, however, gave a hint of trouble when he reported to the Viceroy that six Afghan regiments of infantry had arrived at Kabul from Herat in a mutinous mood, being owed three months' pay.

On August 16 Sir Frederick Roberts, as General Roberts had now become, and his wife came to Simla. Lytton had appointed him to act on a Commission of Inquiry into Army Reform which he had set up, and of which Sir Ashley Eden (he had been knighted the year before) was President. General Roberts and his wife were welcomed as honoured guests at dinner at Peterhof on their first evening. Bonsard produced 'Croquettes à la Roberts and Fillets à la Koorum with bullets of truffles, both new and good dishes'. The Viceroy made Roberts a most flattering speech which he answered very modestly. Nicknamed 'little Bobs' from his diminutive stature, his officers and men all loved him and would have followed him anywhere, Cavagnari had told Edith. Edith recorded in her diary that Haines had not written a line to Roberts to congratulate him either on his victory at the Peiwar Khotal or on his knighthood. Haines was apparently jealous of Roberts's success and popularity.

On August 30 Sir Louis Cavagnari, as he now was, wrote to the Viceroy, 'I have nothing whatever to complain of on the part of the Amir or his ministers that I can really lay hold of.... There is no doubt that his authority is most weak throughout the whole of Afghanistan. This is not to be wondered at after the years of misrule and oppression on Sher Ali Khan's part. But if he keeps straight with us he will pull through.'[16] On September 2 Cavagnari sent a telegram, ending with the words 'all well'. It was his last message.

At two o'clock on the morning of September 5, General Roberts at his house, Snowdon, at Simla was woken by a man with a telegram from the Kuram Valley outpost, announcing that a native messenger had just arrived there from Kabul with the news that on the morning of the 3rd the British Residency had been attacked and that the Englishmen were still defending themselves when he left. Roberts sent his aide-de-camp with the telegram to the Viceroy and as soon as possible went himself to Peterhof where, early as it was, he found the Council, including the Commander-in-Chief, already assembled. It was of immense help to Lytton to have Roberts on the spot at this crisis.

Edith Colley wrote to her husband next day:

This is a terrible day; all seems one terrible time since yesterday afternoon when Lady L. told me the dreadful rumour that the Residency at Kabul had been attacked by the populace, that the man had left Kabul at that stage and did not know the end. At dinner came a telegram confirming this. We were a small party—the Barnetts and Colonel Stansfeld [serving on the Army Commission]—no A.D.C.s and Sir Michael Kennedy the only guest. But he and the others knew nothing of what was going on, so we had to keep up appearances, even when the look which passed over H.E.'s face when he read the telegram told us pretty well there was little hope left. Then just at the end of dinner (which was half an hour early for the theatre), in came Z. [Alfred Lyall] talking in gallant style—but with a look about his eyes which to me made it ghastly. Nothing was to be shown as yet, so Lady L. went to the theatre with Mrs Barnett and Sir Ashley [Eden]. I was so thankful I had declined before; I don't think I could have sat through it. I heard no more until this morning when a letter came from Lady L. telling me it was all true; when she was coming home last night, about one o'clock, she met Z., he passed her without a look or a word or a bow, and she knew worse news had come.... Oh, Geordie, it is all too dreadful! I sometimes think I feel it more than anyone except Z. Cavagnari's face haunts me, and all our last talks and the poor little wife at home.[17]

Poor Edith had had to sit through the play and behave as if nothing had happened. Robert, she tells us, 'stayed at home with Mr Alfred Lyall who had also received the same bad news. When I returned home I met Mr Lyall at the door, which I thought must mean that worse news had come. [This tells us that Z. was Alfred Lyall.] I at once went to R.'s room and he exclaimed, "Oh, they are all lost, it is too true." He could hardly speak for five minutes. All had been massacred and the Residency burnt. Oh, that was such a night of agony.'

What had happened, piecing together the accounts of eye-witnesses, including two sepoys from the escort, the only two survivors, was that the disaffected troops from Herat, coming to the Bala Hissar to claim their pay and being given only a quarter of what was due to them, had started throwing stones at the Residency. One of the guards inside the gates began to fire, whereupon the troops ran to get their weapons. The mob of the city then joined in the attack. All day the small garrison had defended themselves although they could never have had much hope of survival. The Amir, when appealed to for help by a messenger who managed to get through, sent his Commander-in-Chief, Daod Shah, to try to restore peace. He was unhorsed by stones and spears and was said to be dying of his wounds. The Amir then sent his small son with the Koran; he escaped injury but was unable to stop the attack.

Over and over again the British officers charged at the head of some twenty-five of the garrison, whereupon the Afghans ran away, only to re-assemble and re-attack. Cavagnari was the first to be killed. The splinter of a ricocheting ball hit him in the head; with the bloody flap of his forehead hanging down over his eyes he managed to lead a bayonet charge until he could no longer stand. Dr Kelly then helped him inside where he soon died. After some hours only two of the British came out, Hamilton and the civilian, Jenkyns; then only Hamilton, and finally the last sally was made by a Sikh *jemadar* [native lieutenant]. Hamilton was said to have died sword in hand, though not before he had killed five Afghans while badly wounded. The Residency was looted and partly burnt. Cavagnari's body seems to have been consumed in the flames. The other bodies were left unburied for three days and then shovelled into a mass grave with the dead horses and mules. Over six hundred Afghans were killed, proof of the desperation with which the small garrison had defended themselves.

The telegram which had arrived during dinner on September 5 with the news of the burning of the Residency and the destruction of everyone in it had been transmitted from a letter from the Amir himself, addressed to General Roberts at Alikhel, the Kuram outpost. Another telegram came next day, also transmitted from a letter from the Amir to Roberts, ending, '... my kingdom is ruined. After God, I look to the British Government for aid and advice. My true friendship and honesty of purpose will be proved as clear as daylight. By this misfortune I have lost my friend the Envoy, and also my kingdom. Am terribly grieved and perplexed.'[18]

It was a huge relief to Lytton to receive a telegram from the India Office at this juncture giving him full powers to act as he thought best 'with warm assurance of unreserved support in taking vigorous measures'.[19] He was, in consequence, able to act quickly.

The Treaty and the Massacre

A Council of War on the 5th settled the campaign. The rescue of the Amir as well as the avenging of the massacre had to be considered. Lytton, therefore, informed Yakub Khan that a strong British force would march as speedily as possible from the Shutargarden to his assistance.

On September 6 General Roberts left Simla for the Kuram Valley with instructions from the Viceroy to march upon Kabul with 5,000 picked troops. (This occasioned another row with Haines who wanted Roberts to wait until a larger force could be assembled.) General Stewart was ordered to re-occupy Kandahar as swiftly as possible, and the Khyber troops were reinforced. Colonel Baker, the Viceroy's new Military Secretary, was appointed to command one of General Roberts's brigades; he left Simla with Roberts on the 6th, taking Fred Liddell with him as aide-de-camp. The management of transport and supply was entrusted to General Sir Michael Kennedy. Also on the 6th Lytton telegraphed to Colonel Colley asking him to return in this emergency, the Zulu war now being over. (For some reason this telegram did not reach Colley for three weeks.)

Disraeli told the Queen that he was 'quite overcome' by the disaster, but that he had faith in Lytton—'It is a situation which befits his courage, resource and imagination'.[20] The Queen urged immediate action. Lytton received 'a most kind, patriotic and manly letter' from her. 'She is really a better Englishman,' he wrote to Stephen, 'than any of her subjects and never falls short in a national crisis where the interests and honour of her Empire are at stake.'[21] Lytton and the Queen had been in perfect sympathy ever since his appointment, and were to remain so.

Roberts and his small army reached Alikhel, the Kuram outpost, on September 22. Meanwhile General Bright was advancing up the Khyber with a force of nearly 16,000. At Alikhel Roberts found the Amir's two chief ministers awaiting him. They appealed to him on the Amir's behalf to halt his advance: the Amir was restoring order; he had discovered who the murderers were and was going to punish them himself; any further advance of the British would only lead to more trouble. Roberts sent the ministers back to Kabul with a letter to the Amir saying that the British Government could not entrust to anyone else the punishment for the massacre or the restoration of order.

Colonel Baker, going on ahead of the main column, had by the 29th advanced to the village of Kushi, only about forty-five miles from Kabul. He received there a message from the Amir asking whether he would receive him in his camp, and a few hours later Yakub Khan arrived with his eldest son, all his ministers and Daud Shah, his Commander-in-Chief, who was said to have gone to the rescue of Cavagnari and to be dying of his wounds, but who showed little sign of injury. At the same time, the Amir's chief rival, Wali Mahomed, and all the other Sirdars who had been out of favour with Yakub Khan, arrived at Baker's camp. It seems to have been this move on the Sirdars' part that had prompted the Amir to put himself under British protection.

The next day General Roberts himself arrived at Kushi and saw the Amir who pleaded with him not to advance further: all his womenfolk had been left at the Bala Hissar at Kabul with several regiments and were all bound to be massacred if the British refused to halt. (It afterwards came to light that Yakub Khan had already sent all his womenfolk away from Kabul.) Roberts replied that the advance could not be delayed but that a proclamation was to be issued warning all non-combatants to clear out of the city.

The Amir and his suite then asked to stay on at the British camp, a request which was courteously granted. The next day the Amir's uncle, Nek Mahomed, rode out from Kabul and requested permission to speak to the Amir. This was allowed, and he had a long secret interview with his nephew before riding back to Kabul.

On October 2 Roberts's force left Kushi. On the 6th, near Charasiab, only eight miles south of Kabul, a reconnoitring party reported that enemy troops were gathered in great numbers on the heights of a crescent of hills between Charasiab and Kabul. It transpired that there were thirteen trained regiments of Afghan troops on the hills reinforced by tribesmen and fighting men from the city, determined to stop the British advance, and that their commander was Nek Mahomed, the Amir's uncle.

Roberts realised that it was essential to carry the heights before nightfall, for enemy reinforcements were arriving every moment. This task was entrusted to Colonel Baker who accomplished it with small loss of life and without the loss of a single officer. Nek Mahomed's horse was shot from under him but he himself escaped. General Roberts was now in no doubt that this resistance had been ordered by the Amir, and planned with Nek Mahomed during their long secret interview. The Amir all this time had remained in Roberts's camp and had followed the course of the battle with keen interest through his 'opera glasses', but remained calm when told of the British victory. Roberts continued to treat him with extreme courtesy.

Roberts arrived before Kabul on October 8 and here again he met with fierce opposition which he overcame. This second defeat of the Afghan troops was the end of all Yakub Khan's hopes. Roberts had achieved all this in a little over a month since leaving Simla. 'The troops have worked splendidly,' he telegraphed to the Viceroy on October 10. 'For several days we have been without tents, and rations had to be carried for want of transport.'[22] The speed of this advance could never have been achieved if Roberts had gone by the Khyber route. It proved the wisdom of Colley's advice to hang on to the Kuram Valley.

One of the first things Roberts did on entering Kabul was to go to the Residency. 'The walls,' he wrote, 'closely pitted with bullet holes, gave proof of the determined nature of the attack and the length of the resistance. The floors were covered with blood-stains, and amidst the embers of a fire were found a heap of human bones. I had a careful but unsuccessful search made for the bodies of our ill-fated friends.'[23]

Roberts found Russian influence everywhere in Kabul—Russian guns, the soldiers wearing uniforms of a Russian pattern, and 13,000 Russian gold pieces in the treasury. He felt certain now of Yakub Khan's treachery, especially as reports had come in from several sources that far from going to Cavagnari's rescue he had incited the troops to attack the Residency by failing to pay them on the pretext that they had not performed any religious act or protected the honour of their country. On hearing this, it was reported, they had attacked the Residency, declaring that they would earn their pay straightaway by slaughtering the infidels.

On October 12, Yakub Khan, who was still a guest in Roberts's camp in Kabul, went to the General's tent and informed him that he wished to resign the Amirship. He begged that his tent might be pitched next to that of the General 'until he could go to India, to London, or wherever the Viceroy might desire to send him'.[24] Having nothing more to lose he now owned that his father had entered into a treaty with the Russians, the draft of which had been brought by General Stoletov and which had been signed *after* the signing of the Treaty of Berlin. This treaty had remained in his possession for months until he had destroyed it when he heard of the British advance. It was now written out from memory by two Afghan ministers who had participated in the negotiations, and Yakub Khan confirmed the text. It gave Russia complete control over Sher Ali's foreign policy and promised Russian assistance in the suppression of rebellion or invasion by any foreign power. The last clause was a promise by Russia to restore at some time to the Amir 'the ancient country of Afghanistan'.[25] This meant the re-conquest of the Peshawar Valley, the Upper Punjab, which had been taken from the then Amir by Ranjit Singh, and annexed by the British in 1848.

Roberts also found letters from Kaufmann and Stoletov to Sher Ali and his Prime Minister, and letters from Sher Ali to Kaufmann and Stoletov, and one to the Tsar, which showed that Sher Ali had been guided entirely by Russia in her dealings with the British, and that General Kaufmann from 1870 to '75, at a time when the Russian Government had given assurances that Afghanistan was entirely beyond her sphere of influence, had been using every means in his power to form the closest possible connection with Sher Ali, and that from 1875 to '78 confidential agents had passed continually between Tashkent and Kabul. The letters showed conclusively that this friendship had been going on between Russia and Sher Ali for eight years and had *not* merely been provoked by the sending of Indian troops to Malta.[26] It also showed that Sher Ali had relied on Russian promises to defend him. In October 1878 he had written to Kaufmann appealing to him to send the troops which Stoletov had promised, basing his appeal not only on the treaty he had signed but on 'the duration, intimacy and fidelity of his previous friendship with Russia'.[27] Kaufmann had replied, '... the Emperor's desire is that you should not admit the English into your country; and, like last year, you are to treat them with deceit and deception until the present cold season passes away'.[28] *Last year* could only mean the Peshawar Conference between Syud Noor and Pelly.

Stoletov, in a letter to the Afghan Prime Minister, dated October 8, 1878, had advised Sher Ali 'to make peace openly, and in secret prepare for war'.[29] After the Peiwar defeat of December 2 Sher Ali had again written to Kaufmann begging him to send immediately the 30,000 Russian troops which Stoletov had promised would be in readiness at any time they were required.[30]

As General Roberts wrote to Alfred Lyall, 'Our recent rupture with Sher Ali has, in fact, been the means of unmasking and checking a very serious conspiracy against the peace and security of our Indian Empire.'[31] On receiving the translation of the Viceroy's summaries of these Russian-Afghan papers, the Queen asked for them to be published immediately, but Disraeli advised postponement. Relations with Russia were now peaceful; he wanted them to remain so. This was a great disappointment to Lytton, for their publication would, he felt, have fully vindicated his policy.

As well as this proof of Sher Ali's treachery, Roberts found at Kabul that the Maharaja of Kashmir had been corresponding with both Russia and the Amir. At the time when war between England and Russia had seemed inevitable and the outcome uncertain, the Maharaja had wanted to remain on good terms with both sides, but in the eyes of the Indian Government a friend of Russia was an enemy of England. To Lytton, what seemed like the Maharaja's double-dealing was a bitter pill. He had trusted him, had raised his personal salute to twenty-one guns at the Delhi Assemblage and been given, as he thought, firm evidence of his loyalty with his offer to guard the North-West Frontier when Indian troops were sent to Malta. Although there was no proof of actual treachery, Kashmir was deprived of all the extra power, responsibility and territory Lytton had given him during the visit to his camp at Mudhapur in November 1876, and Biddulph was removed from Gilgit. A Russian invasion through the Pamirs was no longer considered a danger.

The Viceroy instructed Roberts to be stern but not cruel in avenging the massacre; he could not 'too carefully avoid the fatal mistake,' Lytton told him, 'of prolonged executions or anything like a reign of terror'.[32] Roberts set up a military tribunal to try the suspects. This did not close until the middle of November. Lytton was greatly dismayed when he heard that nearly a hundred men had by then been condemned and executed. He did not think that the members of the tribunal had been capable of collecting and sifting evidence,[33] and, indeed, it is hard to see who could have accused or defended the suspects considering there were no European eye-witnesses to the massacre. Lytton immediately proclaimed an amnesty and warned Roberts that he would be attacked in Parliament for undue severity. Compared to the appalling atrocities perpetrated by the British army in the Mutiny, not only on the mutineers but on anyone who was thought to have assisted them, Roberts's 'undue severity' seems negligible.

The Court of Enquiry left no doubt of Yakub Khan's moral guilt, though the evidence against him was not conclusive. It was ruled, however, that his conduct had been such that he could never again be restored to the throne of Afghanistan. Having been compelled to give up some of his personal treasure, he was escorted on December 1 to Ootacumund as a state prisoner. There he lived with his wives and his own servants in considerable comfort until his death in 1924.

16

'*A Pauper Earldom*'

Lytton suffered from violent headaches after the September crisis, often sitting up till 4 a.m. to write his long reports to London. At the beginning of October the Lytton family had the joy of welcoming Lord William back from South Africa. He had already written to them an account of the Battle of Ulindi at which the Zulus had been finally defeated in July:

They were indeed two days worth living for and never to be forgotten, I was lucky in the day's reconnaisance, inasmuch as I helped to save a poor man's life whose horse fell with him at about 200 yards from 3,000 Zulus. He was half stunned and bleeding a good deal. I galloped back to him with difficulty, got him up, and away behind me on my pony (even more exciting than the Gymkana races, two to one pony). The Zulus had come to within fifty yards of us, when I managed to start off at a gallop with him, never thinking the pair of us would get away alive.

For this exploit Lord William was awarded the V.C.

No reply had come by the third week in October from Brigadier-General Sir George Colley (to give him his new rank and title) in answer to the Viceroy's telegram of September 6 asking him to return. According to Edith, Robert said, 'He has given me up and won't return I'm sure, and Edith Colley was wretchedly low' when a telegram arrived from Aden to say that he would be arriving at Bombay on October 27. 'Edith Colley was nearly wild with delight, and so were we all, and R. looked happier than he has done ever since Colley left.'

The doctors had recommended that the children should remain at Simla that winter—Victor had been ill with his liver. This made Wellham, the nanny, so cross that Edith was particularly miserable to part from them when she and Robert left on November 20 for a tour of four native States in Rajputana. Their party went first to Delhi, then on to Alwar on the 25th where they were received by the seventeen-year-old Maharaja. The next stop was the pink city of Jaipur where they stayed a few days. (The Hindu princes, and the four the Lyttons visited were all Hindus, did not eat with their guests—they would have lost caste had they done so. They and their staff sat behind the guests and talked over their shoulders at meals.) Robert and Edith were both enchanted by Jaipur with its wide clean streets, like Paris boulevards, lit by gas of the Maharaja's own manufacture.

On the way to the next State, Bhurtpore, they stopped at Ajmer for two days, one of the most ancient cities in India and an isolated British possession in the Rajput States. There they saw William Loch again who was now Principal of the Mayo College—a college for young native princes, opened by Lord Northbrook in 1875 and largely endowed by the princes. 'It is so nice,' Edith wrote, 'to see Captain Loch with all the little native gentlemen round him, so happy and running and playing games like English boys almost.'

It was little native gentlemen from the best schools and colleges all over India whom Lytton hoped to recruit to the new Statutory Civil Service he had recently introduced and which it had taken him more than two years to formulate. This was the nearest he had been able to get to giving the Indians a fairer share in the Government of their country. The new Service allowed for one sixth of the posts hitherto held by the Covenanted Service, and some of the more important posts in the subordinate Service, to be filled by natives. The examination system was in their case to be abolished; instead they were to be nominated by the local Governments. Thus Indians would have a Service of their own, midway between the Covenanted and subordinate Services, but with the same legal status as the Covenanted Service. Instead of attracting the best elements in India as Lytton had hoped, this new Service attracted only those who would in the ordinary way have gone into the subordinate Service, for the Indians realised that the scheme was a compromise, and that the British were still determined to keep them out of the higher Service. After only eight years it was abolished.

At Bhurtpore Robert read in the London *Times* the report of a speech Disraeli had made at a banquet at the Guildhall on Lord Mayor's day, November 10, in which he had praised the Viceroy and deplored the mean way in which he had been attacked while in a distant land. This public expression of confidence in him gave Lytton renewed energy to carry on.

This was just about the time that Gladstone was touring Midlothian, making impassioned pleas in packed-out halls to the conscience of the people, denouncing Disraeli's 'immoral' policies and rising to the heights of eloquence in that famous passage: 'Remember the rights of the savage, as we call him. Remember that the happiness of his humble home, remember that the sanctity of life in the hill villages of Afghanistan, among the winter snows, is as inviolable in the eye of Almighty God as can be your own.' These thrilling words might not have aroused quite the same response in his applauding audience if they had seen with their own eyes some of the appalling mutilations inflicted by the Afghans on British soldiers while they were still alive.

The Lyttons' last stop was at Gwalior on December 9, and so to Calcutta on the evening of the 12th.

There was more trouble in Afghanistan during December. Yakub Khan's departure for India had sparked off a *jehad*, or holy war, in which all the Afghan tribes were for once united, and General Roberts in the Sherpur cantonment just north of Kabul, where he had moved his forces and supplies as being a more defensible position, had several fierce attacks to counter. Lord William had to leave the Lyttons before Christmas to go to Kabul because so many officers in his regiment, the 9th Lancers, had been killed. It was not until the end of the month that Roberts finally defeated the Afghans and was able to move back to Kabul.

It had been decided to split up Afghanistan; the Kandahar province was to be separated from Kabul and placed under an independent ruler who had already been chosen from among the Sirdars. It was now essential to find a new Amir for Kabul so that British troops could be withdrawn as soon as possible. He must be strong enough to govern his people, yet staunchly loyal to the British. There were several claimants to the throne. The legitimate heir was Abdur Rahman, the son of Sher Ali's eldest brother, who had a secret following in Afghanistan. Abdur Rahman had taken a leading part in the battles of succession after the death of his grandfather, Dost Mohomed, in 1863, and had even managed to put his father

169

on the throne for over a year, but since his final defeat by Sher Ali in 1869 he had lived in exile at Samarkand in Russian territory, under the protection of General Kaufmann who had obtained for him a pension from the Tsar. Long awaiting his opportunity to claim the throne, he had been restrained by Kaufmann who was quite satisfied with the subservient Sher Ali. Now, with the abdication of Yakub Khan, Abdur Rahman had been urged to establish his claim, Kaufmann believing that after eleven years of Russian hospitality he would become a vassal of Russia. In January it was reported that he had crossed the border into Afghanistan with Russian funds and was collecting supporters.

Surprisingly, Lytton, as soon as he heard this, recommended to Cranbrook the recognition of Abdur Rahman as the new Amir, and instructed Lepel Griffin, in political charge at Kabul, to contact him and discover what his attitude was towards the British. Abdur Rahman, strong, intelligent and astute had no intention of becoming a vassal of either Great Power. He believed, however, that England would be of less danger than Russia to his independence if he could reach an agreement with the Indian Government on his own terms. He was, therefore, quite willing to send a friendly reply to Griffin's overture, whereupon Griffin was instructed to enter into negotiations with him. These went on until July.

But before that a great deal was to happen. Parliament was opened by the Queen on February 5, 1880, and in the debate on Afghanistan which followed in the House of Lords, Lytton was vilified as usual. The Duke of Argyll for the Liberals tried to force Disraeli to produce the correspondence discovered by General Roberts between Russia and Sher Ali. The Government's refusal to do so was naturally suspect. Their reason for not complying was the same as had been given to the Queen when she had wanted the correspondence published: they did not wish to arouse Russia's hostility. (The Afghan correspondence was not made public until February 1881. See p. 184.)

Stephen wrote to Lytton after the debate: 'You are the first Indian Viceroy or Governor-General whose policy has been the leading party question in England, and of course you have been attacked as hardly anyone in my memory has been attacked.'[1]

But, as Lytton had warned, General Roberts came in for his share of abuse during the debate for ordering the execution of men whose only crime, it was said, had been to defend their country. Roberts, who had already been informed by Cranbrook of the accusations of cruelty against him, defended himself in a telegram which was published in *The Times* on February 6: no one had been executed for merely defending his country, he stated; ninety-seven men had been executed in all—fifty-eight for attacking the Residency, seven for dishonouring the bodies of officers of the Embassy in their possession and fifteen for mutilating wounded soldiers.

Later in February Colley was offered the appointment of Governor of Natal and Commander-in-Chief of the Natal and Transvaal troops in succession to Wolseley. This was promotion which could not be refused, and, of course, he would be able to take his wife with him. But for Lytton the loss was immeasurable, especially at a time when the situation was still so uncertain in Afghanistan. On February 27 the Lyttons gave a farewell dinner to the Colleys. Edith herself arranged the dinner table and had a bouquet made for Edith Colley of all the loveliest flowers from the Botanical Gardens. 'R. who had been saying he should go mad at the thought of Colley leaving but for his absorbing work, made the most touching, feeling little speech I have ever heard him make, his voice was perfect and it quite haunts me.'

'Adieu, my dear and true friend,' Robert wrote to Colley a few days later. 'I miss you every hour more than I can say, but—good heavens! how much one must be resigned to miss more and more as life goes on! Like Falstaff I wish it were bed time and all was over.'[2]

Exactly a year later, on February 27, 1881, Colley was killed at the battle of Majuba Hill while fighting the Boers. His men had run away, which would have broken his heart had he lived. He was killed by a single bullet. The surgeon's report showed that it had entered his forehead while he was facing the enemy.

Colley's place was to be taken by Colonel (afterwards General Sir Henry) Brackenbury, who had been with Wolseley at Natal, but he did not arrive for a fortnight. Captain Rose now went to Kabul where Fred Liddell was still on military duties, so the Lyttons had no old friends left on the staff. Robert was feeling more and more isolated. He had written to Stephen even before the debate in the House of Lords:

You have no idea what a help your letters are to me ... when I read the newspapers (which I avoid reading as much as I can) a horrible sensation creeps over me that, after all, such a unanimous and unqualified condemnation of all I have done, and am doing, must have some solid foundation, and that perhaps, with the best will in the world to do what is right, I have done nothing but blunder and sin since I set my hand to the task entrusted to me.[3]

All Edith's relations were Liberals, and the expressions of their sentiments in letters to India this year caused Robert and Edith great pain. Edith was particularly indignant with her sister Theresa Earle at this time:

She might have abused the policy set down for him but allowed that he could be working out the details well, or at any rate have kept silent over his public acts and tried to praise and uphold him in his private character. Whereas she always seemed to believe every trifling story put in by his enemies.

It was not in Robert's nature to bear a grudge and after an initial coolness he and Theresa Earle formed a close confidential friendship after his return to England. Theresa was plain and dumpy but had a very lively, amusing mind. Edith was more jealous of this friendship than she had been of any of his flirtations.

A week later Edith was writing in answer to a compliment her mother had passed on:

I never find out that I am popular in India, *no one* helps me to be friends, no one dares say they are pleased or the contrary with all the trouble one takes, and I don't suppose there is one in India more truly lonely than I am, but I believe that the way to be praised in a public position is to appear to all outsiders as standing quite alone, and I make a point of never showing that I have any preference for one person more than another, but then *I* can see them sometimes in *private*. I believe R. has sometimes made himself noticed and unpopular by being cordial to people he knows in *public*, when he had *no* other opportunity of speaking to them. It is all difficult to describe and a strange unnatural position and I for one don't care how soon it is over.

'A Pauper Earldom'

Just as they were feeling most forlorn, who should turn up un-expectedly from Afghanistan but Lord William, and this time they heard, to their joy, they would be allowed to keep him.

Shortly after this, on March 9, the agitating news arrived that there was to be a dissolution of Parliament, followed by a General Election. Encouraged by the result of two bye-elections, Disraeli had decided that this was the moment to go to the country. Parliament was dissolved on March 24. The Lyttons' future hung in the balance. If the Liberals were returned the Viceroy would almost certainly be recalled although his term of office was not up for another year.

It had been exceptionally cold that winter at Simla with thirteen inches of snow. The children had been constantly ill, so on March 2 they had been sent down to Ambala where Edith joined them on the 16th. Robert did not want to leave Calcutta until he heard the result of the election. While waiting he had time to look into his own financial position with the help of Brackenbury whom he had already come to like very much and to depend on. He was dismayed by what he found. He told Edith that £30,000 was all that Bracken-bury estimated they would have saved by the end of 1881, and that this was not, as he had at first thought, savings in India, but total savings including those in England.

There had been a slump in England and the value of all his investments had gone down. To his 'inexplicable horror' he had been told that the Calcutta theatricals alone had cost £2;000. And then his Knebworth agent had written to inform him that he had not received more than £2,000 a year from the estate since he had been in India and nothing at all in 1879. Because of bad harvests all tenant-farmers had demanded a 25% reduction in rents for the past three years.

Edith had frequently mentioned in her diary theatricals in Calcutta as well as at Simla. In February that year *The School for Scandal* had been performed at Government House. Rehearsals, which Robert had supervised, had gone on for a whole month. Mrs Plowden had taken the part of Lady Teazel, Lady Strachey of Mrs Candour and Mrs Batten of Lady Sneerwell. Edith had declared that Mrs Plowden was the best Lady Teazel she had ever seen.

A few days later Robert wrote again that the situation was even worse than this. His total investments were now worth only £12,000

173

and nothing more could be expected. Sales of wine, provisions, horses and carriages to his successor would increase his Indian bank balance only to the extent necessary to pay outstanding bills in India. Knebworth could not be expected to produce more than £2,000 a year, so the 'utmost income' they could look forward to when they got home, including 5% on investments, would be £2,600 per annum. 'When we came to India,' he added, 'our private income was nearly £11,000 per an. Pleasant! I shall have to fag and toil like a dragon to repair this disaster.'

The General Election was on March 31. By April 3 it was known that the Conservatives had suffered a disastrous defeat. The Liberals were in by a majority of 108. Lytton immediately sent in his resignation by telegraph. He received a reply from Cranbrook asking him to hold his office until his successor came out unless his 'policy was thwarted by the incoming Government'.[4] 'What a collapse it has all been,' he wrote to Edith. 'What India has cost us! I feel very low and restless—with a great longing to be back with you at Simla.' Edith had gone up to Simla with the children on April 3. She found it 'torture' to be parted from Robert at such a time, but experienced 'a growing feeling of delight at going home'.

Lytton left Calcutta on the evening of April 12. Lord William telegraphed to Edith: 'Viceroy started in excellent spirits. Large assemblage of friends, European and Native. Road to station brilliantly illuminated. Enthusiastic cheering along route on leaving.' This was very different from his arrival four years before. When Edith sent on this message to John Strachey who was in Simla, he replied, 'I am delighted to hear of my dear Viceroy's departure from Calcutta. It is a sign of the future verdict of history.' Edith repeated this to her mother, adding, 'and he [Strachey] is a good Radical, so if R. has fresh attacks on him don't be too ready to join'.

On his way to Simla Lytton heard by telegram that the Queen had bestowed an Earldom on him. In sending this news to Edith he added, 'I think Lord Beaconsfield has behaved very handsomely and loyally from first to last and I am very grateful to him.' Disraeli, in asking for this honour for the Viceroy, had written to the Queen, 'Never was a Viceroy so ill-treated by an Opposition. Lord Lytton is a first-rate man, and, being a real orator, his presence in the House of Lords will be invaluable.'[5]

Edith wrote to her mother:

We are very pleased that darling Robey should get the honours which mark his hard work having been approved, and especially glad are we that he has got the honours from his own party. It will be but a pauper Earldom but still in many ways perhaps it may be an advantage to the girls. As you say we must be very careful. I assure you I shall be *very* stingy and would rather have only a tallow candle in the smallest room than run risks—but dear R. had extravagant tastes, and though he may go to London as a Bachelor he may yet spend a good deal. I do so agree with your theories in educating girls—*charm*, and a power of adapting themselves to their husbands, *we* consider far more essential than great study which might only ruin their healths. But I consider grounding in everything is very necessary, and a power of being able to learn what they wish to take up later in life.

The three girls grew up to be not only very nice-looking but to possess great charm and intelligence.

17

The End of the Story

It was not until Lytton had telegraphed to the Queen for instructions that he heard officially that his successor was to be the Marquess of Ripon, and that he would be arriving at Simla on June 8. (His wife would not be joining him until the cold weather.) Although Lytton fully realised the awkwardness of having two Viceroys in Simla at the same time, he did not intend to travel to Bombay, three days and nights in the train from Ambala, at the height of summer. He told the Queen in a letter of May 4 that Lord Ripon had been sent out in haste at a time when it was impossible for him to leave the country until three weeks after the date of Lord Ripon's arrival without risking the lives of his children. He saw very clearly the hand of Gladstone in this lack of all consideration for him. Lord Ripon's arrival could easily have been postponed until the monsoon broke.

In this same letter to the Queen Lytton explained why he had resigned although he strongly believed that for the good of India the Viceroyalty should not be a political appointment: 'the language of denunciation' of the Liberals had 'gone too far'. Lord Hartington had twice declared in Parliament that the Viceroy was 'personally, as well as politically, unfit to exercise that high function "being everything a Viceroy ought not to be"'. Gladstone had 'publicly imputed' to him 'financial dishonesty, trickery, treachery, tyranny and cruelty', while the Duke of Argyll had charged him with 'a deliberate desire to shed blood, systematic fraud, violence and inveracity of the vilest kind'. So long as these charges were repudiated by the Government, no great injury had been done to British prestige in India, but the result of the election had given credence to them, and he felt that definite harm would be done to the dignity of the Viceroyalty if he waited to be recalled.[1]

The Queen replied most sympathetically:

The End of the Story

Balmoral Castle, 3rd June 1880.—The Queen Empress has to thank the Viceroy for his kind letter of 4th May. She is much grieved but *not* suprised to see by it how much pained and hurt he is at the violent and unjust way he has been attacked, but she hopes he will set it down to the (in her opinion) unpardonable heat and passion of *party* which, alas! seems to blind people, and certainly had exceeded, on the Liberal side, all limits.... The Queen has already expressed her warm thanks to Lord Lytton for his most valuable services, and she trusts he will not move a day sooner than is safe for himself and family to do so.[2]

The Queen herself was miserable at having to exchange Disraeli for Gladstone as her Prime Minister. She considered just as much as did Lytton himself that he had '*caused* the Afghan War'.[3]

But now a new catastrophe was to strike Lytton. Early in May it was discovered that an astonishing miscalculation of several million pounds had been made in the estimates for the Afghan War prepared by the Military Department, headed by Sir Edwin Johnson. These estimates had been adopted by Strachey's Financial Department and presented in the Budget at the end of February. It was eventually found that the estimates had been exceeded by the enormous sum of nearly twelve million pounds, the total cost of the war being £17,490,000 instead of the estimated £5,750,000. A further five million had been spent on frontier railways. The error was due to an outworn system of account-keeping used by the Military Department. The figures, though, had not been questioned by the Finance Department although they had appeared suspiciously low; Strachey, therefore, could not be absolved from blame, and this Lytton minded more than anything. 'The whole thing is the cruellest stroke of mischance that has ever befallen me,' he wrote to Cranbrook, 'and has caused and is causing me unspeakable distress.'[4]

Naturally Lytton took the entire responsibility on himself; nevertheless, Strachey as well as Edwin Johnson felt obliged to resign. Strachey's financial reforms had so improved Indian finances that fifteen million could be paid out of Indian revenue; the balance fell on the British tax-payer. (Strachey and his wife retired to Florence for three years. He then became a member of the Indian Council in London.)

Lytton was greatly comforted at this wretched time by a letter from Disraeli written after the discovery of the error: 'I am sure

177

you have never doubted my entire confidence in yourself and my approval of all you have done in dealing with some of the most considerable and critical affairs which have ever engaged the solicitude of a statesman.'[5] It was also a comfort to him to receive dozens of letters from the Indian princes regretting his departure.

While awaiting Lord Ripon's arrival, Lytton had a fresh anxiety to take his mind off the disaster of the war estimates. While negotiations with Abdur Rahman were near completion (he had reached an agreement with the British and was to be declared Amir on July 22) there was a flare-up at Kandahar where the British had set up a native ruler under the title of Wali. Ayoub Khan, a brother of the deported Yakub Khan and Governor of Herat, was challenging the Wali's rule. The Lyttons were on their way back to England when British troops, fighting for the Wali, whose own troops had deserted to Ayoub Khan, were completely routed on July 27 at Maiwand, about fifteen miles west of Kandahar, one of the worst defeats of native troops in British history. Of the 2,500 men engaged at Maiwand on the British side, 934 were killed and 174 wounded or missing.* The defeat was followed by General Roberts's famous march from Kabul to Kandahar. He covered 320 miles in twenty-one days in temperatures varying 80° between night and day and over some of the worst terrain in the world. His whole force of nearly 10,000 men of all ranks, 8,000 camp followers and over 2,000 horses and mules reached Kandahar on August 31. The next day he defeated and dispersed Ayoub Khan's troops at the Battle of Kandahar. It was from this battle that Roberts took his title when he was made a peer in 1892—Earl Roberts of Kandahar. Roberts in his memoirs acknowledged his deep indebtedness to Lytton for the confidence he had shown in him from the first.

Abdur Rahman had done all he could to help Roberts's advance. Having thus proved his loyalty to the British, Lord Ripon was empowered to reward him with an annual subsidy of Rs. 12,000,000. In the agreement he had come to in July with Lepel Griffin, who had then become the representative of the Liberal Government, Abdur Rahman was not asked to receive a British Resident any-

---

* It was rumoured that Russia had helped Ayoub Khan to defeat the Wali. (The *Daily News*, February 10, 1881.) The total number of casualties among officers in the Afghan War of 1878–80 was recorded as 215—79 killed, 72 wounded and 64 dead of disease or exposure. (These figures included Cavagnari and the officers with him.) There was no official record of the total number of casualties.

where in his territory, though he was required not to have political dealings with any foreign power except the British Government.

By the following year Kandahar had been given up and Abdur Rahman was ruling wisely and firmly over a united Afghanistan, which he continued to do until his death in 1901. So much courage shown, so many lives lost, so much money and anguish expended—what had it all been for? Certainly Afghanistan benefitted in the end by exchanging the weak, shifty, rapacious Sher Ali, and the even weaker Yakub Khan, for the strong, shrewd, just, albeit savagely cruel Abdur Rahman.

The Russians were to continue their creeping advance. In 1884 they took Merv, and the following year war with England was again imminent when they tried to annexe some Afghan territory. Abdur Rahman then showed the British that his strength and loyalty could be relied upon.

As Viceroy, Lytton's name will always be associated with the Afghan War which overshadowed the benefits of his internal policies, such as the reduction of the Salt Tax, the reform of the Army, the Famine Code. In order to assess the extent of his responsibility for the war one must first ask whether it was he or the Liberal Government's policy of *laisser-faire* that caused the alienation of Sher Ali. Whatever the answer, one must then ask whether he created an unnecessary war by risking the Amir's refusal of the Chamberlain Mission or merely brought to a head a situation which was bound to have erupted in war sooner or later. There are strong indications that Sher Ali had fallen irretrievably under Russian domination before Lytton arrived in India and that if the British had remained inactive in 1878, whoever had come to the throne after Sher Ali's death would not have been able to extricate himself from Russia. Moreover, with Russia on the doorstep of Afghanistan, as she was in 1885, and an Amir at Kabul hostile to the British, war with Afghanistan, it seems, would have been inevitable and England would have been in a far worse position to fight it, having lost all prestige in India and among the border tribes for having passively put up with the Amir's insults.

It will probably never be known whether the Russians had designs on India itself (Abdur Rahman publicly declared that they aimed at the possession of India[6] and he might be supposed to know after living amongst them for eleven years) but it seems fairly certain that they had planned to retain their hold on Afghanistan in order to use the invasion of that country as a threat in the event of war with England in Europe, and that Abdur Rahman's defection to the British frustrated that plan.

The aggressiveness Lytton showed in carrying out his policy for Afghanistan was alien to his nature. As he saw it, he had played a cardinal role at great personal sacrifice to keep India within the Empire. Whether India was worth keeping was not a subject for much discussion in those days when the Empire was generally considered to be worth every sacrifice. Whatever we may think of Empire today, Lytton's conception of it was certainly an inspiring one:

I feel very bitter doubts whether England any longer deserves to keep India [he had written to Stephen]. John Morley, who is a representative man, writes to me in a tone of great superiority 'we sober-minded, steady-going folk at home no longer care for Empire'. Surely it is the paramount duty of every great Empire, of every noble people, to maintain above all things else, its own moral character—that is to say, the confidence of other nations in its courage, its energy, its high spirit, and its unimpeachable good faith.[7]

Ironically, John Morley was to become Secretary of State for India in 1905.

During their last weeks at Simla the Lyttons managed to live very frugally. They were no longer required to entertain, and had got rid of Bonsard. Bonsard ran the Grand Hotel at Simla for a season and then opened the Hotel de Paris at Aurramotollah, Calcutta, in partnership with the Lyttons' coachman, Wilson. Edith's treasured maid, Ozzie, had, like Mlle Feez and the German governess, who had married a man she had met on the voyage to Bombay, found romance in India. She returned with her mistress to England and then went straight back to India to marry Wilson.

When Lord Ripon arrived the Lyttons were to move to Snowdon, General Robert's house, let to a Maharaja who was lending it to them. Lord William went to Bombay to meet Lord Ripon and accompany him to Simla. Leaving him at Ambala he came on ahead to spend the last evening alone with the Lyttons at Peterhof. He told them that the heat during the journey had been worse than anything he had ever known—it was 112° in the shade at Ambala but Lord Ripon and his party had not complained or been ill. Lord William also told them about Colonel Gordon ('Chinese Gordon', afterwards killed at Khartoum), who had come out with Lord Ripon as Military Secretary but had resigned after two days to Lord Ripon's great inconvenience. 'Lord William says the world is not big enough for him [Gordon],' Edith wrote, 'and that there is no king or country big enough. He hit Lord William on the shoulder, saying, "Yes, that is flesh, that is what I hate and what makes me wish to die".'

Gordon's reason for resigning, according to Lord William, was because he was told to write a letter to a Parsee in Bombay informing him that Lord Ripon had read with much pleasure and interest a pamphlet sent to him by that gentleman. 'You know perfectly well that Lord Ripon has never read it and I cannot be made to tell lies,' Gordon had declared, and promptly sent in his resignation. His departure meant that Lord William was taken on by Lord Ripon as Military Secretary, a post he also held under the two succeeding Viceroys, Lord Dufferin and Lord Lansdowne.*

Lord Ripon and his party arrived at five in the afternoon of the 8th. Lytton had provided tents for them on the *tonga* road so that they could lunch and change before the official reception at Peterhof and the dinner the Lyttons were giving for them. Salutes were fired, a guard of honour was drawn up and the band played. 'Lord Ripon has very cordial manners,' Edith recorded, 'and will, I am sure, be popular though not a shining light of the earth. Our dinner party went off well but when it came to starting off from the old house, I felt it a good deal, and very nearly broke down.' She had changed for dinner in her old room but never returned to it.

Lord Ripon was full of apologies for being sent out in such haste. He gave a farewell dinner for the Lyttons on June 23. Although Robert said while driving from Snowdon to Peterhof, 'This is like returning to *Hell*', the dinner 'went off very cheerily'.

When the day of departure came, June 28, the monsoon had fortunately just broken. All the society of Simla assembled at the gathering place near the church and Lord Ripon led the cheers as

---

*Lord William married in 1895 an American, Lily, née Warren, widow of the 8th Duke of Marlborough whose second wife she had been. They settled down at Deepdene near Dorking and he became a very successful owner of race-horses. He died of peritonitis in December 1900, aged fifty-three. He had one son who died young, unmarried.

the Lyttons drove away in what had been Edith's pony carriage. Barbara Lyall was able to take a private farewell of them by walking some way down the *tonga* road. The last of their friends to say good-bye was the faithful Lord William who accompanied them as far as Ambala. The special train which had brought Lord Ripon to Simla took them back to Bombay and they were treated with Vice-regal honours throughout the journey.

The Barnetts, Captain Rose and Colonel Brackenbury, and Robert's beloved Japanese dog, Budget, travelled back with them on the troopship, the *Himalaya*. Many years later Brackenbury was to write to Robert's daughter, Betty, about her father: 'The stars in their courses seemed to combine against him, but his courage never failed, he never lost his dignity. It was then, even more than at the time of his prosperity, that I was so intensely attracted to him.[8]

The *Himalaya* was met at Portsmouth on August 7 by members of Edith's family and by Colonel Burne and Wilfred Blunt among others. 'Oh, the dear drunken people in the streets, how I love them!'[9] Edith exclaimed as they drove away from the docks to the Southsea Hotel. For dinner they chose fried soles, the greatest treat they could imagine.

The next day the Lyttons went to Osborne to see the Queen at her invitation. She received them with the utmost warmth and kindness; then in the afternoon they proceeded to Knebworth by a special train laid on by Colonel Brackenbury. The sight of the neo-Gothic towers of the house from the railway was one of the happiest moments of their lives. The station platform at Stevenage was carpeted in red and decorated with flags, and all the Knebworth tenants were lined up to meet them. They drove off through a triumphal arch. At the Park gates the horses were taken out of the shafts and the tenants dragged the carriage up to the house where Robert and Edith proudly held up their two little sons. Victor, who now had the courtesy title of Viscount Knebworth, would be four next day.

It is indeed like a dream to me [Robert wrote to Barbara Lyall two days later] that I should be writing to you on this delicious afternoon, under the oak-tree on the lawn of my grandmother's garden—the bees humming, the birds hopping, and the children capering about me—the sheep-bells drowsily tinkling from the distant Park—and Budget dozing in the mossiest turf at my feet, and the air bathed in the manifold scents of an English August.[10]

Epilogue

For seven years after his return from India Robert Lytton was free
from official duties and lived in England for the first time since he
had gone to Bonn at the age of seventeen. Although he was
encouraged by Disraeli to take part in politics he was sickened with
political life as exemplified by the personal attacks on him. He knew
he was not fitted for such a game; he was too thin-skinned, and
then Edith felt his health would never have stood it. He spoke only
three times in the House of Lords, each time on Afghan affairs.
After his maiden speech on January 10, 1881, Disraeli wrote to the
Queen:

Last night, Lord Lytton made his *début* in the House of Lords, and at
once mounted to the first rank of present Parliamentary orators. This
is a most important adhesion to our debating bench. The Duke of Argyll
had expected from the new peer, who had never addressed either House
of Parliament, a personal and egotistical address, and of a florid character.
His Grace was much disappointed. He had to reply to an admirably
practical address on the surrender of Candahar (which never must be surrendered); and this in a tone severely chaste, and in the best style of
Parliamentary debating. The Ministers had so depreciated and under-
rated Lord Lytton that his success was to me proportionately gratifying.
They have found their master....[1]

After this speech, Disraeli told Lytton, as they left the House
together, that he felt as if he had won the Derby.

On February 7, 1881, Lytton asked in the House of Lords for
the secret papers to be produced which General Roberts had found
at Kabul. 'These papers,' he said, 'were forwarded by the late
Government of India for the information of Parliament, but Her
Majesty's late Government thought, that while diplomatic and military questions were still pending, the time for the issue of those

documents had not arrived'; now, however, the situation was entirely different. Lord Granville, the Foreign Secretary, was quite willing to lay the documents on the table of the House of Lords, though he pointed out that they had been written at a date when there had been strained relations between Russia and England. The Duke of Argyll, the Lord Privy Seal, stated that there was no evidence of the Amir being hostile before Lytton went out to India. It was 'the triumph' of Lytton's policy 'to wound the susceptibilities' of both Russia and Afghanistan and 'throw them for the purpose of defence, and possible aggression, into each other's arms'. His policy had 'written its failure in bloody letters on the face of Afghanistan'.

The next day, February 8, before the documents had been produced, the full text of the Afghan-Russian correspondence as well as the text of the treaty signed between Russia and Sher Ali was published in the Conservative daily, the *Standard*, together with a leading article which described the documents as 'a plain exhibition of systematic and unblushing duplicity' on the part of Russia and Sher Ali. A leading article on the subject also appeared in *The Times* next day, regarding the correspondence 'as evidence of a plot to strike at the very heart of the Indian Empire'.

The Liberal press naturally had a very different point of view. It did not impugn the authenticity of the documents; it belittled their importance. The *Pall Mall Gazette* declared that it was the Duke of Argyll and not Lord Lytton who would find his position strengthened by their publication. It stressed the point that the first letter had not been written until June 1878, at a time when relations between Russia and England justified 'some hostility of action' on the part of the Russian authorities in Central Asia against England. The fact that one of the most incriminating letters (the one from Stoletov to Sher Ali telling him to make peace openly and in secret prepare for war) was written on October 8, three months *after* the Treaty of Berlin, was lamely attributed by the *Pall Mall* to the difficulty of breaking off 'the course of negotiations in remote regions with semi-savage tribes'.

The *Daily News* took the same line but emphasised the fact that Lord Beaconsfield himself, in the debate on December 10, 1878, had expressed entire satisfaction with the conduct of Russia and had had no complaints to make about the Russian Mission still being at Kabul. On February 10 the *News* published the report of an article from the *Journal de St. Pétersbourg* in which it was stated that the Russian Government had no objection to the publication of the documents; the Government claimed that there was nothing hostile in them to British interests and that if they should appear to be in part of a political character this was because at the time the possibility of war with England had justified Russia in taking up a position of self-defence.

The Conservatives' hopes that the publication of the documents would irresistibly strengthen their case for the retention of Kandahar were not realised. On March 3 Lytton moved a resolution that Kandahar should be retained. The resolution was passed by a majority of more than two to one, only to be reversed in the Commons. Kandahar was given up.

The Lyttons managed to live at Knebworth House in spite of their financial straits; indeed, under a new agent the estate yielded more than Robert had expected. Edith was determined to remember only the pleasant side of their life in India, whereas Robert, she tells us, could never recall it except as a nightmare. He felt a constant regret that he had ever left Lisbon where he had been happy, and peaceful. While Edith remained at Knebworth with the children, Robert travelled a great deal by himself. He contributed regularly to various periodicals and began to write his father's biography, but the leisure he had longed for in which to devote himself to poetry had come too late: inspiration had dried up—for ever, he believed. Then in 1884, laid up with an attack of sciatica, came a sudden creative flowering which resulted in a 300-page narrative poem, *Glenavril*. It met with mixed reviews when it was published the following year, most of them favourable. For the rest of his life he was engaged in revising that other long narrative poem, *King Poppy*, a satire on courts and courtiers, which was published posthumously.

When at home, Robert began to find his children 'more and more fascinating'. None of them remembered his ever scolding or punishing them. His eldest daughter, Betty, became his chief confidante as she grew up. He once took her alone to Florence and Venice. 'He was often ill,' she tells us, 'often melancholy, but always intimately loving, indulgent, and the object of my unqualified adoration.'[2]

Epilogue

In 1883, when he was fifty-two, Robert met the young American actress, Mary Anderson, who was appearing in London in his father's play, *The Lady of Lyons*. He was soon to fall passionately in love with her. This was the only real infidelity of his married life, and then it was not a physical one since Mary Anderson, who was a Catholic, would not become his mistress.[3] This last love was in many respects a repetition of his first love in Florence—a reciprocated passion frustrated by insuperable obstacles. Edith knew of the attachment and was as hurt by it as one can imagine. When at the end of 1887 Lord Salisbury, who had become Prime Minister after the election of 1886, offered Robert the post of Ambassador in Paris, he grasped at this solution to his problem.*

Robert was ideally suited to this post. He had a treasure of a chef, gave dinner parties at which the talk was as good as the food and wine, entertained all the most distinguished and interesting men and women of the day in every walk of life, and made full use of his box at the *Comédie Française*. His eccentricities of dress and manner were as popular in this cultured society as they had been outrageous in Calcutta and Simla. He was more loved by the French than any British ambassador before or since. His duties were light and perfectly suited to his abilities. 'I devoted my life to India,' he said, 'and everybody abused me. I come here, do nothing and am praised to the skies.'[4]

Robert died in Paris on November 24, 1891, shortly after his sixtieth birthday. He had been suffering for some weeks from such a painful inflammation of the bladder that he had been obliged to stay in bed, though the actual cause of death was a cerebral haemorrhage. He had had his bed moved into the private sitting-room so as not to be separated from his family. Edith was sitting beside him and he died in her arms. He had written a letter to her to be delivered by his valet in the event of his death. In it he expressed all the love he had always felt for her. He did not deny that he had loved one woman, 'M. A. deeply and too much' but she was the only one who had ever 'come between' him and Edith in his 'heart of hearts' in the whole of their married life, and even then he had never ceased

---

* By 1885, when Salisbury had briefly become Prime Minister, he and Lytton had so far made up their differences that he had considered Lytton the only possible candidate for the Foreign Office, but realising that his colleagues would never accept Lytton because of his lack of parliamentary experience, he had kept the Foreign Office in his own hands.

to love and revere Edith; and now, as he was writing this last letter, his whole heart was filled with 'unspeakable love' for her.

Robert was given a state funeral in Paris, after which the coffin was taken to England and interred in the family mausoleum in the Park at Knebworth. An elaborately sculpted memorial tablet by Alfred Gilbert was erected to him in the crypt of St Paul's Cathedral. It was his old friend Wilfred Blunt who wrote the most heartfelt obituary: 'How shall we perpetuate the memory of his personality...? This was more wonderful and rare than all his works ... for in truth he was the brightest, best and most beloved of men.'[5]

In 1895 Edith became a Lady in Waiting to Queen Victoria, and after the Queen's death to Queen Alexandra. She retired from Court in 1905 and thereafter lived quietly in a house at Knebworth designed for her by her son-in-law, Edwin Lutyens. The people she liked best to see were those whom Robert had loved, and she even urged her daughters to visit Mary Anderson.[6] Edith died in 1932 at the age of ninety-five and was put to rest in the only place she had ever wanted to be since she had first met Robert—by his side.

Acknowledgments

Material from the Royal Archives is published by the gracious permission of Her Majesty the Queen. Transcripts of Crown-copyright records in the India Office Records appear by permission of the Controller of Her Majesty's Stationery Office.

I wish to thank Mr Neil Raymond for most generously giving me full use of his as yet unpublished biography of Robert Lytton, *Victorian Viceroy*, and Lady Longford for allowing me to quote some of her own transcripts of passages from Wilfred Blunt's unpublished diaries at the Fitzwilliam Museum, Cambridge, before her own biography of Blunt was completed. My thanks also to the Syndics of the Fitzwilliam Museum for permission to publish these extracts. I am also most grateful to Lady Cobbold and to the Hon. David Lytton-Cobbold for their co-operation and the loan of family letters and photographs. To the late Mr Prakash Nayer and his son, Ashok, of Calcutta, all my thanks are due for the information they have sent me. I also wish to thank Dr Dinshaw of Bombay, Mrs Rosemary Seton and Mrs Pauline Rohatgi of the India Office Library, the Archivist and his staff at the Hertford Record Office and the Librarian of the Cambridge University Library for their kind help. My thankfulness for the London Library and its incomparable staff is too vast to be encompassed in words.

Source Notes

The chief source material for this book is Edith Lytton's diary, kept while she was in India, her weekly letters home and her letters to her husband and his to her when they were parted in India. (The diary and letters are in the author's collection.) In 1899 an expurgated version of the diary was privately printed. Although much was left out, it contains some extraneous material, such as letters from friends and from the Viceregal staff, and a few useful annotations. All quotations in the book not linked by numbers to the Source Notes come from the above sources.

Abbreviations for unpublished sources

Cambridge	Papers of Sir James Fitzjames Stephen, University Library, Cambridge, 14 Add. 7349 (C)
Hertford	Lytton Papers, County Record Office, Hertford
IOR	Lytton Papers, India Office Records, MMS EUR. E 218/522/1–4, 16–17
Knebworth	Lytton Papers, Knebworth House, Hertfordshire
ML	Lytton Papers, Author's Collection

Abbreviation for most used published source

BL	*Personal and Literary Letters of Robert, 1st Earl of Lytton*, 2 vols, ed. Lady Betty Balfour, 1906

See Bibliography for other references

1. DISRAELI'S OFFER

page	Note	
1	1	BL, I, 339
1	2	Royal Archives, March 20, 1875
2	3	BL, I, 340
2	4	ibid, 342–4

Source Notes

2. PREPARATIONS FOR INDIA

Source Notes

3. VOYAGE TO INDIA

page	Note	
22	1	Butler, p. 146
25	2	BL, II, 6
27	3	ibid, 7

4. THE NEW VICEROY

31	1	Chuck
32	2	BL, II, 11–12
32	3	ibid, 12–13
32	4	ibid, 24, letter to Salisbury, July 23, 1876
33	5	The *Friend of India*, August 13, 1876
35	6	IOR/1, pp. 359–63, letter from Lytton to the Queen, August 6, 1876, *Annual Register* 1876 and Chaudhary, pp. 14–39 where the case is very fully discussed
35	7	*Annual Register* 1876
35	8	Buckle II, 482n, August 6, 1876
36	9	Chaudhary, p. 25, September 13, 1876
36	10	*The Times*, October 31, 1876
36	11	ibid, March 22, 1876
36	12	Young, II, 148

5. SIMLA

41	1	IOR/1, August 20, 1876
41	2	BL, II, 19, April 30, 1876
41	3	Buckle, II, 461, May 4, 1876
42	4	IOR/1, pp. 349–51, August 5, 1876
42	5	Knebworth
43	6	Blunt, *Ideas on India*, p. xvii
44	7	BL, II, 16, April 30, 1876
44	8	Cambridge, May 7, 1876
44	9	ibid, May 29, 1876
45	10	ibid, June 24 and August 7, 1876
45	11	BL, II, 23–4, undated
47	12	IOR/4, p. 95, to Cranbrook, February 8, 1876
49	13	Balfour, p. 63

Source Notes

page	Note	
50	14	IOR/1, p. 346, to Sir Henry Rawlinson, August 5, 1876. Rawlinson's book *India and Russia in the East* (1875) had been a cardinal factor in alerting Disraeli to the danger of Russian encroachment in Central Asia. Rawlinson was a member of the Indian Council in London

6. THE RUSSIAN MENACE

55	1	IOR/1, pp. 316–24, July 30, 1876
56	2	BL, II, 30, to John Morley, September 9, 1876
57	3	IOR/1, p. 355, August 6, 1876
58	4	Balfour, pp. 82–3
59	5	IOR/1, p. 614, Lytton to the Queen, November 15, 1876
61	6	BL, II, 94, November 14, 1876
61	7	IOR/1, p. 569, October 26, 1876
61	8	ibid, p. 570
62	9	ibid, pp. 611–13, Lytton to the Queen, November 15, 1876
63	10	BL, II, 32, September 9, 1876
64	11	IOR/1, pp. 108–16, November 15, 1876
65	12	BL, II, 36, November 22, 1876

7. THE KHAN OF KHELAT

68	1	IOR/3, p. 857, to Henry Loch, November 25, 1878
71	2	BL, II, 39, December 12, 1876
72	3	ibid, 41, November 29, 1876

8. THE IMPERIAL ASSEMBLAGE

75	1	Burne, p. 219
76	2	Quotations from Prinsep in this chapter come from his published journal (see Bibliography)
80	3	IOR/2, pp. 41–51, diary letter to the Queen, December 23 to January 10, 1877
80	4	ibid, quoted in BL, p. 44
81	5	ibid, omitted from BL
81	6	BL, II, 20, April 30, 1876
81	7	Temple, I, 289

Source Notes

page	Note	
86	8	BL, II, 53, Lytton to Ponsonby, January 12, 1877
87	9	IOR/2, pp. 41–51, diary letter to the Queen, December 23 to January 10, 1877
87	10	IOR/2, p. 16, January 22, 1877

9. CALCUTTA

93	1	P. E. Roberts, p. 432
93	2	ibid, p. 434
93	3	Monypenny, VI, 379, April 7, 1877
94	4	IOR/2, p. 155, to Sir Bartle Frere, March 2, 1877
96	5	BL, II, 56, January 31, 1877
96	6	IOR/2, p. 386, May 17, 1877
96	7	ibid, p. 447, June 4, 1877
97	8	Blunt's Diary, from transcription by Lady Longford
98	9	Cambridge, June 15, 1877
98	10	ibid, July 17, 1877
99	11	ibid, August 2, 1877
99	12	Hertford, D/EK 038, undated letter by unknown person, first and last pages missing
99	13	BL, II, 259, name not given
99	14	Buckle, III, 29, July 20, 1879
100	15	BL, II, 393, letter to Theresa Earle, February 16, 1890

10. FAMINE

103	1	Cambridge, June 24, 1877
103	2	Cecil, p. 154, June 22, 1877
103	3	ibid, p. 159, August 10, 1877
104	4	Hansard, June 11, 1877
104	5	Cecil, p. 159, August 10, 1877
104	6	ibid, p. 160, October 25, 1877
105	7	Prinsep, p. 250. All quotations from Prinsep in this chapter are from his published journal
107	8	The *Madras Times* and the *Madras Mail*, July and August 1877
108	9	BL, II, 71, July 29, 1877
108	10	ibid, 72, August 12, 1877

Source Notes

Source Notes

page	Note	
133	13	Monypenny, VI, 381
133	14	ibid
134	15	Gathorne-Hardy, p. 83
134	16	Cowling, p. 64
134	17	IOR/3, p. 749, letter from Lytton to Cranbrook, October 11, 1878

14. WAR AND PEACE

135	1	Cowling, p. 70
137	2	Forrest, p. 481, September 22, 1878
137	3	BL, II, 121–2, September 26, 1878
137	4	IOR/3, p. 676, September 26, 1878
137	5	Gathorne-Hardy, p. 96
137	6	IOR, L/P & S/7/257, p. 173
138	7	Kazemzadeh, p. 48
138	8	ibid, p. 49
139	9	Monypenny, VI, 382
139	10	Cotton, p. 169
140	11	Balfour, p. 291
140	12	Forrest, p. 485
140	13	IOR/3, p. 774, October 24, 1878
141	14	Monypenny, VI, 383
142	15	IOR, L/R3/9, vol. 9
142	16	IOR/3, p. 740, October 10, 1878
142	17	ibid, p. 774, October 24, 1878
142	18	Cecil, II, 341–2
143	19	Blake, p. 761, November 21, 1878
144	20	Monypenny, VI, 387, October 26, 1878
144	21	ibid, p. 358, October 10, 1878
146	22	IOR/3
147	23 -	Correspondence discovered by General Roberts at Kabul in October 1879

15. THE TREATY AND THE MASSACRE

148	1	BL, II, 139, January 30, 1879
148	2	IOR, MSS Eur. F. 127, Mrs Strachey to her husband January 18, 1878

Source Notes

page	Note	
150	3	IOR/16, April 3, 1879
152	4	IOR/4, June 1, 1879
152	5	ibid
152	6	Cecil, II, 343, May 23, 1879
152	7	Monypenny, VI, 476, August 14, 1879
153	8	Quotations from Blunt's diary in this chapter are from transcripts by Lady Longford
153	9	Lady Anne Blunt's Diary, British Library, Add.MS 53903
154	10	Butler, p. 221, January 22, 1879
154	11	BL, II, 152–3
155	12	IOR/17, letter of August 31, 1879
156	13	Lytton, p. 111
157	14	Roberts, II, 178
157	15	ibid
158	16	Balfour, p. 348
159	17	Butler, p. 239
160	18	BL, II, 167
160	19	Balfour, p. 360
161	20	Monypenny, VI, 479
161	21	BL, II, 172, October 12, 1879
163	22	Balfour, p. 366
163	23	Roberts, II, 232
163	24	ibid, p. 235
164	25	ibid, p. 178
164	26	Hertford, D/EK/036, letter from Lytton to Disraeli, September 18, 1880
164	27	ibid
164	28	ibid, D/EK/W119, speech by Lytton for debate in House of Lords January 10, 1881, but never delivered
164	29	Roberts, II, 247 and *Standard*, February 9, 1881
165	30	*Standard*, February 9, 1881
165	31	Roberts, II, 470, November 29, 1879
165	32	IOR/4, letter to Cranbrook, December 5, 1879
165	33	ibid

16. 'A PAUPER EARLDOM'

170	1	Cambridge, April 1, 1880
171	2	Butler, p. 248

Source Notes

page	Note	
172	3	BL, II, 191, January 10, 1880
174	4	ML, cipher telegram, decoded April 8, 1880
175	5	Monypenny, VI, 527, April 8, 1880

17. THE END OF THE STORY

176	1	BL, II, 209
177	2	Buckle, III, 107
177	3	ibid, p. 75, letter from Queen to Ponsonby, April 8, 1880
177	4	BL, II, 217, June 1, 1880
178	5	Blake, p. 721, May 31, 1880
179	6	S. E. Wheeler, p. 136, from State paper by Abdur Rahman read in Durbar at Kabul in June 1886
180	7	IOR/3, p. 737, January 28, 1878
182	8	BL, II, 218
182	9	Blunt, *Secret History*, p. 3
182	10	BL, II, 218, August 10, 1880

EPILOGUE

183	1	Buckle, III, 182
185	2	BL, II, 305
186	3	Information from my mother, Emily Lutyens. Betty Balfour was her father's chief confidante in the affair.
186	4	Dictionary of National Biography
187	5	*Nineteenth Century*, June 1892
187	6	Information from my mother

Bibliography

The Afghan War, Causes of: a Selection of Papers Laid Before Parliament (1879)

Alder, G. V., *British India's Northern Frontier 1865–95* (1963)

Balfour, Lady Betty, *History of Lord Lytton's Indian Administration* (1899)

Blake, Robert, *Disraeli* (1967)

Blunt, Wilfred Scawen, *Ideas on India* (1885)

—— *Secret History of the Occupation of Egypt* (1911)

Buck, E. J., *Simla Past and Present* (Bombay, 1925)

Buckle, G. E. (ed.), *The Letters of Queen Victoria*, 2nd Series, 1862–85, 3 vols (1928)

Burne, Sir Owen Tudor, *Memories* (1907)

Butler, Lt-General Sir W. F., *Life of Sir George Pomeroy Colley* (1899)

Cambridge History of India, Vol. VI, 1858–1918

Cecil, Lady Gwendoline, *Life of Robert, Marquis of Salisbury*, 4 vols (1921)

Chakravarty, Sunash, *From Khyber to Oxus, a Study in Imperial Expansion* (Delhi, 1976)

Chaudhary, V. C. P., *Imperial Policy of British India, 1876–1880* (Calcutta, 1968)

Chesney, Sir George, *Indian Polity* (1868 and 1894)

Chuck, N. A. (ed.), *The Imperial Bouquet of Flowers, Including a Collection of Lord Lytton's Speeches in India* (Calcutta, 1877)

Cotton, Sir Henry, *Indian and Home Memories* (1911)

Cowling, Maurice, *Lytton, the Cabinet and Russia, August to November 1878* (*English Historical Revue*, January–October 1961)

Dufferin and Ava, Marchioness of, *Our Viceregal Life in India*, 2 vols (1889)

Duke, Joshua, *Recollections of the Kabul Campaign 1879–1880* (1883)

Earle, Mrs Charles, *Memoirs and Memories* (1911)

Bibliography

Egremont, Max, *The Cousins* (1977)

Forbes, Archibald, *The Afghan Wars 1839–42 and 1878–80* (1892)

Forrest, C. W., *Life of Field-Marshal Sir Neville Chamberlain* (1909)

Gathorne-Hardy, A. E. (ed.), *Gathorne Hardy, 1st Earl of Cranbrook*, 2 vols (1910)

Hanna, Colonel H. B., *The Second Afghan War*, 3 vols (1899)

Harlan, Aurelia Brooks, *Owen Meredith* (New York, 1946)

Hibbert, Christopher, *The Great Mutiny: India 1857* (1978)

Hussey, Christopher, *Life of Sir Edwin Lutyens* (1950)

India List 1876–80

Kazemzadeh, Firuz, *Great Britain and Russia in Persia 1864–1914: A Study in Imperialism* (1968)

Keay, John, *The Gilgit Game* (1979)

Kennedy, A. L., *Salisbury 1830–1903: Portrait of a Statesman* (1953)

Lee, Sir Sidney, *King Edward VII*, 2 vols (1925)

Lethbridge, General Sir Roper, *The Golden Book of India: A Genealogical and Biographical Dictionary of the Ruling Princes, Chiefs and Nobles of the Indian Empire* (1893)

Longford, Elizabeth, *Pilgrimage of Passion, A Life of Wilfred Scawen Blunt* (1979)

Lutyens, Lady Emily, *The Birth of Rowland: an Exchange of Letters in 1865 between Robert Lytton and his Wife* (1956)

Lytton, Neville, *The English Country Gentleman* (1925)

Magnus, Philip, *Gladstone* (1954)

Martin, Frank A., *Under an Absolute Amir* (1907)

Marvin, Charles, *The Russian Advance Towards India* (1882)

Menzies, Mrs Stewart, *Lord William Beresford, V.C.* (1917)

Miller, Charles, *Khyber* (1977)

Monypenny, W. F. and Buckle, G. E., *Life of Benjamin Disraeli Earl of Beaconsfield*, 6 vols (1910–20)

Morley, John, *Recollections*, 2 vols (1917)

Morris, James, *Pax Britannica* (1968)

Murray's Handbook for the Punjab (1883)

Murray's Handbook for Travellers in India, Burma and Ceylon (1913)

North, Marianne, *Recollections of a Happy Life*, 2 vols (1892)

Paget, Walpurga, Lady, *Embassies of Other Days and Further Recollections*, 2 vols (1892)

Prinsep, Val C., *Imperial India—an Artist's Journal* (1879)

Rait, Robert S., *Life of Field-Marshal Sir Frederick Paul Haines* (1911)

199

Bibliography

Rawlinson, Major-General Sir Henry, *England and Russia in the East* (1875)

Roberts, General Sir Frederick, *My Forty Years in India*, 2 vols (1897)

Roberts, P. E., *History of British India under the Company and the Crown* (1923)

Shiva Rao, B., *India's Freedom Movement* (Delhi 1972)

Singhal, D. P., *India and Afghanistan, 1876–1907* (1963)

Smyth, Sir John, Bt., V.C., *Story of the Victoria Cross 1856–1963* (1963)

Stephen, Sir Leslie, *The Life of Sir J. F. Stephen* (1895)

Temple, Sir Richard, Bt., *The Story of My Life*, 2 vols (1896)

Wheeler, James Talboys, *The Imperial Assemblage at Delhi* (1877)

Wheeler, S. E., *The Ameer Abdur Rahman* (1895)

Woodruff, Philip, *The Men Who Ruled India*, 2 vols (1954)

Young, J. R., *Around the World with General Grant*, 2 vols (1879)

Younghusband, Major G. J., *Indian Frontier Warfare*, 2 vols (1898)

Index

Index

Index

Index

Lytton, Robert (1st Earl); appearance, 1, 4, 14; character and personality, 11, 12, 92–3, 99, 100, 153, 186–7; administration, 2, 43–4; and Afghanistan, 20, 40, 49, 50, 52–8, 93–4, 138, 152, 180; and Anglo-Indians, 32, 36, 47, 86–7, 96–8; and anonymous letters, 112, 155; congratulated and praised, 14, 22–3, 27, 44, 81, 99, 111, 117, 145–6, 152, 168–9, 175, 182–3; criticised and abused, 36, 47, 87, 94–5, 99, 105, 138–9, 143, 148, 169–70, 174, 176, 184; and his Council, 12, 23, 26–8, 30–2, 43–5, 49, 50, 97, 108; depression, 4, 8, 102, 155, 172, 177; Earldom, 174; on Empire, 180; and famine, 60–2, 72, 78, 85, 106–13; and finance (private), 6, 8, 9, 10, 25, 113, 173–4, (public), 27, 31, 41, 55–6, 91, 113, 152, 177; and fear of Russia, 20, 57, 92, 103–4, 138, 147; and fire balloons, 48–9, 156; flirting, 10, 50, 63, 94, 96, 98, 155, 177; and friendship, 7, 9, 11, 15, 27, 99, 109, 116, 148, 157; G.C.B., 117; health and habits, 2, 7, 40, 45, 47–8, 51, 60, 97, 105, 126–7, 186; operation, 101; on Indian Council in London, 124–5; and Indian princes, 40–1, 50, 55, 59, 81, 86, 123, 178; levees and investitures, 32, 45, 82, 90, 94–5, 98, 117; in love, 4, 7, 8, 10, 11, 15, 186; and the massacre, 159–60, 165–6; as poet and writer, 2, 4–6, 8, 10, 11, 185; and presents, 62, 65–6; as public speaker, 30–1, 71, 81, 84–5, 94, 183–5; reproved by Cabinet, 142; resignation, 174; and Salisbury, 17, 63, 102–3, 132–3, 186 & n; shocks proprieties, 32, 40, 86, 96, 100, 155; on Society, 10, 45; and his Staff, 13–4, 24–5, 42–3; and theatricals, 48, 123, 173, 186; on tour, 51, 59–72, 101–2, 115–6, 121–2, 167–9; at work, 43, 92, 102, 105, 116

Letters and telegrams: to Blunt, 61; to Buckingham, 111; to Bulwer-Lytton, 5; to Colley, 118, 154, 171; to Cranbrook, 123, 124–5, 128–30, 131–2, 142, 154, 177; to Disraeli, 2, 41, 81; to Edith, 13, 14, 30, 31, 52, 109–12, 135–6, 173–4, 186; to Forster, 10, 11; to Lady Holland, 32, 64; to Morley, 11, 44, 63, 96, 148, 149–50; to Salisbury, 31–2, 41, 96, 104, 107–8, 152; to Lady Salisbury, 45;

to Sher Ali, 31, 40, 49, 58, 129, 130; to Stephen, 44, 96, 98, 102, 108, 152, 161, 172, 180; to Strachey, 140, 142; to the Queen, 14, 25, 41, 62, 63–4, 79–81, 87–7, 112, 130, 176; to Prince of Wales, 40, 42

Lytton, Rosina, Lady, 3, 6
Lytton, Victor (2nd Earl), 53, 76, 81, 117, 149, 155n, 167, 182

Madras, 2, 16, 60; famine at, 78–9, 106–7, 109–13
Maiwand, Battle of, 178
Malleson, Colonel, 96 & n
Mallet, Sir Louis, 23
Malta, troops sent to, 122–3, 164–5
Mandi, 62
Margy, 30, 52–3, 59
Mashroba, 45, 47, 51, 60, 104, 109
Massacre at Kabul, 159–60
Mayo, Earl of, 13, 49
Mereweather, Sir William, 70–1
Merv, 92, 103, 179
Miliutin, General Dimitri, 138
Millais, Sir J. E., Bt., 14
Morley, Viscount, 9, 11, 12, 96, 116, 148, 180
Mudhapur, 65, 68, 165
Muir, Sir William, 27, 49, 94, 126
Mussaks, 64
Mussorie, 116
Mysore, 17, 60, 96, 106, 112; Maharaja of, 76, 81, 96n

Nabha, Raja of, 50
Naini Tal, 101–2
Napier, Lord, 26, 31, 42
Narkanda, 51–2, 60, 62, 135–6, 139
Nawab Ghulam Hassan, 129–30, 135–6, 143
Nepal, 17
Norman, Sir Henry, 60–1, 71, 94, 125
North Marianne, 126–7
Northbrook, Earl of, 1, 15, 18–9, 29, 31, 34, 42, 56–7, 116, 168
North-West Frontier, 18, 20, 31, 59, 114, 123; L's policy for, 68, 115, 125
North-West Provinces, 16, 27, 35, 55

Ootacamund, 112, 166
Opperman, Mlle, 118, 180
Osman Pasha, 109
Oswald (Ozzie), 46, 65, 83, 101, 180
Oudh, 16, 55, 101

Index

Index